FALSTAFF'S COMPLETE BEER BOOK

Frederic Birmingham

AWARD BOOKS NEW YORK · TANDEM BOOKS LONDON

PREFACE

When Sir Edmund Hilary, the conqueror of Mt. Everest, had finally scaled the unscalable, he was asked why he had attempted to climb the peak in the first place.

His answer is now a classic: "Because it was there."

It could be that Sir Edmund was enigmatic by choice or simply that he had no better reason to offer at that moment. At any rate, it added another mystic twist to an already quixotic adventure.

Our own project—this little book on beer—was motivated by more down-to-earth reasons. To begin with, the people of the Falstaff Brewing Corporation of St. Louis, Missouri, had been favoring for some time the idea of sponsoring a book that would express for all of the great brewing industry an abiding pride in its centuries'-old craft. Meanwhile, I—as an ardent beer lover—had been intrigued by the incredibly ancient role of the brew as a buttress to the Spirit of Man. Further, although the literature of almost all nations abounds in references to beer and its traditions, these tidbits are scattered across library shelves around the world, and nowhere could I find a single volume telling the full story for our time.

So it was that these two motivating impulses came together in this one volume. The effort represented a towering challenge, and I hope that we have scaled it together in all its imposing and yet intimate intricacies. Should anyone still ask why it was attempted, I shall look affectionately at the glass of beer at my elbow and answer: "Because it is here."

I do wish to mention with especial admiration, however, the gentlemen of Falstaff who, early in the game, established some kind of an all-time record for good manners and restraint in their consideration of this book that they are sponsoring. They did not provide me with a retouched portrait of The Founder to run as a frontispiece. They did not enrich me with a composite photograph showing the original brewery in dramatic contrast to one of their gigantic plants of today. And although they are devoted to the concept that beer is the very staff of the good life, and Falstaff beer most of all, they made a point of requesting that their trade name be played down as much as possible in the book and the generic story of beer itself played up as much as possible. And lastly, with virtually unprecedented nobility, they took the stand that their business is brewing and mine is writing and that the twain should meet in the pages of this book, but never in supervisional pressures. Their cooperation was illimitable, their instructions nil. A toast to them, good reader.

My second pleasant experience was the seductive quality of the subject itself. I like beer and I have drunk it in the past with enjoyment and frequently with gratitude for its refreshing and sturdy presence, although not to the exclusion of other alcoholic beverages. But now I find a quality about beer that seems to transcend all the others.

This is no mere beverage, this glass of beer. It is a small miracle. It is the drink of worship in millions of grottoes, forests, temples and secret grounds that have now receded into the dark thousands of years before man's recorded history.

It is the laughter and fighting boasts of a million fighting men from the Norseland. It is the chanting of a million monks of the church who reverently thought of bread and beer as one. It is the jollity of songs and toasts bellowed in a million taverns and flung to the stars in a thousand tongues across the centuries.

It is the grains of the earth growing in the ground under the blazing sun and the night mists of the plains girdling the planet, and of barley seed grown rich and golden.

And it is the men who turned to the craft of brewing—at first with awe and then with growing art and science and love —and made it into one of the great achievements of man's accommodation to his natural environment.

I found myself becoming ever thirstier and thirstier as I researched this book. Locked in the public library in New York City, it would come over me like a wave at intervals that what I needed was a glass of the brew to refresh my dusty gullet, to pick up my flagging energies and to keep me in actual physical rapport with my topic. The guards at the entrance began to know me as the guy who reads for only an hour at a time before he dashes out into the streets on some mad, mysterious errand, then to return with clocklike regularity for another session, a new man.

I don't care. An author has to keep his mind on his subject. And this book is a question of taste. I hope you have the same problem as you read along. And I certainly recommend the same treatment.

F.A.B.
Buck Hill Falls, Pennsylvania

TABLE OF CONTENTS

BIBLIOGRAPHY AND ACKNOWLEDGMENTS

Beer is a word threaded through all the histories and languages of man. Its story is so intertwined with the general story of man that all references to its past seem to be shared by all writers on the subject.

This writer, like the others, is indebted to ancients such as Herodotus, Pliny, Archilochus, Dioscorides and Tacitus, as well as to chroniclers in medieval and recent times who were equally taken by the subject of beer. But these small adventures for the student are offshoots from the main body of the research, which may be guided by special authorities in the field. Recommended basic reading should by all means start with various encyclopaedias that have substantial entries on the subject of beer and then proceed to the following: "Beer Has a History" by Frank Alfred King; "The Book of Beer" by Andrew Campbell; "Brewed in America" by Stanley Baron; and the all-knowing "Grossman's Guide to Spirits, Wines & Beer" by Harold J. Grossman.

The New York Public Library and the St. Louis Public Library have other listings that will draw the student deeper into his subject, but to these basic books I feel an especial debt. Something of an oddity, but an overwhelming piece of scholarship on the subject is "Origin and History of Beer and Brewing" by J.P. Arnold, if history is your dish.

For material on American colonial life and taverns, I am indebted to many sources and chiefly among them are "Everyday Things in American Life" by William Chauncey Langdon; "Little Pilgrimages Among Old New England Inns" by Mary Caroline Crawford; "The Colonial Tavern" by Edward Field; and "Stage Coach & Tavern Days" by Alice Morse Earle.

Special acknowledgment is made to the following for the use of specific material contained in this book:

1. To the book, "History of the Brewing Industry and Brewing Science in America," begun by John P. Arnold and completed by Frank Penman and containing speeches delivered at the Century Of Progress Exposition held in Chicago in 1933, from which the remarks by the late Dr. Max Henius, page 22, are quoted.

2. To Hill & Knowlton, Inc., for original preparation of the cooking recipes appearing on pages 104 to 109.

3. To the United States Brewers Association for statistics of the industry, appearing in Chapter Eight.

4. To the American Can Company for marketing and packaging data from "A History of Packaged Beer and Its Market in the United States," appearing in Chapter Eight.

5. To the Master Brewers Association of America for definitions included in "The Language of Beer," pages 125 to 129, and quoted from the book, "The Practical Brewer," published by the Association.

6. To the MacMillan Company for permission to reprint the first stanza of "Laugh and Be Merry" by John Masefield, from Collected Poems, Copyright 1912 by The MacMillan Company, renewed 1940 by John Masefield, as subtitle for Chapter Three of this book.

7. To Mr. J.V. Fort, author of "Let's Talk Beer," published by the Mycroft Press, copyright 1958, for permission to utilize source material from his book describing the steps in the brewing process, appearing in Chapter Nine.

8. To Small, Maynard & Co., for the reprinting of lines from "Dartmouth Lyrics" by Richard Hovey, from his "Hanover Winter Song," which appear at the opening of Chapter Seven.

For courtesies and assistance on too many fronts to detail, I am indebted to the staff of the United States Brewers' Association, which was unfailingly courteous and helpful in providing necessary data and reference suggestions.

Above all, I am grateful to the many people at Falstaff, at the home office in St. Louis and in the field, whose suggestions and guidance were valuable contributions to this book. Material of especial interest was gleaned from the pages of *The Shield*, the company publication of Falstaff, and additional information was graciously provided by the curator of the Falstaff International Museum of Brewing in St. Louis.

A NOTE FROM THE SPONSOR

An effort was made in the preparation of this book to provide its author with all that he needed in the way of information relating to the brewing industry and its unique heritage.

Since it was hoped that this book would afford entertainment as well as serve as a form of reference for lovers of the golden brew, the author was given his head in matters of style and personal viewpoint. Thus it could be that from time to time the reader may take issue—at least in part—with his observations and points of view. In this area we stand aside officially in the belief that such excursions promise only lively and enhanced reading pleasure.

We believe this book to be technically accurate, and we are sincerely gratified by the generous cooperation of all who contributed to it.

Falstaff Brewing Corporation
St. Louis, Missouri

Chapter One

THE MYTH, MYSTERY AND MEANING OF BEER

*Work is the curse of
the drinking classes.*

In these United States, according to the records, no less than 3,604,410,920 gallons of beer went down the hatch during a recent year.

Trained investigators, zeroing in on the facts, have found no clues such as strong-arm squads or infiltration by seductive dancing girls to account for the disappearance. A special committee appointed to look into all aspects of the case has only just released its final findings in a report that puts an end to any conjecture once and for all as to why all this beer disappeared in just one year.

Their conclusion: beer just tastes great.

Sociologists, who by nature will never let well enough alone, have come up with their own explanation. And that is that the case of the disappearing beer is a heartening indication of the general youthful bent of this nation. There is something about beer, according to exhaustive field tests made on the subject at selected and well-appointed bars and taverns, that brings out the youth in all of us, especially if we are youths.

A friend of mine who is a research specialist has put a head on the whole matter by a nifty little survey among college students as to their favorite areas of conversation. Being a student himself, he got the straight answers. And these, friends, are the first topics of discussion in dormitory bull sessions, in order of preference: motorcycles, beer, sex and *Playboy* magazine.

Now that should please almost everyone. Certainly brewers. Surely girls—who may have been suspecting that they have slipped more than that. Indubitably, Mr. Hugh Hefner. And possibly even professional pessimists, who may now refresh their dreary refrain by groaning that we're all going to hell on a Honda instead of in a handbasket.

Beer has this way of getting us to see the bright side of things. It was helping a long time before Noah's Ark, as we shall see. And it bids fair to continue at least for centuries to come; as we enjoy the 21st Century, visiting nearby galaxies over the long weekends, we can take along with us our battery-chilled hampers of the companionable brew.

I can't find anyone who has a word against it, although I suppose that voices are raised somewhere in remote pockets of the land against such a useful and pleasant drink. In that case, I could envy the Lincoln-esque good humor of a politician who was called upon to make a speech to a group of voters in an area of the country where strong feelings pro and con alcoholic beverages were running high at that very time. A few careless words on either side of the fence might ruin his entire career, yet running away from the subject was equally unthinkable. In effect, he seized the nettle with a firm grasp and escaped unscathed with these ringing words:

> I had not intended to discuss this controversial subject at this particular time. However, I want you to know that I do not shun controversy. On the contrary, I will take a stand on any issue at any time, regardless of how fraught with controversy it might be. You have asked me how I feel about whiskey. All right, here is how I feel about whiskey . . .
>
> If, when you say whiskey, you mean the devil's brew, the poison scourge, the bloody monster that defiles innocence, dethrones reason, destroys the home, creates misery and poverty, yea, literally takes the bread from the mouths of little children; if you

mean that evil drink that topples the Christian man and woman from the pinnacle of righteous, gracious living into the bottomless pit of degradation and despair, and shame, and helplessness, and hopelessness, then certainly I am against it, But;

If, when you say whiskey, you mean the oil of conversation, the philosophic wine, the ale that is consumed when good fellows get together, that puts a song in their hearts and laughter on their lips, and the warm glow of contentment in their eyes; if you mean Christmasy cheer; if you mean the stimulating drink that puts the spring into the old gentleman's step on a frosty, crispy morning; if you mean the drink which enables a man to magnify his joy, and his happiness, and to forget, if only for a little while, life's great tragedies, and heartaches, and sorrows; if you mean that drink, the sale of which pours into our treasuries untold millions of dollars, which are used to provide tender care for our little crippled children, our blind, our deaf, our pitiful aged and infirm; to build highways and hospitals and schools, then certainly, I am for it.

This is my stand, I will not retract from it, I will not compromise!

Fortunately we are not compelled here to take any such bold stand. There are no "sides" to a glass of beer. So that leaves us only the top and the bottom to explore, in the old-fashioned way.

BEER GROWS ORCHIDS

There is something really irresistible about beer.

Like, it grows orchids. We have it straight from a Mr. Yap Chong Beng in the *Malayan Orchid Review* that a quart of beer, mixed with ten gallons of water and applied to the base of the plants, will produce firmer roots and stems and more dazzling blooms. A doctor who is also an orchid grower does not find this surprising, but he also injects into his opinion a note of uncertainty as to the ultimate destination of such a treatment on a hot day: "Beer is a fermentation product, and its carbohydrates, proteins, vitamins and minerals are all beneficial to plant growth. Beer also contains diastase, maltase, protease and zymase. Unfortunately for my own orchids, beer also contains alcohol, which is beneficial to the spirits of the orchid grower."

And if orchids, why not ladies' hair? I have not lingered recently in a beauty salon with my head under a dryer, exchanging cozy gossip with the girls, but my spies tell me that for years even the most elegant salons have made a practice of dipping the hair into stale beer to feed it and "fix" it just before setting.

Beer also produces such by-products as should rejoice the human heart, troubled today by wastes, since these offshoots go into a highly useful second life as feed for animals. For example, several notable Kentucky thoroughbred horses have been raised on Falstaff feed. So have innumerable more humble beasts such as cows, beeves and hogs, and even some of the denizens of Chicago's Brookfield Zoo. My favorite animal story concerns an elephant that was booked for a nationwide tour. Everything was fine except that it was feared he might eat so much en route that he would outgrow the van in which he was traveling. The tour was accomplished and the elephant kept down to size when they packed into the traveler's trunk enough of a balanced Falstaff feed to keep his energies up and his weight down, a triumph of quality over quantity.

The point of all this is that the selective process of brewing beer leaves valuable grain ingredients that are utilized in as many as 44 different animal foods in the Falstaff line. These foods contain high-energy concentrated cereal elements, unidentified growth factors, phosphorus, B-complex vitamins, plus residual amounts of carbohydrates, malt and digestive aids. Each by-product is then fortified with the necessary additional vitamins and minerals to properly balance home-grown roughages.

And there is another by-product, "brewer's yeast." Yeast is an important part of the brewing process, and it has a well-known capacity to increase in quantity during the process of fermentation. This results in an excess that is put to very good use as a dietary supplement for both animals and people. Brewer's yeast is also the richest-known source of B-complex vitamins, which are valuable human nutrients, and it is also a useful supplement to livestock feedstuffs and pet foods. "Debittered" yeast is useful in baking processes and is applied in the manufacture of other products such as candy bars, peanut butter and syrups. As a part of certain flavoring compounds, it adds "meaty" flavor to such foods as powdered soups and gravies.

Then there is the great thirst for knowledge engendered by beer.

Men who wouldn't crack a book on a bet, and who avoid using their minds with an ingenuity worthy of a great cause, are greatly given to borrowing a dime in bars and taverns and calling up the nearest brewery to inquire how many beers it would take to float a battleship. (This mental aberration seems to be peculiar to Americans, who are also given to calling up an aquarium and asking for Mr. Fish—a quest for information which, I am told, makes them feel better for weeks afterward.)

At any rate, here is the answer about the battleship for those thousands of interested students of physics: Taking the U.S.S. Missouri as a prototype, weighing 45,000 long tons, a quick flick of the pencil and a lightning review of the laws of displacement reveal that approximately 134,400,000 twelve-ounce bottles or cans of beer would turn the trick and float the ship.

Beer, they say, will also improve your golf score.

This news may not be fraught with such significance that it will send the students of Cairo out rioting in the streets—but the facts are: a Dr. William W. Vollaton, an ophthalmologist of the Medical College of South Carolina and a man whose interest in better living is equaled only by orchid growers, says he has proved that a golfer can see better after drinking a beer. Forty-five per cent of those tested at the links over a month's time reduced their putting scores by at least 10 per cent. Forty per cent of the golfers tested showed no change, and 15 per cent raised their scores. That's golf for you. Of those who increased their scores, however, 10 per cent were not normally beer drinkers, but drank beer as a part of the test.

The youngsters who keep interrupting their fathers at work to proudly announce that they have fewer cavities would do better to turn their tiny steps to Guy's Hospital in London, England, where scientists soaked young, healthy teeth in 14 different solutions, including beer and fruit juices. After six weeks the teeth immersed in the fruit juices developed cavities. Those in the beer were in perfect condition. Never mind the rest of the class, kids—just make up your mind to drink beer as soon as you're grown up.

WOMEN, SAILORS AND BEER

Logicians will also find no flaw in close connections I have noted between women, sailors and beer. Women control most of the money in the United States, and they also own a big share of the corporate stock and real estate. Women are also greatly attracted to sailors as a class. Sailors as a class like beer. There is a great wisdom hidden somewhere in here, if I can only pry it out.

An Assyrian tablet of 2000 B.C. relates that beer was among the provisions taken aboard Noah's Ark. (Who knows, maybe he figured it might do the animals some good, too?) Then we find that when a salvage crew recently brought up a Swedish naval vessel that was sunk in 1628, the log revealed that the daily ration for each sailor aboard was 12 bottles of beer.

Another famous ship's log, aboard the *Mayflower*, reveals that were it not for beer, the Pilgrims would have sailed right on to Virginia instead of landing at Plymouth Rock, which would have raised havoc with the details of all our Thanksgiving Day cards. What happened was that the *Mayflower* made for the nearest suitable landing place because "we could not now take time for further search or consideration; our victuals having been much spent, especially our beere." The Pilgrims had the foresight to invite aboard a young cooper, or barrelmaker, by the name of John Alden, and although he beat out Captain Miles Standish for the hand of Priscilla Mullins ("Why don't you speak for yourself, John?"), Standish did not bear a grudge long and it was later found that a number of beer casks with the Alden touch were included in the old boy's estate.

Another sailor, Rear Admiral Richard E. Byrd, USN, was equally partial to beer when he sallied forth on his famous Antarctic expedition. Of course he did not have to stock his beer for one of the reasons most important to the old-time sailors—that of fighting scurvy—but it amounted to much the same thing, since he declared that the beer provided minerals and other dietetic values decidedly lacking in melted snow, in spite of the latter's plentiful supply. (In addition to the ingredients cited by our orchid-growing medic, beer also contains vitamins such as riboflavin, niacin, pantothenic acid and pyrocidine.) As I said, it's hard to fool a sailor. Ask any woman.

DUBIOUS DOSAGES

Such faith in beer therapy has a long and lovely pedigree. For one "fiend-sick," the Anglo-Saxon prescription was to "sing seven masses over the mash, add garlic and holy water, and drink the liquid out of a church bell." For hiccups: "Take the root of jarrow, pound it, and put it in good beer, and give it to the patient to sup lukewarm."

Ale was also recommended as an outward application; for pains in the knees, woodwax and hedge-rife were pounded and put into ale—the patient was to rub some on his knees and drink the rest.

A recipe for the black jaundice: "Take a gallon of ale, a pint of honey, and two handfuls of red nettles, and take a penny-worth or two of saffron, and boil it in the ale, the ale being first skimmed, and then boil the honey and nettles therein all together and strain it well, and every morning take a good draught thereof, for the space of a fortnight. For in that space (God willing) it will clean and perfectly cure the black jaundice."

For cough or shortness of wind: "Take a quart or more of beer and put to it a good piece of fresh butter, sugar candie an ounce, of liquorice in powder, of ginger grated, of each a dramme, let it boyle in the quart . . . and who so will drinke it as hot as he may suffer. Some put in the yolke of an egge or two towards the latter end, so making it the more strengthfull."

Perhaps the very first anesthetic was suggested by a Dr. Solas Dodd some centuries ago: "Take the oil pressed out of fresh herrings (a pint), a boar's gall, juices of henbane, hemlock, arsel, lettuce and wild catmint, each six ounces, mix, boil well, and put into a glass vessel, stoppered. Take three spoonfuls and put into a quart of warm ale, and let the person to undergo any operation drink of this by an ounce at a time, until he falls asleep, which sleep he will continue during the space of three or four hours, and all that time he will be insensible to anything done to him."

Henry Jenkins, a salmon fisherman who lived in 1670, took his ale wherever he could get it, and proved its efficacy, for he died at the age of 165 years. A tombstone in Great Walford attests to a similar faith.

> Here John Randall lies
> Who counting of his tale
> Lived threescore years and ten,
> Such vertue was in ale.
>   Ale was his meat,
>   Ale was his drink.
> Ale did his heart revive,
> And if he could have drunk his ale,
> He still had been alive.
> He died January five.

Two other splendid examples of the uses of beer in survival come to mind.

One concerns William Lewis, late of Llandismaw, Wales. He continued two excellent practices during a long life: one was to read extensively from his Bible

Here John Randall lies
Who counting of his tale
Lived threescore years and ten,
Such vertue was in ale.
Ale was his meat,
Ale was his drink.
Ale did his heart revive,
And if he could have drunk'his ale
He still had been alive.
He died January five.

every morning, the other was to drink eight gallons of
ale every evening. It was calculated that he had
drunk enough during his life to float a seventy-four gun
ship of the line, and I suppose he might have been
able to handle the *Missouri* had he lived long enough.
Unfortunately, he expired from an ill-advised
change of pace, although in a happy mood, when he
mixed a cup of Welsh ale with a quart of wine. William, who weighed 560 pounds, was derricked into his
grave with admiring solemnity by his countrymen,
who had dubbed him, at his request, "The King of
Spain."

Followers in his foamsteps are such guzzlers as
Auguste Maffrey of France, who drank 24 pints of
beer in 52 minutes in 1950; and J. H. Cochrane,
upholding the honor of Princeton University at
Harry's Bar in Paris in 1932, drank two litres of beer
(amounting to 4.22 pints) in 11 seconds.

The second happy use of ale in quantity was during
a devastating fire in London in the 17th Century. The
Temple, which is the court of law, was in flames, and
the Templars, aroused from their beds, could not get
an adequate supply of water from the frozen Thames.
In this difficulty they brought up barrels of ale from
the Temple "butteries" and fed the fire engines
with the malt liquor, at which—I cannot help pre-
suming—the flames licked.

And finally, the Germans, who should know, have
always said: "*Die Brauerie ist die best Apotheka*," i.e.,

the brewery is the best drugstore.

Beer also works its therapy on our national economy, pouring billions of dollars annually into purchases, payrolls and taxes.

Yes, beer is big. Very much at the head of its class.

THE ART AND MYSTERY OF BEER

Beer is also unique. A mineral is something to pluck out of the ground, to refine, and that's that. A gigantic plane is a scientific marvel, but once you have it in the air, all that is left is to pilot it. But beer has a "mind" of its own. Beer is a living thing.

We touch on great matters when we look closely at how beer comes about. A leading authority, the late Dr. Max Henius, said: "That the art of brewing remained a 'mystery' all through the ages may be in part due to the fact that it includes one of the most remarkable and recondite processes in nature, which was not understood until very recent years. The process of fermentation has ever been a mystery to man. It filled him with awe and reverence, so much so that he called its product—the animating essence—by the same word which he used to designate the supreme essence of his own being. The word 'spirit' designates both the mysterious element in the product of fermentation and the highest faculty of man."

And now, even at this writing, comes the whisper over the radio of the creative possibilities in yeast—not the human body this time—to produce living genes.

BY ANY OTHER NAME

Each language has its tribute to that spirit we call beer and also what is within ourselves. Listen:

Piwo *(Poland)*	**Bir** *(Indonesia)*
Alus *(Lithuania, Latvia)*	**Bierra** *(Italy)*
Biere *(France, Belgium)*	**Birre** *(Albania)*
Bier *(Germany, Holland)*	**Ubhiya** *(Africa, Zulu)*
Bere *(Moldavia, Romania)*	**Cerveza** *(Spain, Mexico)*
Sor *(Hungary)*	**Olut** *(Finland)*
Ol *(Denmark, Norway)*	**Biru** *(Japan)*

Ol *(Sweden, Iceland)*   **Biyar** *(India)*
Pivo *(Russia, Czechoslovakia)*   **Bior** *(Israel)*
Bira *(Greece, Turkey, Bulgaria)* **Serbesa** *(Philippines)*
Mai Chiu *(China)*   **Cerveja** *(Portugal)*

Our own word, *beer*, can be traced back to the Latin word *bibere*, meaning "to drink." It is first encountered in the 8th century in the old High German form of *peor* or *bior*, from which evolved the English "beer."

The encyclopedia, that cold-blooded armory of pure fact, without so much as a side-glance at Dr. Henius, states that: "Brewing is the preparation of beer from carbohydrate material, chiefly malted barley, by means of the action of yeast and usually with the addition of hops."

THE TYPES OF BEER DEFINED

And from there, as our best starting point, we should understand exactly what we are talking about when we say *beer*, since there are quite a number of types, although the one most popular with Americans is called "lager" and we shall discuss it later on.

The beer drunk in America today has evolved first from the English ales and beers that were drunk in our early years as a colony and then a nation, and then, somewhat later on, from German immigrants who brought their craftsmanship in the arts of brewing to this country. American taste eventually took a swing in their favor, which we have retained. But let us stay with the calendar in examining how we have progressed from our first brewing adventures.

THE BEERS OF ENGLAND

English beer has not changed in basic characteristics for many, many years, and so when we quaff a bit of the brew from a British tap, we are experiencing what generations of Englishmen have found inspiring in their course of empire.

Ale originally differed from beer in England in that each was made from malt derived from barley, but the beer was prepared with hops and the ale was not. Originally English ale had about three times the potency of beer, but beer was apt to keep better. At length they met in the middle; hops were put into the ale and the beer made stronger, so that in time they became more or less indistinguishable. But ale today has a different fermentation process, one that involves the use of what is termed a "top-fermenting" yeast, which adds a distinctive character. It is paler and more tart than beer and has a more pronounced flavor.

Porter is a variation of ale, with a sweeter and less "hoppy" taste. It developed early in the 18th Century as the answer to two other popular drinks—"half-and-half," which was a mixture of ale and two-penny "small" beer (just another way of saying weak beer); and "three shreads," which combines ale, two-penny and regular beer. This kind of thing made barkeeps busier than a one-armed paperhanger, and it was not long before a brew was worked out in which the three elements were mixed. It was first called "entire butt" or "intire," but eventually it picked up the nickname of "porter" because so many of the London porters went for it. It had a brief notoriety in America in a stage and movie appearance in "The Barretts of Wimpole Street" as the stern father (Charles Laughton or an unreasonable facsimile thereof) tries to force his delicate daughter, Elizabeth Barrett, to down some porter for her own good. Unfortunately the old boy was right, but porter is a dark, bitter drink made of several kinds of malt—black, dark, amber and pale— and Liz was much more partial to listening to handsome poet Robert Browning, who taught her to pay no attention to either her old man or his porter. That apparently finished porter for good, at least as far as Americans are concerned.

Stout is similar to porter, but sweeter, and is stronger, darker and heavier, with a marked flavor of malt. This is for dyed-in-the-wool beer drinkers; it is of a general consistency more heady than any ale.

GREAT GERMAN BEERS

This brings us to a consideration of the classic German beers that have contributed so much to our brewing literature and sprinkled many familiar names across the bar, which we should do well to sort out here with some accuracy.

Perhaps of all of them there is more misinformation, or at least conjecture, going the rounds about *bock beer*. So let us boil down some of the conflicting claims. The most likely explanation for the name is that it was one of the principal products of the city of Einbeck, in Germany, and that the "bock" part of it came from reference to the city. In the Middle Ages, Einbeck beer was also exported from its home on the banks of the Ilm River, about 40 miles from Hamburg, to all parts of the world—England, the Netherlands, Denmark, Norway, Sweden, Russia and even Jerusalem. When we consider that the English managed to name the wine *sherry* that they imported from Spain, simply by mangling the name of the city of its origin, *Juarez*, it is not too far-fetched to imagine what they could do to Einbeck beer. Then again, the German city was sometimes spelled "Einbock." And now we reach the point of realizing that in German this is how that bearded character got into the ads staring at you every spring. "*Ein bock*" means "a goat."

Incidentally, if you run across the canard that bock derives its distinction from being an end-of-the-season residue in the brewers' vats, scrub it as absolutely untrue.

All of this sage reasoning, however, blurs slightly when we look at a Mesopotamian privy seal of about 2000 B.C., which shows a queen and her nobles sipping beer through golden straws from a common jug, and there, prancing around them, is a goat. Further confusion: the word for goat in Hindustani is "bok." You may take it from there.

Bock beer is usually prepared for consumption in the spring, around Easter time, which is simply a carrying-on of the German custom of brewing beer in either October or March, when temperatures were most favorable. The brew is a special one, rather heavy in flavor, usually darker in color and richer in taste than our regular beers. It is made from both regular barley and caramel malt or burnt malt.

Weiss beer is another very popular German beer. In Europe it is brewed mostly from wheat rather than from the barley that we think of as the chief grain ingredient of beer. It has a very pale color, a distinctly tart taste, and it is especially rich in carbonation, so that it foams strongly when poured. These characteristics are chiefly those of Berlin Weiss; there is another called *Broyhan*, a Weiss made in Hanover and first brewed there as far back as the 16th century. It has its own special character—the appearance and bouquet of young wine and a sweetish-tart taste. Other beers similar to Broyhan are *Kofbusser* beer and Goslarer *Gose*.

Weiner beer stands somewhere between the very light Pilsners and the Bavarian. Among the Bavarian beers, *Munich* is a great favorite, light brown but with a strong flavor. *Kulmbacher* is another Bavarian type, just as strong but with a dark brown color.

Each of these German beers influenced American tastes as it was brought into our country by the brewers who had learned, each in his own home area, to make their special beer with differing characteristics of taste and appearance. But gradually they all began to filter down into the one general type of beer, German inspired, that we classify under the overall name of lager. The chances are—unless you are a great experimenter and have the fortitude to make taste excursions into the stouts and porters and bocks—that this is the type you prefer and regularly drink.

I might mention at this point a common misapprehension that often arises among dedicated beer drinkers, involving the relative alcoholic contents of American and European beer labels, that Continental beer has more alcohol in it. This is not quite the case. The problem arises from the fact that in the United States the alcohol content of the *finished* beer is the criterion. Thus the American consumer asks how strong the beer is and expects an answer in terms of the alcohol content of the beer. The European asks what quality the beer is, or how strong it is, and is told how concentrated the beer was before it was fermented. . . not in terms of alcohol, but in terms of all the complex solubles in the wort (unfermented beer). So beers of comparable alcoholic content are found in most countries. American beers are actually equivalent to, and in some cases exceed, the alcoholic content of foreign beers.

Steam beer is a name you may run across, a kind of invention that was born out of necessity in our own West around 1850, where it was not always possible to obtain the ice needed to provide the low temperatures at which regular beer can be fermented. So brewers went ahead anyway at higher temperatures and this worked out to their advantage, at least in terms of speed, since the steam beer could be processed much more rapidly than regular beer.

Pilsner is an old, old favorite. In the early 19th Century the great beer-producing areas in Germany competed with no holds barred for the world market, and some of the keenest rivalry was between neighboring cities. The Munich-type beers of Bavaria held the scepter for a long time, but by the end of the century the city of Pilsen (now in Czechoslovakia, but then in Bohemia) had come on fast and was considered the champion brewing center.

Pilsner is world-famous for its lovely, light taste and golden appearance, and this beer is often referred to as Bohemian beer. It has a paler appearance than the dark Bavarian beers and a more pronounced hop flavor. *Dortmunder* (a very pale beer) is also one of the best known of this type. Other famous Bohemian names are *Abzug* and *Schenk* beers. Both are light, with a dry, vinous and sharp taste. *Graetzer* is another favorite in the Pilsner group. The Pilsner glass was created, in fact, to dramatize the special, light qualities of this excellent brew at a time when most beers were heavier and darker and their aroma was unmistakably more robust. The Pilsner glass is tall, wide at the top, offering the drinker a fine view of his brew, and its delicate bouquet rises the more freely.

Malt liquor is a relative newcomer on the brewing scene. It is strictly defined as a malt beverage, but it lacks both the malt and the hops taste of lager beer and has a higher alcoholic content—over four per cent by weight and with no upper limit. It bears the same relationship to beer that "stock ale" bears to ale. Both have higher alcohol, and more volatile flavoring components. In terms of flavor it may be compared to the British porter or stout, although its proportion of dissolved solids is lower than in either one, and its processing is, in fact, different from that of both porter and stout, just as it is different from regular beer. It has a delicate and aromatic flavor that some connoisseurs prize quite highly.

ALL HAIL TO LAGER

Lager is effervescent, light amber to dark in color, with a mild hop aroma and flavor. The ales, porters and stouts, as we have seen, were products of British tastes and techniques in the 19th Century, while German brewers were doing things in another way—especially "lagering" the beer, which means "to store" and comes from the word *lagern*. After brewing, the beer was *lagered* for months until it was mellow and sparkling. October beer was easy to cool over the winter; the March beer was hidden away in cool mountain caves during the summer months when the heat decreed a suspension in brewing.

A good 90 per cent of the beer made in America today is lager. Englishmen, while still retaining a taste for their own beers and ales, are beginning to consume more and more lager. They like their flavor so much, however, that they drink it warm in order to give the aroma fullest play. On the other hand, Americans like their beer very cold, perhaps colder than it should be served; but then, we are like that in everything—cocktails, air-conditioned rooms, milkshakes and the rest. However, it could also be said to be a conditioned reflex on our part; the first commercial air-conditioning system in this country was installed in an Alexandria, Virginia, brewery in 1880, the first patent in the field going to a brewer, Robert Portner. Thank your lucky stars for beer when you sit in cool comfort everywhere you go now during the dog days.

There remains only the debatable issue about the difference between draught and bottled-canned beer.

I say "debatable" because the land is full of voices professing to find draught superior to bottled-canned and laying loud claims to being able to tell the difference. Well, fellows, the only difference is that most draught beer is put into barrels directly from the storage vats, while most bottled-canned beer is pasteurized by heat after being packaged. This is on the general assumption that draught beer is to be kept refrigerated and drunk almost immediately upon delivery in bars, restaurants, taverns and the like, which have the equipment to tap it on the spot. (There are home "Tappers" available now, too, for the fellows who really enjoy draught beer: and make no mistake, it's fun drawing your own brew.) In addition to the pasteurization, the packaged beer tends to be a trifle more carbonated, but not even enough to help beer connoisseurs who have been put to the blindfold test—and failed.

Be that as it may, you'll enjoy good beer *either* way.

Chapter Two

THE INCREDIBLE ANTIQUITY OF BEER

Stale beere, with good store of
sugar, eyther in the morning or
before meales, it rejoiceth the
heart, cleareth the complexion,
and cureth melancholy.

from William Vaugh's
Directions for Health,
Naturall, and Artificial
(1598)

The story of beer cannot be told without dipping into its past, and beer's past is such a whopping dip that the awful word "history" may crop up into the conversation. I do not, certainly, propose to drag you through ten thousand years of brewing, bubble by bubble, with the merciless glee of an anthropologist describing the left tibia of a caveman he excavated in a pile of rocks in Zamboanga. But history ceases to be history when it applies directly to the present.

And so, let's see beer in that light.

A bunch of boys were sitting around a bar one night sipping beer, and they began to kick because it wasn't strong enough. And, went the familiar refrain, it certainly wasn't as good as it had been in "the good old days!" What *they* might have been I leave you to imagine, since this little conversation was reported on a stone newspaper of 3000 B.C., found in the city of Ur. The boys signed off, or the roof fell in on the newspaper, just as they were getting warmed up to the problem of whether having barmaids might help the taste of the beer! Times do not change as much as we like to think they do.

But over in Mesopotamia, about a thousand years before our bull session in Ur, the girls had already made it, since they were officially the master brewers of their day. (By the way, a nice little point to tuck away in your noggin is the fact that the female of "brewer" is "brewster." Although you are not likely to run into any such around this country today, Brewster is not unknown as a name for various American settlements, there being 11 in as many states in my atlas.)

Such little tidbits only hint at the antiquity of beer, which may well have been one of the first inspirations of the caveman, already mentally exhausted by having invented the wheel and fire and much in need of a relaxing drink—due to certain stirrings in the furthest reaches of his mind that were to start by the addition of two stones to another two to make four and end up as the computer.

The truth is quite a simple one. Civilization as we know it evolved in the great river valleys such as the Euphrates and the Tigris in Asia Minor and the Nile in North Africa, where the nomads and cave-dwellers gave up the idea of chasing their dinner all over the countryside every evening and fighting every human being on sight, and took to growing grains, domesticating animals and poultry for instant feeding, and throwing up protective walls around their communities to hold off invaders. And where there was grain, sooner or later there was beer.

Some of the most remarkable archaeological dis- coveries have been in the realm of beer. That Assyrian tablet found in Nineveh and dating to 2000 B.C. men- tions Noah's Ark, and we are indebted to Professor Paul Hapt of Johns Hopkins University for an exact translation: "For our food, I slaughtered oxen and killed sheep—day by day. With beer and brandy, oil and wine, I filled large jars . . . ." The Bible, which is the chief source of our acquaintance with Noah, does not mention his proclivity for beer, possibly because the translators did not find it respectful to do so in view of his advanced age. But there are other Biblical references to beer, and there is the likelihood that the

Hebrews learned much about the drink during their periods of captivity in Assyria and Egypt.

Scholars of the University of Chicago's Oriental Institute and of Catholic University in Washington came up with some remarkable finds about beer on a tablet of fire-baked clay. Written in Sumerian and Akkadian around the fourth or fifth centuries B.C., it is a copy of a text that was itself older by more than 1500 years. It seems possible that the Babylonians had more kinds of brew than we have today— dark beer, pale beer, red beer, three-fold beer, beer with a head and one without. Some types of beer were reserved exclusively for certain temple ceremonies in honor of the goddess Siris, patroness of beer, although she was supplanted later by Ninkasi. So important was brewing that the women brewers were actually the temple priestesses.

University of Pennsylvania scientists unearthed a golden straw used by Queen Shu-bad of Mesopotamia for sipping beer, and they also found in "the cradle of civilization" evidence that baking and brewing were companion arts in the everyday kitchens of the people. They knew what they were doing, too, even by modern standards. They prepared malt from barley and evidently also developed strains of yeast for fermentation. And just as our modern brewers sell protein products back to the farmer for livestock, as by-products of brewing, so in old Babylon the mash was used for "fattening cattle." The brewers then also turned out a kind

of small cake as a by-product of the beer making, and it was not uncommon for temple overseers to pay their workmen with these cakes—which would be a little like a furniture manufacturer of today paying his workmen with sawdust, a fine practice if you can get away with it.

ON TO EGYPT

But Egypt was the true home of beer, just as it was the originator of so many other arts and institutions. There the patroness of beer was the goddess Isis, and beer was literally the national beverage. A high official was appointed "superintendent of breweries" and charged with the quality of the nation's beer. If he caught any retailers watering their beer or adulterating it in any way, the man was nailed by the ears to the door of his shop as a warning to customers, and he himself got the message after a couple of days.

Egyptian beer was made from lightly baked barley bread. The bread was crumbled, put into jars with water and allowed to ferment, after which the liquid was strained and consumed or bottled. This method worked out very handily on long journeys across the desert; the bread was light to carry and when water was reached at an oasis, the beer was made on the spot as a kind of instant brew. Date sugar or honey was often added for sweetening and probably to induce what we now call fermentation, but which action to the Egyptians was a mysterious intervention of the gods. Tart herbs might also be tossed in to spice up the flavor. This was called "bousa," and the method has persisted until today in parts of North Africa.

Most Egyptians, even children, drank beer and esteemed it so highly that it was regularly offered as a libation to the gods. Ramses III sacrificed 30,000 gallons yearly from his royal brewery. He may well have taken the idea from his father, Ramses II, who lived about 1250 B.C. This Ramses was a better politician than his son in that he distributed yearly 500,000 gallons of his beer to his subjects on the sensible theory that the glow thus induced inside of them came from him personally. Rich and poor, nobles and fellaheen, downed the brew with relish. "Here's beer for your ghost!" was a favorite toast!

And an old Egyptian tomb bears the inscription: "Satisfy his spirit with beef and fowl, bread and beer." The exquisite Queen Tiy, wife of Amenhotep III, was wont to delight and impress her king and guests with dazzling dinners of roast duck, gazelle, porcupine and beer; and porcupine—as I have discovered for myself when eating them on mountain-climbing expeditions—provided both very succulent meat and toothpicks for after-use.

The Egyptian beer, called Hek, meant even more to those people than a religious offering and a merry party. The famous Ebers papyrus, compiled by Egyptian pharmacists 3500 years ago, listed 700 prescriptions of which 100 contained beer.

And finally, Egyptians had a surefire way of predicting the sex of an unborn child through beer. "Make two holes in the ground. Throw barley into one and wheat into the other. Then pour into both the water of the pregnant woman, and cover them again with earth. If the wheat shoots up first before the barley, it will be a boy, but if the barley comes up first, thou must expect a daughter."

BEER CROSSES THE RUBICON

Egypt gave beer its big start; the Greek and Roman conquerors took that special knowledge of brewing with them and spread it in the wake of conquest all over the world. When Caesar crossed the Rubicon, he toasted his troops with beer, and he always took plenty of it on long marches to keep the legionnaires happy. The oldest beer mash in existence dates to about that time. In the town of Alzey in Germany, excavators found, in 1911, amid the ruins of a Roman house that had long since crumbled, a stoppered jug containing a dark brown substance. Chemical analysis revealed that this was actually beer mash, and also—thanks to the tight closure—that it had retained its character unaltered for 16 centuries. The old Roman who set it under his cellar stairs to ferment, just before the Alemanians roared in on him and burned his house to the ground, had never figured to age it that long.

WESTWARD WITH BEER

As beer followed the path of Western civilization, it held on to its character as a beverage, and it also managed to push along in front of it some of the old traditions. If priests made beer for Mesopotamians, so did medieval monks become the official beer makers of their communities as a part of their bread-making routines. If Egyptians sent along beer with those departing this life, so did the Norsemen. The latter ate six meals a day and drank a soup of bread and beer with each one from a bull's horn that contained a full gallon, and therefore held quite logically that a good drinking hall was a necessary establishment in their Valhalla!

Funeral feasts of the Danes were actually called "grave ales"— the ale being drunk on the spot to keep the ghost of the departed at arm's length. The Anglo-Saxons had their "bride ale," which was a wedding celebration with much quaffing of ale, and so we now have our word "bridal" for the nuptial feast. We pass the wassail bowl during the Yule season because the old Anglo-Saxon greeting "*was hael*" meant "be well" and was accompanied by the drinking of the traditional wassail beverage—spiced hot ale with an apple and a piece of toast floating in it.

Beer had moved just a small step from its original

status as part of religion, but the cachet clung just the same. The Magna Carta, defining British liberties, evidently considered good beer one of them, for it established the kingdom's first standard measurement for ale. According to Norse law, contracts made in church, court, or beer house were favored, and there was even a legal term of "beer-house testimony." The Saxon nobles of the 6th and 7th Centuries would not deign to sit in council considering questions of high importance until they had drunk their beer, which they downed in common from large stone mugs. The gesture was a symbolic one, as if to say that beer were a measure of all true men of good will as well as a fine and refreshing aid to judgment. Charlemagne himself was the personal tutor and trainer of the brewers of his realm; he intended to have no inferior brew for the people who were soon to call him The Great.

THE LEGEND OF GAMBRINUS

These solemn rituals reached a fine climax in the creation of Gambrinus, patron saint of beer for all Christendom, who is said to have invented the beverage. Chiseled in stone on the Andecho Monastery in Bavaria was the legend: "Holy St. Gambrinus, pray for us!"

However, there was considerable confusion as to what religion old Gambrinus really belonged to. His earliest biographer, Aventinus, writing in his *Annales Bojurum* in 1554, avers that Gambrinus was born in 1730 B.C., exactly 2234 years after the creation of the world. The Egyptian god Osiris is also believed to have invented beer, but Aventinus smooths this over by saying that Gambrinus was the consort of Isis, who was the wife of Osiris, and that this bit of mild adultery gave him some claims on the beer invention of her husband, not to mention the lady.

The truth of the Gambrinus legend seems to point more precisely to a man who actually lived: one portrait of Gambrinus labels him as "King of Flanders and Brabant." We do know that a famous Baron of Brabant was a certain Jan Primus, who was not only a noted warrior and a local hero, but also renowned for his

capacity. He is said to have quaffed 72 quarts of beer at
one sitting. In addition, he was President of the
Brussels Guild of Brewers from 1261 to 1294, with his
portrait hanging in the great hall. If you say Jan
Primus fast enough and figure out that a man of that
name was the champion drinker of his time, you have
the right kind of start to launch a patron saint of beer
called Gambrinus.

Thus beer has been an important part of German
culture from the earliest times, and it is through the
small principalities of that era that we trace our own
beer lineage. We got the habit, of course, from the
English, but it has been the German influence on the
product—all the way through to our day—that brings
us the kind of beer we have.

The North German cities of the Hanseatic League
were famous for their beer, Rhine wine and linen, and
the first days of Germany's greatness in brewing
stems from those places—at first as many as 85 towns,
including Hamburg, Luebeck, Bremen, Einbeck,
Rostock, Dantzig, Cologne, Hanover, Muenster and
Nuremburg. Hamburg was considered the queen of
them all as a beer center in the Middle Ages. Later the
accolade fell to the southern cities—Munich,
Nuremburg, Frankfurt, Dortmund and others. If a city
did not have adequate production facilities for
brewing, the government imported beer from more
fortunate areas and sold it under the cellar of the city
hall—or rathskeller.

It seems to be a common aim of most drinking men at
one time or another to try to out-drink the other
fellow. The Germans were a sturdy, well-knit lot
whose ancestors had emerged from their dark forest
homes to terrorize the countryside from time to time,
and in those days one did not become a terror without
going in for some pretty rough-and-tumble tactics.
The descendants of these ferocious Huns liked to pass
time by indulging in three-hour drinking bouts. The
contestant was required to drink continually, and
under no circumstances was he permitted to leave
his seat. Beer drinkers will immediately perceive
that this seemingly involves a contradiction in pur-

poses if not in terms—the more drinks of beer, the greater the need for some form of natural relief. The Bavarians who indulged in these lengthy drinking bouts either punished their kidneys with excruciating muscular control or they wore tightly constructed leather pants which were ... er ... waterproof.

Of course it is not fair to impugn the reputation of an entire age with this faintly horrifying story. The Bavarians were simultaneously perfecting their arts of brewing and tightening their grip on the world market by restricting the exporting of their fine malts and by keeping their brewing secrets—well, secret. The abbots of England were in the meantime becoming as famous for their beer as the Trappists for their cheese or the Benedictines for their liqueurs.

HOPS MAKE THE SCENE

Nearly all of these early European breweries were operated as craft enterprises by the monasteries, and we have to thank the Bavarian monks for the first use of hops in beer—a use that was, in terms of our own beer, the turning point of the entire industry toward the flavor we now know.

Up until that time beer must have been as hard on the roof of the mouth as on the seat of the pants. The chief flavoring agents of the brew were the bark and leaves of the oak, ash and tamarisk, which, as you know, were also used extensively in tanning the hides of animals. (The effect on the stomach lining may have been similar.)

But a charming little plant, *humulus lupus* by precise appellation, changed all that for the better. Its entrance on the brewing scene, in fact, was a high point in our little drama.

Lupus is the hop plant, a twining vine with three- or five-lobed leaves related to the mulberry. It bears flowers in cone-shaped clusters, which when dried and ripened are used to impart that piquant-bitter flavor to our beer. Hops have evoked their own poetic outbursts in the literature of beer and have been hailed as "a sedative, a meditative and digestive tonic,

a stimulant to breathing, song and story, a fragrant re-
sin . . . ." They have become the special favorites of
the taste buds of the world ever since their first introduction into the brewing of beer.

Actually, the Bohemians have always stoutly maintained that *they* were the first ones to use hops, and it
is also rumored—mostly by the people who live in
these places—that the plant came originally from Fin-
land or perhaps from France. I, myself, being perfectly content to believe that Shakespeare wrote the
plays of Shakespeare and that Columbus discovered
America, although vehement objections have been
raised from time to time against such accepted traditions, am content to say that the Germans first used
hops. At least they used them best, and that's probably
how the tale got started.

Hops traveled from Germany to Norway and the
Netherlands and at length reached England with a
group of Flemish immigrants who settled in Kent
during the reign of Henry VIII. They began the culti-
vation of the famous English hop gardens.

The German and the British who have admired
and hated each other for centuries, do have common
points of temperament and one of them is a kind of
phlegm, to use the old word, which in the British is
recognized as staunchness and in the Germans as
stubbornness. This goes well with the drinking of
beer, as opposed to the more volatile flights of
temperament found in the Latin countries. What also
put them together in the same beer vat, gastro-
nomically speaking, was that Italy and France were
blessed with climatic and soil conditions that encouraged viniculture, and the exuberant wines thus
produced were temperamentally very much at home
in these countries. Barley could be grown far better
than grapes in both Britain and Germany; their national futures were written in the waving fields
rather than on the climbing vines.

Not that England took hops, the German discovery,
to its bosom immediately. The British were accustomed to serving beer both hot and cold, dosed
with cinnamon; strong, weak, bitter and sweet, and

sometimes all together; and they favored a dollop of
melting butter floating on the top. Also, if you ever
come across the word "gruit" or "grut," you will be
close to what was a mixture of aromatic herbs that
actually preceded hops as a flavoring agent and that
was commercially recognized while, at the same time,
the secret of all of its ingredients was never divulged.
The grut boys had the knife out for the hops boys, naturally, since the latter were invading a firmly en-
trenched commercial territory, but we know now who
got in the last slash.

BEER FOR GOOD QUEEN BESS

Some of the old recurrent patterns in brewing take
place all over again in England. Queen Tiy of Egypt de-
lighted her dinner guests with beer, but so did Queen
Elizabeth I of England. What is more, she liked the
brew herself. She had a couple of tankards of beer
every morning, and she carried her favorite brand
along with her when she traveled as well as sending
couriers out to test the brew in the towns ahead of The
Royal Progress. Some harsh remarks have been made
about the way Good Queen Bess did in the more
glamorous Mary, Queen of Scots, but Bess at least
understood what Mary was saying when the Scottish
beauty demanded her own supply of beer when she
was imprisoned in Tutbury Castle. She was willing
to cut off Mary's head, but she was not up to cutting off
Mary's supply of the brew.

The English passion for ale was so widespread at
the time, however, that we must not conclude that
these two queens were overdoing things at all. Children were permitted a quart of beer each at breakfast. The Earl and Countess of Northumberland were
willing to eat assortments of fish for breakfast
during Lent, but they continued to share a quart of
beer and a quart of wine as eye-openers. Lady Lucy, a
Maid of Honor in the lusty court of Henry VIII, was allowed for breakfast a chine of beef, a loaf of bread
and a gallon of ale; for dinner a piece of boiled beef, a
slice of roast meat and a gallon of ale; and for supper—porridge, mutton, a loaf of bread and a gallon of

ale. In those days if Lucy felt like sloshing down a little more ale during the period between meals, it was called a "russin"; a "potatio" is something she drank in the evening after supper. Such regal customs anent beer are reflected in our own day, when the coronation of Queen Elizabeth II in 1953 was distinguished by special brews prepared for the great occasion.

THE ALE CONNER

History repeated itself again in England, where a superintendent of breweries—just as we have seen in old Egypt—headed a crew of beer inspectors in every borough of the land. In fact, one of the oldest public offices in England is that of the ale "conner," or taster. The post was created by William the Conquerer in order to keep ale prices and quality in line, and the job still exists, paying about $40 a year, with free beer thrown in. William Shakespeare's father is believed to have been an ale conner, which was a post of some importance in Elizabethan England. He was not only an expert judge of ale, but he had the power to condemn a batch or order its sale at a lowered price if it did not meet his standards.

Every person who brewed ale or had it for sale was compelled by law to set out the ale stake (originally the ale bush, after the ivy of the Romans, who used it as a signboard of a drinking shop) as a signal to the local ale conner that his expert services were required before the public should be served from the new batch of the brew. Many retailers were women, and these were the "ale-wives" of song and stage, mostly cast in the role of villainesses who fleeced honest English yeomen by watering or adulterating the beer. For their efforts, if caught, they were not nailed to their shop doors by the ears, Egyptian fashion, but they were given a ride in the ducking stool at a nearby pond, preferably muddy.

There is hardly any way in which we can appreciate or understand the omnipresence of beer in English life, just as the role of the horse in the last century seems unreal to us today (the Union cavalry, for example, used up 30,000 mounts every week during the Civil War). Ale was used as the baptizing liquid, and sometimes it substituted for the Communion wine. Ale was sold to the church by its parishioners, awarded back to them as a form of jolly receipt when they paid their tithes; it also was the official drink of celebrations in honor of a whole series of church holidays, as well as the first appearance of the cuckoo in spring.

Besides the Cuckoo-Ales, there were Help-Ales, Lamb-Ales and Midsummer-Ales. The English just couldn't get enough of the brew. They washed their choicest horses' hooves in ale, and they even invented an ale potion that very cleverly dyed the fisherman's line a pale and watery green.

LUSTY APPETITES OF OLDE ENGLAND

It was an age of excess in food and drink. While we now have our central heating units in our homes and office buildings, and because we favor the slender figure for both sexes for reasons of health or vanity, we must not forget that people in the old days had to eat by way of stoking the only furnaces they had—and these were the ones inside. And, of course, the necessity soon became a pleasure. When the Archbishop of York was enthroned, the eatables that burdened his festive board on that occasion included 104 oxen, 6 wild bulls, 1,000 sheep, 304 calves, 400 swans, 2,000 geese, 1,000 capons, 2,000 pigs, many thousands of such lesser fowl as quail, plovers and pigeons, plus 4,000 cold venison pies, 500 stags, 603 pike and bream, 12 porpoises and seals, and other delicacies so esoteric as to be unrecognizable. All of this was washed down the gullets of the faithful with 604,800 pints of ale and an equal quantity of wine.

And the most English thing of all was that beer was knighted in the person of Sir John Barleycorn, a whimsey that lent nobility to the high gesture of swigging down a pint and wiping the foam from the lips with the back of a horny hand. The wine countries never found a way to equal that; their Bacchus is just a silly fellow with vines in his hair, playing on his pipes and chasing the girls.

Chapter Three

BEER COMES TO AMERICA

*Laugh and be merry, remember, better the world with
a song.
Better the world with a blow in the teeth of a wrong.
Laugh, for the time is brief, a thread the length of a
span.
Laugh, and be proud to belong to the old proud pageant
of man.*   John Masefield

The way of the brewer was the way of our very
first colonists. America's first "Help Wanted"
advertisement appeared in London in 1609,
calling for brewers for service in Virginia. It pulled
two Frenchmen, loitering away from home across the
Channel, and they worked out just fine in the new
country.

The first white child born in the new land was Jean
Vigne, of New Amsterdam, who grew up to be a brewer. Not far from where he was born, the first brewery
in Colonial America rose up in 1633 on the spot where
Wall Street now is (make what you can out of that) and
the order promptly went out to pave the street first in
order to keep the brew wagons rolling.

The big cats of that day all cared for their brew. Johann Rising, last governor of New Sweden, which was
a Swedish colony along the Delaware River from 1638
to 1655, in writing to the old country and asking for
someone to pick him out a wife, cared not a whit about
her looks but put it down in black and white that she be
skilled to "make malt and brew the ale."

GREAT COLONIAL BREWERS

And many of the greats were brewers themselves.
Samuel Adams of Boston was one, as we shall see later.
James Oglethorpe, founder of Georgia, another.
William Beekman of New York was both burgo-
meister and brewer.

Down in Bucks County, Pennsylvania, in 1633, William Penn erected his great manor house, "Pennsbury," and the brewhouse adjoining it. The rare old patriot and diplomat was accustomed to reaching this country estate, some 20 miles up the river, by way of a six-oared barge, and there "Pennsbury" still stands—manor house, gardens and brewhouse—as a tribute to Penn's taste and capacity for the fine gesture.

Farther south other great men of our country's past, such as Thomas Jefferson and George Washington, both of Virginia, followed Penn's lead. Jefferson, holding a glass of beer to the light, declared: "I wish to see this beverage become common," and he went so far as to send to Bohemia for brewers who could teach their art to the Americans, which may yet be a point on their side in the argument about the hops.

George Washington liked beer well enough to have his own recipe, which follows:

TO MAKE SMALL BEER

Take a large snifter full of Bran Hops to your taste. Boil these three hours, then strain out 30 gallons into a cooler. Put in 3 gallons molasses while the beer is scalding hot or rather draw the molasses into the cooler and strain the beer on it while boiling hot. Let these stand till it is little more than blood-warm, then put in a quart of yeast. If the weather is very cold, cover it over with a blanket and let it work in the cooler 24 hours, then put it into the cask. Leave the bung open until it is almost done working. Bottle it that day when it was brewed.

Always a leader who was concerned for the welfare of his troops, Washington saw to it that each of his men had a daily supply of beer, and during the hard days at Valley Forge, when he was writing imploring letters to the Congress for more arms and supplies, beer was one of the tools of war he specifically requested.

Dr. Benjamin Rush, Washington's own physician-general to the Continental Army, signer of the

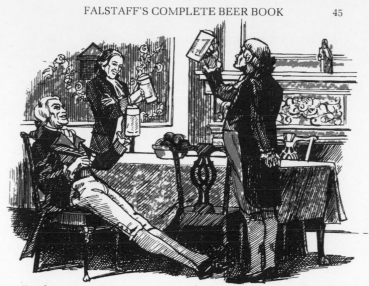

Declaration of Independence and one of the most re-
vered scientists in the annals of American medical
history, was in whole agreement with the Command-
er-in-Chief's high regard for the brew. Rush, who in
1784 was to publish a study of the effects of alcohol
upon "the human body and mind," came to these conclusions about malt beverages: "Fermented liquors
(i.e., beer and ale) contain so little spirit, and that so
intimately combined with other matters, that they
seldom can be drunken in sufficient quantities to produce intoxication and its subsequent effects. They
are, moreover, when taken in a moderate quantity,
generally innocent and often have a friendly influence upon health and life."

The colonial rank and file were also in full agreement with their Chief on beer and its delights. At first
their beer was of an amateur variety, not having the
hops immediately on hand from European gardens.
Spruce twigs, birch bark, pumpkin and apple parings
were added to the water and malt and sweetened with
molasses to make the brewing mixture, and the song
went, "Oh, we can make liquor to sweeten our lips, of
pumpkins, of parsnips, and walnut-tree chips."

In the old country, the men sometimes made a "Flap
Dragon" which consisted of pouring alcohol over the

top of the beer, lighting it and then drinking it flames
and all. This took drinkers who were *drinkers*!

THE PATRIOTIC BREWERS

Brewers themselves had a share in the ratification
of the new country. In parades dramatizing the infant
republic, brewers played a lively part. In Philadelphia, for instance, there were ten of them, headed by
Reuben Haines, with ten ears of barley in their hats,
and they carried with them branches of hops, malt
shovels and mashing oars, and bore a standard aloft
that read, "Home brew'd is best."

This loyalty of the brewers was rewarded. Both
James Madison and Alexander Hamilton believed
that moderation could be encouraged among the
people by reasonable taxes on beer in order to keep
its price down. The Massachusetts legislature went
even further in 1789 by exempting brewers from
taxation for five years. During the same year,
Madison, as a member of Congress, urged a duty of
eight cents a gallon on foreign beer. This was the kind
of encouragement the domestic brewers could understand, and before Madison died, beer was being
brewed in every original state of the Union and was
proving itself a valuable factor in the nation's
economy.

The next influences in the growth of beer in the
United States were, once again, the re-entry of the
German touch with the introduction of lager beer
around 1840 and the development of scientific principles somewhat later that moved brewing into the
modern picture.

Another mid-century footnote to brewing was written in 1865 when Mathew Vassar, a brewer of Pough-
keepsie, New York, endowed Vassar College,
America's first privately endowed college for
women, and established for it such standards of ex-
cellence that its daughters consider with some reason that there's Vassar—and then you can start talking
about the other women's colleges. (As a matter of fact,
you might have to talk fast because by now every one
of the great women's colleges of the Seven Sisters, in-

cluding Vassar, has conceded to the co-ed theory in
one form or another, or is considering the move.)

LAGER BEER COMES TO AMERICA

We have noted that lager means "to store," but there
was another difference about the German *lager bier*,
and that was its fermentation, which for reasons not
wholly understood at the time was accomplished by
a type of yeast that settled to the bottom after fermentation in contrast to ale yeast, which rises to the top of
the brew. Therefore, this particular yeast had to be
brought to America before anyone in this country could
make lager. One theory is that it was made possible
only by the speed of the Baltimore clipper ships, which
made the voyage from Germany to America in three
weeks—fast enough to keep the yeast from losing its
strength en route. A second theory persuades us that a
brewer in Philadelphia, one Wagner, had brought
some of this yeast with him from a brewery in Bavaria
where he had been brewmaster and that he introduced
the old-country arts and techniques into our country in
this way. It was not much of a start. Wagner had a very
primitive little plant on St. John Street in 1840, and his
brewery had a capacity of eight barrels, hardly production enough to start a brewing revolution. But apparently it did. Perhaps it was the yeast that branched
out, which is the very nature of yeast, when various
employees of the Wagner plant branched out for themselves, and then their employees branched out again,
and the yeast multiplied for all.

The story of Wagner was a microcosm of what soon
began to take place on a larger scale. The German en-
gulfment of the brewing industry was technically
due to their proficiency but sociologically due to the
great tide of German immigration that swept to
American shores in the 19th Century.

The earliest Germans had come for religious freedom. The later Germans often came to the land of
golden opportunity to improve their lot financially,
and still others felt they could improve their lives by
placing as great a distance as possible between themselves and the draft, compulsory for all citizens, into

the German army. After the 1848 uprisings many left
Germany for social or political reasons.

GERMAN COLONIES IN THE UNITED STATES

The English-oriented communities of the Eastern
seaboard were not particularly hospitable to the suc-
cessive waves of Irish, Jews and other nationalities, the
general keynote of their attitude being taken from the
nobly intended words on the Statue of Liberty that refer to the immigrant as the "wretched refuse" of his
homeland.

Quite naturally the newcomer's response was to
hole up in pockets of self-protection where he
nostalgically clung to the habits of his former life. The
Germans followed this tendency all over the country.
A "Germantown" sprang up in Braintree, and there
was one in Philadelphia. Brooklyn had its
"Dutchtown," and Cincinnati its own district called
"Over The Rhine." In Chicago it was "The Dutch
Settlement." So many German immigrants had
settled in Ohio by 1817 that the State Constitution and
part of the General Laws had to be printed in a
German version. Even before the State of Texas came
into being, Germans settled in San Antonio in 1844
under the leadership and idealistic patronage of Carl,
Prince of Solms-Braunfels, a cousin of Queen
Victoria. The Prince returned to Germany but his
people stayed, and it is reported that by 1856 almost
a third of San Antonio's citizens were German-born,
drawn to the far-flung community and ready to brew
their lager brew there; they even published a
German-language newspaper, *Freie Presse*. In St.
Louis, perhaps drawn by the caves and the water (in
those years a brewery was limited by the size of the
storage caves, and St. Louis had plenty of them),
brewer Adam Lemp made his appearance in 1838 and
introduced the first *lager beir* in the West. There, too,
was a German-language newspaper, the *Mississippi
Handels-Zeitung*.

And where there were Germans and lager beer,
there were the delightful beer gardens. Each was a
community gathering place, scene of wedding re-

ceptions, club meetings, political gatherings and other neighborhood social events. They were usually immense buildings fitted out in imitation of a garden, often with a capacity of over a thousand guests. It was a homey kind of place, the music lilting and good, a touch of nostalgia for the old country ever present. Not far away there inevitably would be the *Turnvereine*, or gymnastic club; and then nearby the Singing Society for male, female and mixed voices. (This Teutonic predilection for muscle and music was never outgrown. Parallel bars and 3/4 bars continue on today in many of the same German-oriented communities that have become an integral part of the larger community in so many other ways.)

What had happened was that brewing now belonged to the whole world in the 19th Century. From the beginning brewing had been a batch process, as it still is, but there was growing on all sides of the ancient craft scientific methods that were to modernize its packaging and establish certain controls that ultimately led to a standard product of outstanding quality.

Joseph Priestley's theories on oxygen, the life-essential of air, were formed while he was actually observing bubbles rising to the surface of a vat of beer in an English brewery. Two other renowned nationals, Lavoisier and Scheele, were brewery workers who transformed their working curiosity into scientific discovery. Magdeburg's theories of air pressure evolved from his experience as a brewmaster. Sorensen, who developed the pH scale of hydrogen ion activity, and Kjeldahl, famed for his work on nitrogen, linked observations in the brewery with those in the laboratory.

Behind the scenes science was providing an important answer to a traditional problem of the brewing industry as refrigeration became a fact rather than a hope. Brewers found that controlled temperature techniques enabled them to turn out a stable beverage. But perhaps the most glittering contribution of all was made by the great French scientist, Louis Pasteur, with his *Studies on Beer*, published in 1876. His observations led to present-day food processing in all kinds of categories, and his theory of applying heat to achieve a biological stabilization of a given product—to be called forever thereafter "pasteurization"—laid the foundations of beer that could be stored without the dangers of organic action taking place after it had been fully brewed and was ready in all its glowing perfection for the table of the consumer.

There is the wry supposition that Pasteur was influenced perhaps more by patriotism than by philanthropy in turning directly to the study of beer to apply his theories; it has been said that he was motivated chiefly by a desire to make the French beer at least as good as the German, following the Franco-Prussian debacle on the battlefield that proved Teutons were very much the masters in the arts of war.

But the result was far more noble than the motive. As Alexander Dumas said to Pasteur before the Academy of Sciences: "You have discovered a Third Kingdom—the kingdom to which those organisms belong which, with all the prerogatives of animal life, do not require air for their existence, and which find the heat that is necessary for them in the chemical compositions which they set up around them." He was describing the "mystery" of yeast fermentation.

After Pasteur came Emil Christian Hansen, a Danish scientist who worked in Copenhagen in laboratories established again by a brewer. He showed that "wild" yeasts can contaminate the kind of "pure" yeast most needed by the brewer, destroying carefully guarded flavor. His discoveries gave brewers the means of conducting a controlled type of fermentation, giving to the beer predictable characters of taste, aroma and body. Fermentation became for the first time an expert manipulation, and although the mystery still lingered, it was now a process that could be handled.

When one considers the close affinity between these gigantic minds of science and the laboratory of the brewery—especially in the test laboratories set up on the premises to examine the theoretical possibilities—it might be judged that more harm than good was about to be dealt mankind by an emerging social philosophy presented at that time as "beneficial and necessary." I refer, of course, to an idea called "prohibition," which in time spelled the doom of the brewing industry for more than a decade and simultaneously put a temporary end to the partnership of the brewing industry and pure science.

The events that led up to prohibition in the United States—the controversies, the debates—if fully explored here, would fill many times the space available in this relatively slender volume. Thus for the serious student of the era we can only recommend the study of one or more of the many references available on the subject. To mention just a few: Fisher's *Prohibition at its Worst*; McBain's *Prohibition: Legal and Illegal*; *Temperance or Prohibition* by Tresort; *Prohibition in America* by Newsholme; Krout's *The Origins of Prohibition*; and Colvin's *Prohibition in the U.S.: A History of the Prohibition Party and of the Prohibition Movement.*

Suffice it to say that the 18th Amendment to the Constitution, ratified on January 16, 1919, and effective one year thereafter, lowered the boom on the alcoholic-beverage industry for a long, dry spell.

Thus began the crime-ridden era of "The Noble Experiment." The nation, plagued by underworld violence spawned by illegal bootlegging gains, lost billions in tax revenues and in the costs of a vain enforcement of an unworkable law. Today's historians can possibly trace the origins of much of our current organized crime to the Prohibition Period.

Brewers had to live through 13 long, lean years by producing near beer, soft drinks and even—as did Falstaff—by curing hams and bacon. It was a struggle, and many of them fell by the wayside.

AFTER REPEAL

But on the cool, clear night of April 7, 1933, legislated prohibition came to an end and beer was back. It was back—but in order to avoid past excesses, federal

and state legislatures played it safe with the voters by
imposing regulations on beer-processing require-
ments, on the alcoholic content of beer, on the types
and sizes of packages; they determined where alcoholic beverages could be made, sold and consumed;
the hours and conditions of sale; terms of labeling
and advertising; and permissible real estate.

Thus harnessed, the brewers did not have an immediate new lease on life. Granted, those who clung to
their plants were besieged on April 7th with
gargantuan orders they could not possibly fill. The
trucks rolling out of the breweries with the goods
were, in many instances, guarded by police riding
alongside to protect the product from a thirsty
populace.

Then, as beer became more plentiful, the habits of
the consuming public began to change and there
was no going back now to the heyday of the saloon. At
first, in 1934, 75 per cent of the beer sold was in draught
form. But by 1937, 44 per cent of all beer sold was in
bottles, and the first can appeared in 1935.

The full story of the complete revolution in drinking habits brought about in the years following is explored in greater detail later in this book, because for
those who really revel in the romance of pure fact, the
analysis of who drinks what, how much, where and in

what form is an intriguing study.

This opening glance at the pageant of the golden brew over the span of its existence—span? the history of mankind to date!—reveals its glory, its touches of absolute mania, the unconscious humor and the conscious search for the perfect beer. It has been possible only to skip along on the peaks, trying to catch the high points that make some sense out of the valleys. For me, the great moments took place in the warmth and companionability of ancient and storied taverns. I have captured some of that, I hope, in the next chapter, because I could not bear to pass by the hum of conversation therein, the sound of oaths and the bursts of laughter, and the great eloquence of thoughts and dreams unspoken.

Chapter Four

THERE IS A TAVERN IN THE TOWN

Landlord, fill the flowing howl,
until it doth run over,
for tonight we'll merry be,
tomorrow we'll be sober.   18 Century Song

There's a touch of true magic in the word tavern. Let's go to a bar?—well, maybe. Let's go to a tavern? You can't say no.

The place is snug, the atmosphere and the decor masculine. The talk is small, but the dreams are big. The bartender's hands are busy, but the hands on the clock momentarily stand still. There is an unspoken fraternity to the place. A man may down his drink with a chuckle or a roar or a sigh, but that's his business and his alone.

Said Dr. Samuel Johnson, who was seldom wrong, and if he were, would find a way of not admitting it:

> There is nothing which has yet been contrived by man, by which so much happiness is produced, as by a good tavern or inn. There is no private house at which people can enjoy themselves so well as in a capital tavern. Let there be ever so great plenty of good things, ever so much grandeur, ever so much elegance, and ever so much desire that everybody should be easy, in the nature of things it cannot be; there must always be some degree of care and anxiety. The master of the house is anxious to entertain his guests, the guests are anxious to be agreeable to him, and no man but a very impudent dog indeed can as freely command what is in another man's house as if it were

his own; whereas, at a tavern there is a
general freedom from anxiety. You are sure
you are welcome, and the more noise you
make, the more trouble you give, the more
good things you call for, the welcomer you
are. No servant will attend you with the
alacrity which waiters do who are incited by
the prospect of an immediate reward in
proportion as they please.

A relaxed picture indeed.

The aristocracy of ancient Egypt gathered in com-
munal drinking places over 3,000 years ago and asked
each other the riddle of the Sphinx or read the
morning papyrus over a glass of their Hek. Socrates
met with his fellow Greek intellectuals in Athenian
taverns to discuss philosophy, although it is an
eternal loss to the world that he switched from drinking pimos to hemlock.

The Romans and Persians were partial to taverns and
set up hostelries along the byways that crisscrossed
their empires. The forerunner of the tavern as we
know it, however, was an import from the Middle
East. During the time of the Crusades some 800 years
ago, thousands traveled to and from the Holy Land
every year, and it must be confessed that the cultural
impact of these pilgrimages was not so much a giving
as a taking. The Crusaders, both armed and peace-
ful, thought of the Saracens as infidels although they
could not help but admire their splendid trappings,
their works of art, and their seductive women; and the
crude Westerners took mental note of much of this
and brought it back to imbed into their own culture,
which lacked such civilizing sophistries at that time as
the Easterners had achieved centuries before. The
concept of the "inn" was one of the ideas brought back
from the East, where conversation and the gentle art
of wasting time profitably has long been brought to a
point of perfection.

ENGLISH STREETS OF RED LATTICES

The English, being English, set out to improve the

Saracen tavern. And it must be confessed that they succeeded. The tavern of Elizabethan days, and for about two hundred years thereafter in England, was the source spring of much of her greatness, for it was in taverns that her most illustrious sons chose to gather.

What a place the Falcon Tavern must have been, by the Bankside in London, when Will Shakespeare, rare Ben Jonson, Kit Marlowe (he was killed in a tavern brawl while just a youth, and many thought he could have gone on to outdo the Bard of Avon had he lived), Ford, Beaumont, Fletcher, Drayton and Herrick met there to exchange shafts of wit! They would all sit back and listen, though, when Jonson and Shakespeare crossed words—for those two were the champs. One who was there, Fuller, says it was like the clash of a great Spanish galleon and a British man-of-war. "Master Jonson, like the former, was built far higher in learning; solid but slow in his performances. Shakespeare, like the English man-of-war, lesser in bulk but lighter in sailing, could turn with all tides, talk about and take advantage of all winds by the quickness of his wit and invention." What a stage, that tavern, where the greatest playwright of all time improvised his lines over a glass of ale!

The Mermaid Tavern, over on Bread Street, is far better known today as one of Will's haunts. It was there, according to Beaumont, that the talk ran into the clouds:

—What things have we seen
Done at the Mermaid! heard words that have been
So nimble and so full of subtle flame,
As if that everyone from whence they came
Had meant to put his whole wit in a jest,
And had resolved to live a fool the
rest of his dull life . . . .

Well, I for one believe it. Sir Walter Raleigh, back from buccaneering over the seven seas, established a club at the Mermaid in 1603. Will Shakespeare was a member, of course, and Ben Jonson and the others, and now we add the name of John Donne, the cleric

who wrote some of the most passionately erotic poems in the English language. The man who invented the tape-recorder, dammit, was only 350 years too late—think of what Walter and Bill and Ben and John would talk about when their hair was down. Worlds of conquest, worlds of men, worlds of love!

The Boar's Head, near "London stone," was another playground of Will Shakespeare's, and of course he made it immortal by making it the scene of the wild pranks of Prince Hal and "honest Jack Falstaff" in several of his plays. The tavern actually lasted until 1831, when "progress"—as we always seem to term it when we are tearing down some irreplaceable landmark to make way for a shopping center—doomed it to be razed to make way for the approaches of London Bridge. Now the bridge itself is falling down and is being shipped to an American park as a curiosity. Could the Boar's Head have been preserved, we might have been able to purchase from the British not a curiosity, but a shrine. Ah, well.

Such taverns came in time to be recognized by their red lattices. The windows were left open so the drinkers within could peep out and get some fresh air, but lattices and trellises were put up to somewhat shield the customers from prying eyes.

We can see how well the Lord Mayor made out when we read a report made in 1632: "A whole street is in some places but a continuous alehouse, not a shop to be seen between red lattice and red lattice." At about that time, by the way, the innkeeper was known as an "ale draper." I have no way of telling what a female innkeeper was, other than a hostess, but I can tell of the demise of one, Ann Collins, as reported on her epitaph in Gloucestershire:

> *Twas as she tript from cask to cask,*
> *In at a bung-hole quickly fell,*
> *Suffocation was her task,*
> *She had no time to say farewell.*

The political role of the taverns carried over to the British colonies in America, and the whole atmosphere and presence of the tavern is closely interwoven with our Revolutionary period.

The very first American tavern is generally acknowledged to have been The Blue Anchor, obviously a safe haven for seafaring men, which opened its hatches in Philadelphia early in the 1600s.

Sam Adams, often called the father of our Revolution, was himself a brewer, and so was his father before him. The man who became Governor Chittendon of Vermont was originally a brewer. He was among the Green Mountain Boys, led by the Allen brothers, Ethan and Ira, who frequented the Catamount Tavern in Bennington, Vermont. It was Ethan who carried a barrel of beer on his back up Mt. Washington in order to have proper refreshment on hand when he reached the summit. And it was he who threw in the lot of the Green Mountain Boys with the American army after the news came through from Lexington that the British had fired upon colonials in a stand-up confrontation. He later was to capture Fort Ticonderoga for the rebels, and history books have staunchly declared ever since that he pounded on the entrance to the fort with his fist and called upon the commandant to deliver the fort "in the name of the great Jehovah and the Continental Congress." Actually,

according to those who were there, the British officer
appeared in his nightshirt, vastly perturbed at the
noise, with his mistress, also in disarray, at his elbow. Because what Ethan had thundered out into the
night was: "Come on out of there, you British sons of
bitches!" And while the Redcoats might be willing to
admit that there were a lot of people who thought of
them in that way, they weren't quite sure who *these*
guys were.

The U.S. Marine Corps, by tradition filled with le-
gions of Ethan Allen types, had its own beginnings in a
tavern, The Tavern of the Tun, in Philadelphia in 1775.
Back in New York City, George Washington made his
headquarters at Fraunces Tavern, and it still stands
there in the heart of the financial district, and a
mighty good tavern yet. And in the Indian Queen
Tavern, again back in Philly, a man sat, beer in hand
(for, like Washington, he loved the brew), poring over
a paper he had been writing for some time. At length
satisfied, he unknit his brow, smiled, folded up the
paper—and then Thomas Jefferson walked out of the
tavern with the very first draft of the Declaration of
Independence in his pocket.

Such taverns were a wonderfully colorful lot. And
they were one of the most important units in the colonial community, as it turned out.

They had humble beginnings. At first the tavern
might be no more than a lean-to, put up to accommodate travelers passing through a huddle of
cabins nestled in a hacked-out clearing. But then trails
turned into primitive roads, boats appeared on the
rivers and the towns grew larger; the tavern turned into a cabin and then into something more pretentious.
You found them at crossroads, at rope-ferry river
crossings such as the one in Bethlehem, Pennsylvania,
called "The Tavern Over Ye Water." It had been first
erected because the citizens of Bethlehem, being of
the Moravian faith, were not too keen on taking into
their homes strangers who might not respect their
religion or their Moravian ways of life, or, on the other
hand, who should not be compelled to join in. So the
inn flourished for many years on this basis.

A TYPICAL COLONIAL TAVERN

The tavern is worth our affectionate inspection. It was usually built on the style of a private home, with living rooms downstairs and bedrooms above for an overnight stay. As one approached it on the Common, horses were tethered outside, cows grazed about the door, and turkeys, pigeons and chickens roosted on the roof and windows—advertisements of succulent roasts to come. A bench was left outside, next to the door, for thinkers and those who chose to drink in the great outdoors.

Inside, the tavern was hospitable, warm and inviting, both physically and spiritually. The fire room, or main room, was as big as possible, and it was the place that drew the guests immediately. There were racks for their guns, drawers for tobacco, and tongs with which to extract a coal from the roaring fire to light a pipe. Tallow candles flickered close to the walls, their light thrown out by metal reflectors and just strong enough to cast shadows on the great beams of the low ceiling overhead, softened and mellowed by the smoke of many happy evenings. Chairs, chests, benches and stools were scattered about indiscriminately, because this place was intended for many. The flooring was of wide boards, meticulously scrubbed and covered with sand or brookside rushes, or—if the landlord were lucky and had a couple of gifted daughters—with hooked and braided rugs.

The taproom was close by, where the serious drinking took place. There was a combined storeroom and bar, guarded by a portcullis that could be lowered in case the over-thirsty or the light-fingered came too close. There was a roaring fire here, too, and one viewed by its light the liquid treasures in mugs, kegs, barrels and bottles, awaiting the options of the patrons. In one corner was a tall desk where a guest could write a letter if he chose. It also served as the landlord's office. His tallies he kept on the wall, and they were not erased until settlement.*

On the walls of the taproom were notices of coming events: sales, jamborees, auctions and the arrival of peddlers with mysterious things from other worlds.

This was the heart of the colonist's world. Here he exchanged gossip, learned the news of the next town (either from the landlord or someone passing through), argued politics or merely exchanged small greetings with neighbors who worked too hard to visit each other during the week.

---

*Two nice little permanent additions to our language derive from this tavern scene. The first is "minding your P's and Q's." A landlord who failed to tally up the Pints and Quarts downed by his customers (who couldn't care less what their total count was) often found himself short of the moneys coming to him. The second word is "tip," a little something extra for the waiter. In early days one of the accessories of the great room of every tavern was a small box nailed to the wall. At the top was a small opening into which the customers were encouraged to drop money, and on the face of this box was the legend, "To Insure Promptness." The servants of the house would customarily take the money from the box from time to time and divide it among themselves. If a certain guest was giving the money box the go-by, the tavern servant often would give him a gentle reminder of his obligations by whispering the first letters to him—"T . . . I . . . P." The box thus became known as the tip box, and later as a tip. And when the box disappeared in time and was replaced by the outstretched palm, the word lingered on. And so we hand our waiter a tip.

FOOD AND DRINK OF EARLY TAVERNS

And they enjoyed themselves. There was music for a song, perhaps helped along with a creaky fiddle. And to eat, in addition to beefsteak, veal, mutton and bacon, there was wild turkey, bearsteak, venison, squirrel, partridge, quail, plover, snipe, wild pigeon; and if supplies ran short by any chance, a stroll into the woods behind the clearing, gun in hand, would restock the larder. There was shrimp in beer, baked beans and molasses flavored in beer, pilgrim's syrup (beer and brown sugar made into a syrup) to pour over flapjacks, and hot gingerbread, johnnycake, corn pone, and rye and Injun bread. That, good friends, was a day of mighty trenchermen.

And the drinks!

A traveler in Philadelphia recorded in his diary that as a part of the normal hospitality extended to him, he had cider and strong punch (punch was as good as its word, being a mixture of rum, brandy, wine, fruit and other enticements) with his lunch; rum and brandy before dinner; punch, sweet wine, port and sherry at dinner; after which the serious drinking took place, and he downed—from punchbowls big enough for six ducks to swim in—quantities of beer, rum, whiskey and punch until he went to bed.

Gentlefolk were no less thirsty. Water was considered just an invitation to dysentery or worse, and so the answer was almost always in the beer mug or the punchbowl. They used great ingenuity in mixing their drinks. "Calibogus" was basic: cold rum and beer. "Whistle-Belly-Vengeance" was not only the best named but the most nourishing of all—a full measure of beer with crusts of brown bread (rye-and-Injun) crumbled in and the whole sweetened with molasses. There was always a bowl of hot punch, with everything in it, over there in the fire room, smoking away and ready for everyone to dip into. Filled cider mugs stood in a ring around the fireplace, warming up for drinks to come. "Marrathan" was beer with rum and sugar added, and "Tiff" was the same, except that buttered toast steeped in it. (Some of the colonists enjoyed coffee made with beer rather than water, although coffee was hard to come by in those days as a rule.)

But a "Flip" was the big colonial drink. Try one to-day, if you wish, made thisaway:

> *Into two quarts of beer pour a half-pint of gin. Beat four eggs together with four ounces of sifted sugar. Then stir, little by little, the beer and gin together. Then froth by pouring from one large pitcher to another, and serve in thin glasses, with fresh-grated nutmeg on top.*

If you would like to go the whole way, try the colonial loggerhead trick. A loggerhead was a small iron poker hung by the fire, but intended for mixing drinks, not for stirring the fire. With the flip finished, for example, you thrust the loggerhead into the flames until red hot and then thrust it into the drink. There is a moiling and a broiling, while beer, egg and all acquire a slightly burnt, bitter taste that only adds zest to the drink for a man who knows what he likes. You'll recognize from the word "loggerhead" what frequently happened in the fire room, too. A standard flip glass in colonial days held from three to four quarts. Also, it was standard to brace up a flip such as I have described with a couple of sloshes of rum, added at the very end. Thus a man who was tolerably favorable toward his drink of flip might have another, and another, and he might get a little smashed, too, in the end. A roomful of such topers was often "at loggerheads," as the saying now goes. I leave it to you to imagine a bunch of brawny woodsmen and Indian fighters with their flip glasses in one hand, brandishing red-hot loggerheads at each other with the other.

"Rumfustian" was another good beer drink. It consisted of a quart of the brew, a bottle of white wine or sherry, half a pint of gin, the yolks of 12 eggs, orange peel, nutmeg, spices and sugar. Again, when strong hearts were present, another half-pint of rum might be added as a sweetener.

The beer, you will weep to hear, was a cent a quart.

THE INNKEEPER AS A PERSONALITY

The boss of this meeting place, not unexpectedly, was no pinched-faced, skulking, by-your-leave trades-man and would not take any guff from his visitors. He usually was a man of strength and also a man of other substance. The court saw to that before he was licensed and often tempted him with offers of free land, free pasturage or even tax exemptions (how it must have pained them!) when they found the right man for the job.

Even his domain was akin to that of a courthouse. By general custom, for example, an agreement or business contract was binding irrevocably and there was no getting out of it if the deal were closed in town meeting, in a court of law or at the tavern. Sometimes it was all much the same thing. The tavern was often used as a prison. And the Court of General Sessions was held there four times a year. The landlord was very much a part of all this, since he could well be in his own person simultaneously the Collector of Taxes, Selectman, Justice of the Peace, Roadmaster, Sunday Constable, Town Moderator, Recruiting Officer for the Militia (to whom he sold guns and uniforms on the side) and general keeper of the peace. John Adams himself described a typical landlord, this paragon, the host at the Ipswich Inn, as follows:

Landlord and landlady are some of the grandest people alive, landlady is the great-grand-daughter of Governor Endicott and has all the notions of high family that you find in the Winslows, Hutchinsons, Quincys, Saltonstalls, Chandlers, Otises, Learneds, and as you might find with more propriety in the Winthrops. As to landlord, he is as hap-py and as big, as proud, as conceited, as any nobleman in England, always calm and good-natured and lazy, but the contemplation of his sons, his house and pasture and cows, his sound judgment as he thinks, and his great holiness as well as that of his wife, keep him as erect in his thoughts as a noble or a prince.

But all was not feasting, drinking, gaming and affairs of state at the tavern. It was also a meeting ground for enjoyments of every variety. Two-legged cows and six-legged heifers might be brought in from the countryside for other farmers to gape at. A real lion once went the rounds, having by some exhaustive miracle been brought all the way from Africa, as did a polar bear from Greenland. There were bull fights and dog fights and man fights out on the Common Green, and footraces, and courting under the trees.

And before and after, one and all repaired to the tavern. The Americans had outdone the British themselves at the naming of their inns: The Fox Chase Tavern, The Bunch of Grapes, The Beehive, The Moon and Seven Stars, The Man Full of Trouble, The Hard Times Inn, The Battle of the Kegs. There was a nice sense of open country to their names, as well as a touch of philosophy.

LIBERTY AND THE TAVERN

They were to need it, because the British found the colonists far too gruffy to be proper servants of His Majesty the King. And the colonists found the British far too huffy to tolerate as overlords.

As early as 1768 the Sons of Liberty were holding their meetings at public taverns; Captain Olney of Providence dedicated a great elm next to his tavern—with brazen courage for it could be a hanging offense—as The Liberty Tree. It was so large that a platform had been built in the branches which could accomodate ten or twelve people who might choose to drink up there in the shade. This tree started a country-wide fashion in the colonies which sent George III spinning on his throne—and eventually off of it—as every town designated its special Liberty tree or even a pole, where the men would meet, have a drink, and talk against the old country, with toasts to the liberty they meant to fight for. Now each tavern had its meetings of the Committees of Safety. The Councils of War were deliberating the questions of the conflict to come. Recruiting officers had their headquarters in the tap rooms for the new army. The town weapons and stocks of ammunition were secreted in the tavern chambers.

The Green Dragon Inn, on Union Street in Boston, was called the headquarters of the Revolution by Daniel Webster. It was used as a hospital during the war. One of its main functions during the conflicts with the British is described by Paul Revere:

> "In the fall of 1774 and winter of 1775, I was one of upwards of thirty men, chiefly mechanics, who formed ourselves with a Committee for the purpose of watching the movements of the British soldiers and gaining every intelligence of the movements of the Tories. We held our meetings at the Green Dragon Tavern. This committee were astonished to find all their secrets known to General Gage, although every time they met every member swore not to reveal their transactions even to Hancock, Adams, Otis, Warren or Church."

What it all came down to in the end is something I have dubbed—alone among historians, but with proper respect for all the combatants—The Battle Of The Taverns.

On the 18th of April, a good man on a horse, such as Paul Revere, could have gone the rounds and found the answers to what the morrow was to bring—"the shot heard 'round the world" at Lexington—simply by visiting the taverns in the area. At Weatherby's "Black Horse" over in Winchester, John Hancock and Sam Adams were meeting until midnight with other members of the Committee of Safety and Supplies—translation, Safety for the colonists from British arrest and Supplies to shoot at the Redcoats. At the Wright Tavern in Concord, Major Pitcairn, the British Commander, sat in the parlor and swore he would stir the rebel's blood as he now did stir his glass of brandy with his finger. Over at the Monroe Tavern in Lexington, Lord Percy awaited the crushing of the revolt, although the British attempt to catch the Committee over at the Black Horse had failed when the Americans hid in a field behind the tavern. Just a few steps away from Milord stood the Buckman Tavern, and there the Minute Men were rallying.

The famous Green Dragon Tavern was then kept by

one Lieutenant Joseph Winn. On the morning of April
19, 1775, he could stand dispensing drinks no more. At
two in the morning he took off his apron, grabbed his
musket, took a last haul at his beer and answered Paul
Revere's alarm to "every Middlesex village and farm"
by hot-footing it over to Lexington to join the farmers
who were to stand there against the Redcoats. He
stood up with them and then returned that night to the
tavern. But not to stay. When the British marched up
Bunker Hill and the Americans were holding their fire
until they could see the whites of their enemies' eyes,
Lieutenant Winn was there, too, ready with finger on
the trigger.

The salad days of the old-time tavern were to last for
another 50 years or so after '76. By then the French
Revolution had introduced into their own taverns the
practice of "perpendicular drinking" as opposed to
sitting at a table, and it caught on throughout Europe
and America, so that we still have the stand-up bar as
well as a place to sprawl in next to a table. But the great
statesmen and patriots were gone now, quartered at
the more luxurious places called "hotels" that were
springing up all over the East as our lamented urban
sprawl commenced even then to put an end to the
rural nature of our nation, and the taverns moved West
with the covered wagons.

THE TAVERN TODAY

Today, if one is very, very lucky, he may find one of
the old taverns still standing staunch, none of the old
glamour gone. If you have this chance, please do not
hurry along. Linger by and let your mind play over
some of the glorious past these old timbers have seen,
some of the laughter and silences that filled these
ancient spaces. Or perhaps you would like to stop by
one of the restorations, where the tradition visibly
lives on but the air conditioning still manages to put in
a good word for today.

What has actually happened, however, is that the
tavern has adapted to the changing society of each generation. We have our own contemporary versions,
quite as valuable to our own life style as they once

were to that of the colonists.

It was not so very long ago that the tavern was the place to go simply to see TV in a congenial atmosphere; the tavern keepers were alert to realize the attraction offered by The Big Game or a special broadcast. For a period during the '40s they were far ahead of the general public in ownership of the magic box. The figure of the bartender, so long ensconced in his semi-regal privilege behind the mahogany, rose above all as now and then he would mount ladder or stool to make his expert adjustments on wildly shuttering off-tackle runs or upon a speaker's face suddenly assuming the dimensions of a watermelon.

The modern tavern has taken on its own delightful variations. There is the motel tavern, for instance. In a remarkable number of places, even those quite remote, the grand old spirit of the original taproom has often been given the loving attention of builder and decorator, and the result is a restful haven and retreat for the tired traveler in the Olde English or colonial idiom of its progenitor. Many of our proudest urban hotels are known for their handsome so-and-so rooms that are in reality no more than that beloved old spot next to the village Common where the ale flip flowed as free and easy as the conversation.

Then, of course, there is no city too large or hamlet too small not to rejoice in one or more neighborhood taverns that are not far in spirit from The Mermaid. There modern poets and dreamers gather, and the wit—let us say here and now—cannot be any the less barbed and inspired than that of yore. This is a kind of unnamed club for the man of today, a place where he can stop by now and again, see the same faces once in a while, make his special needs known to the host and bartender, and feel that here is a comfortable extension of his very own home.

But even more deserving of a salute than the grand old institution is the man who has fostered it through all these centuries—your host. More than likely he is host and bartender in one, for the skill of the man behind the bar, not to mention his character and personality, is often the very keynote of the entire place.

He is confidante and psychologist in one; defender of the weak and peer of the strong; a listener of infinite patience; and when opportunity offers, a conversationalist of ringing eloquence. The very motion of his hands and measured eye—sure, decisive and muscular—often serves as a show in itself for the sedentary types on the other side of the bar who admire a man of action, especially when they see one bent on such a saving errand.

Hail the tavern keepers, Sir, as members of a great and enduring calling. The man who serves you today is the keeper of a faith, an ally who continues to uphold one of the greatest unsung institutions of mankind.

A Photographic Gallery
of Steins from the
Falstaff International
Museum of Brewing
in Saint Louis

These German character steins are crafted in porcelain, and all were produced in the early 1900's.

1 The green-eyed devil is from the E. Bohne Pottery Works in Rudolstadt, Thuringia (now East Germany).

2 The alligator is believed to have been made in the same plant, due to similarities in material and painting technique.

3 The representation of Prince Otto von Bismarck-Schonhausen, First Chancellor of the German Empire, is of unknown origin.

Pages 74-75

All of German origin, these steins are:

4 An earthenware vessel dating from the mid-1930's. A Third Reich representation of the traditional military commemorative cup, it is inscribed, "Non-Commissioned Officers Corps, Headquarters Company, Armored Force School, Wunsdorf." The pewter lid is crowned with a replica of an army helmet.

5 A porcelain stein of the early 1900's, bearing a handsome transfer print on its face, and a lithopane in the base.

6 Model #1956, by Villeroy and Boch, Mettlach. It bears the cameo representation of a man's head across the eagle's breast, and the rim of the pewter lid is inscribed, "Sunday Bowler's Club—1891."

7 Produced in the late 1800's, this lidless stein is Bavarian in origin, and depicts a noble family in excellent colored miniature portraits.

Pages 76-77

8 Porcelain stein of the late 1700's, produced in Meissen and decorated in the style of Watteau.

9 Stoneware pitcher, Mettlach #2369. Dated 1908, this vessel depicts a scene in Munich.

10 This elaborately styled Mettlach stoneware beaker, #168, was produced in 1911. Standing 16 inches high, it bears relief figures depicting the ascent of man.

11 Stoneware pitcher, fabricated in the Westerwald area of Germany in the early 1800's.

12 Mettlach stoneware stein #2093 is dated 1902. The playing card motif on the sides is repeated in an inlay in the pewter lid.

Page 78

13 Mettlach #1526 depicts a jovial Sir John Falstaff quaffing his brew from a *tranken stiefel*, or drinking boot. Of heroic proportions, this vessel holds slightly more than three quarts.

14 Mettlach #2755 is in the Wedgewood style with bas relief cameo figures and was produced in 1903. These figures were carved from thin white clay, and then applied to the body of the stein and fired.

15 This handsome hunting stein is fashioned of porcelain, and bears a hand-painted scene depicting a stag drinking from a stream. The hunting hound on the lid is carved from the horn of a roebuck, as is the thumb lift.

Page 79

16 This pewter stein was produced in Nurnberg in the early 1900's. The body, cast in five parts, depicts a 17th Century drinking garden.

17 Porcelain regimental stein with pewter lid in shape of cannon shell. Top portion twists off to reveal a drawing of the town of Hammelburg under a glass reflector.

18 Hand painted porcelain regimental stein is proud reminder of the military service of Rifleman Schmidt, 4th Company, 74th Hanoverian Infantry Regiment from 1900-1902.

19 Mettlach #1786 dates to 1897. Detail on body shows St. Florian extinguishing flames of burning city, and handle is fashioned in the form of a dragon.

Page 80

20 Dating from the late 1700's, this cobalt blue glass stein with gold leaf design is believed to be of North German origin.

21 Delicate glass stein with unusual glass domed lid is of the style created by Eugen Cremer of Cologne.

22 Sterling silver tankard by Tiffany & Co. is a reproduction of the original by Samuel Vernon of Newport, R.I., which is on display in the Metropolitan Museum of Art.

4

5

6

7

8

9

11   12

20

21

22

Chapter Five

FROM CUP TO LIP

He who drinks strong ale,
Goes to bed mellow,
Lives as he ought to live,
And dies a jolly good fellow.
(Old Song)

Man was created thirsty. And being thirsty, he drank. No doubt very much in the simple way we ourselves—if we are fortunate enough to create an episode in our lives that involves an encounter with pure running water in the natural state—go about it, either by drinking directly from the surface or by using our hands as a scoop or cup.

Diogenes himself, at the height of the Greek civilization of some 500 years B.C., which prized its drinking vessels of metal and even glass, threw away his cup and drank out of the hollow of his hand in return to the simplicity we often yearn for ourselves today.

In the beginning, of course, the drinking cup was natural and not man-made. A savage might use a broad leaf as a plate, a gourd as a bowl and if the climate permitted, a halved coconut shell as a cup. Even today in tropical climates, the gourd, the coconut and the calabash are prime rivals of the manufactured drinking vessel.

Probably the tribal chief, who merited a cup more than the others, started a trend toward something more refined in drinking vessels. There was the stone, worn away to form a cup and ornamented with his special symbolic devices. There was the clay, found near the river beds, that lent itself into shaping and then hardening in the rays of the sun.

With the discovery of what fire could do, man learned how to bake pottery until it was almost as hard as stone itself, and then he took to its decoration and shaping on the potter's wheel. At almost the same time, the Greeks, Romans, Assyrians and Egyptians were developing pottery into a fine art, while half a world away the Mexicans and the Peruvians were doing the same in their own idiom of aesthetics.

History being somewhat beyond our present ability to control, it pains me to report that certain uncouth tribes—chiefly the Scythians, Tibetans and Danes—favored the skull of a fallen enemy as a drinking vessel. The fashion was abandoned before it could do any lasting harm to civilization, but it did provide us with the Norse word "skoal," which commemorates a rougher day with a word of more gracious connotation in our day, when it offers our wishes of good health to a companion.

EARLY DRINKING VESSELS

Among the earliest kinds of drinking vessels were those made of hides and skins. After all, an animal's skin serves chiefly to hold his liquids together, plus a few bones, and it doesn't take a Neanderthal genius to see that a small container, less the bones, would be a perfect drinking vessel. This device continued on to our time, when many wine vessels are merely bags of skin. Squeeze 'em and you have a drink.

A most interesting reference to the leather bottle is in the Bible. Christ, in one of His parables, speaks against the practice of putting new wine into old bottles. It is at first a somewhat puzzling bit of advice, until we realize that in the time of King James of England, when the Bible was first translated into English from the Latin based on the original tongues, the word "bottell" was understood to be a container made of leather. Christ originally advised against putting new wine into old leather vessels soaked by and redolent with many other fillings, and this was an easily understood figure of speech in His time. So it was in King James' time, but now when we read the word "bottle," we automatically tend to think of a glass bottle, and so the reference has lost its practical meaning to us over the passage of time.

Not that glass was unknown in Christ's day; it was

simply that it was not the usual container for liquids in that humble community. Actually, at least according to Pliny, it was on the coast of Palestine itself that glass was first discovered.

THE EGYPTIANS, AGAIN

Be that as it may, we know for certain that on the tombs of Beni-Hassan, which date from about 2,000 years before the Christian era, there are representations of Theban glassmakers. One is taking glass from a furnace; others are shown blowing a vase with blow-pipes. With such sophistication in glass manufacture growing into great centers in Egypt, such as Thebes, it is not surprising that when Augustus Caesar subdued Egypt just a few years before the start of the Christian era, he should take back the arts of glassmaking with him to Rome and demand tribute in glass as well as gold from the Egyptians. The Greeks, who also invaded Egypt when they were bored for a little excitement, exchanged cultures, too, and frequently even personnel—Ptolemy, who started an Egyptian dynasty, was originally just another officer on the staff of Alexander the Great and was left behind to govern Egypt when the Greek had tired of the southern climate.

A cut-off of the exquisite objects made by these nations came when the barbarians invaded the Roman and Hellenic countries, and the fine arts died in those countries as the forest took over.

In Western Europe, where civilization in Mediterranean terms had barely touched and Britons were still dyeing themselves blue and dancing around trees and worshipping their spirits while Socrates was contemplating the arts of government, the way of the drinking vessel proceeded more slowly. The move was from the skull to the stone and eventually to the fine woods and leathers of Olde England. We learn the following from Heywood's marvelously named book, *Philoxothonista or The Drunkard Opened, Dissected, and Anatomized (circa 1635)*:

> Of drinking cups, divers and sundry sorts we have, some of them elme, some of box, some of maple, some of holly, etc.; Mazers, broadmouthed Dishes, Noggins, Whiskins, Piggins, Crinzes, Ale-bowls, Wassal Bowls, Court dishes, Tankards, Kannes from a bottle to a pint, from a pint to a gill. Other bottles we have of leather, but they are mostly used amongst the shepheards and harvest people of the country; small Jacks we have in many ale-houses of the Citie and suburbs, tip't with silver, besides the great Black Jacks and Bombards at the Court, which when Frenchmen first saw, they reported, at their returne into their countrey, that Englishmen used to drink out of their bootes: We have besides, cups made out of horns of beasts, of cockernuts, of goords, of the eggs of ostriches; others made of the shells of divers fishes. Come to plate, every taverne can afford you flat bowles, prounet cups, beare bowles, beakers; and private householders in the citie, when they make a feast to entertain their friends, can furnish their cup boards with flagons, tankards, beare cups, wine bowles, some white, some purcell gilt, some gilt all over, some with covers, others without, of sundry shapes and qualities.

ENTER THE BRITISH

The British bottell was usually of tanned ox-hide, very thick and very heavy. It was somewhat like our Gladstone bag in shape, being a full skin doubled around and stitched together about two inches from the edge. Straps were passed through the outside edges, and the whole thing could thus be slung over the shoulder or tied to a man's belt, and he could carry his refreshment with him.

A bouget was another form of the bottell, but more sophisticated. It was two leather bags joined together by their necks, and of course you could carry two kinds of potables with this gadget—an excellent traveling companion for a man who likes his beer half-and-half.

The Black Jack, or just plain Jack, was a relative of the bottell. It was a leather jug, made somewhat on the same principle of doubling leather, sewing it around the edges to close it up, and then sewing a strong leather handle on the outside for grasping it. A heavy leather bottom in circular form was afterwards sewn in to give a round shape to the Jack. These were made for the heroic drinkers of Olde England and described even at that time to be of "imposing stature that quite dwarfs all rival pots."

The Black Jack was an especially British creation, one of those things that are particular to that blessed isle and not likely to catch on in the Continent, like roast beef and plum pudding. Perhaps it was because the British raised such good cattle. British grass, watered by the mists of the Atlantic and the cold Channel vaporings, is the best in the world, and Britain's cattle follow suit with such fodder to chomp on. Hence it follows that the British, in making a drinking mug from leather, made it from a hide that was not to be found on the Continent for toughness and heft. Perhaps that is why they were so proud of their Black Jacks. And so when they thought of the old brave days, they were given to the leather drinking mug.

The Bombards mentioned in the *Philoxothonista* were actually even huger Black Jacks than the usual gargantuan affair.

A "mazer," also mentioned in the *Philoxetc.*, was little more than a kind of shallow dish, but it was greatly popular in England from the early 13th Century on for drinking beer. Woodworkers were very proud of their mazers and made them mostly from bird's-eye maple, which is that part of the wood where the branches of the tree start and that has a rather attractive speckled grain (still favored by some for bedroom furniture). When the New World produced new species of hardwoods such as mahogany from the Indies and South America, they were quickly adapted for mazers, as was—for that matter—pewter, silver, pottery and glass. Many of the finer mazers had a silver band around the rim, and at the bottom of the bowl there was a circular medallion and an inscription, known as the "frounce" or the "founce," and sometimes as "the print." The Scotch called their mazer a "quaich" and made it with two or three handles for passing the same drink around to many; it was particularly popular as a family drinking vessel. It was the mazer that took off into giant size and became the traditional wassail bowl, from which our own punchbowl is derived.

The English also had a drinking cup called "treen," meaning simply that it was made from either walnut, pear, cherry, maple or beechwood trees. These were chalice-like in appearance and handily decorated with crests, initials and various ornamentations, many burned into the wood with a branding iron.

The Irish, meanwhile, were having at it with their "Maeddher," an oddly shaped vessel from which to drink mead. It was square in shape with a handle on each of the four sides, and four feet at the bottom were cut out of the solid wood from which the cup was fashioned. When one drank from it, he gulped from the angles of the corners, since there was not even an Irishman with a mouth large enough to catch his mead as it poured over the sides of the square cup.

These gigantic drinking mugs call to mind the realization that our ancestors were really never quite as uninformed as we often give them discredit for. Modern science has revealed that the taste buds for sweet things are situated at the front of the mouth and those created to most appreciate the bitter and tart flavors lie at the back of the cavity. Therefore, the best way to get the full flavor from a drink that is literally bursting with it, such as beer, and to quench your thirst in one grand gesture, is to toss the liquid into the back of your throat in one mighty throw.

MASTERWORKS IN VENETIAN GLASS

Meanwhile, back in the Mediterranean, where once a legendary Greek goblet had been fashioned to the exact curve of the divine breast of Helen of Troy, the creative urge could not be long stilled. The Venetian Republic gathered to its domain the finest artisans of the area and so efficiently contrived a glassmaking industry that around the 13th Century it was the only place in the world where glass was being manufactured; every foreign country was forced to apply to her for the precious stuff.

The Republic took care of its own, too. It severely punished those who would export the primary materials of which glass is made, or even broken glass—in other words, anything that might enable other countries to enter into competition with Venice in the least degree. In fact, the glassmakers were eventually confined to the island of Murano and virtually imprisoned there in order to preserve their art. If they had any ideas of being independent with their skills, the Venetian Council of Ten wrote out a statute calculated to quell such ambition:

> If a workman carries his art into a foreign country to the detriment of the Republic, an order to return will be sent to him.
>
> If he does not obey, his nearest relations will be put in prison.
>
> If in spite of the imprisonment of his relatives, he should persist in remaining abroad, an emissary will be charged to kill him.

That kind of thing made the men on the island real stay-at-homes. It was not bluff, either, on the part of the Council of Ten. The Emperor Leopold enticed a couple of Venetian workmen to Germany. The Council sent out a contract on them and the workmen were duly assassinated, we trust toward the finish of at least one glassblowing stint.

Of course in the end Leopold and the other rulers were not to be put off their pilfering, and the art of glassmaking spread to other parts of Europe. The Bohemians before long excelled in cut glass and beautifully engraved patterns of the most exquisite refinement. The Germans, who had beer on their minds, took a more practical stance and evolved a form of enormous drinking glass called the *wiederkommen*, which was always of an elongated cylindrical shape, usually of a greenish or yellow color. Some of them, it was remarked at the time, "if mounted on carriages, might be taken for cannons." But the truth of the matter probably lies in the name of the glass, since *wiederkommen* means "to come back." A *wiederkommen* containing several pints was presented to the host at the end of the feast, and after drinking from it, he passed it to his right-hand neighbor, who in his turn, after having sipped from it, presented it to the next person, and so on. Eventually, when all of the guests had drunk from the *wiederkommen*, it "came back" to the host, empty.

And then there is the *tranken stiefel*, or drinking boot (illustrated on the cover of this book), whose origin is vague, but whose popularity continues even today—particularly in the German *gast haus*. Fashioned of either clear glass or ceramic material, this drinking vessel is in the shape of a knee boot and usually of heroic proportions. The neophyte is handed the boot brimming with beer, and he is challenged to drain the contents without removing the container from his lips. Woe betide him if he drinks with the toe pointed upward, for as the boot is tilted, a pocket forms at the axis of the ankle and the entire toeful of beer suddenly breaks through the pocket, gushing into the face of the unsuspecting imbiber! With the toe down, he is on safer ground, but to be absolutely sure, turning the toe horizontally to either side is recommended.

THE GERMAN STEIN

But the greatest German contribution to the art and enjoyment of drinking was in the magnificent beer stein. The Germans have been producing steins for nearly 500 years, all the way back to the time when the first steins were created of earthenware or stoneware. In fact, "stein" means "stone" in German. And if you have ever wondered why most steins have hinged lids, this practical bit of ornamentation can be traced back to a 16th-century German law. Because of the swarms of insects that plagued the country, the lawmakers decreed that all food and drinking vessels should have lids.

Although the Germans originated the stein, craftsmen in other countries have created a multitude of these vessesls in a variety of shapes, sizes, colors and materials. Frog mugs, for example, were produced by the English in the late 18th Century, somewhat in the manner of the famous Toby mugs that show the head of a country squire or perhaps that of a particular British hero (the most popular one today is Sir Winston himself). The frog mug had a lifelike replica of a frog molded into the bottom. Since the frog did not appear until the mug had been nearly drained, he often came as a surprise to the drinker, who may have been unaware of the design and thought he was encountering a real croaker. The phrase, "deep in his cups," was coined to describe the reaction of the startled users of this container.

Steins suffered from a variety of superstitions. It was held that, under proper conditions of the Zodiac, a stein would fly to bits if poisonous liquids were poured into it. Another popular belief was that colored glass, when used in mugs or steins, would reduce the intoxicating quality of the alcoholic beverages in them.

The Germans, said to be the greatest brewers and beer drinkers in the world, have in the course of time created their own art form to hold their wonderful beer, and they have lavished upon it the creative and somewhat Gothic artistic instincts of the race.

We see many of these various drinking vessels of yore gathered together in the Falstaff International Museum of Brewing in St. Louis. It contains a large collection of such vessels, and in addition, it also houses a handsome assortment of tavern furniture and brewing related art and artifacts. The collection favors the stein in its many forms, but it is, however, quite international in flavor. There is the classic English "yard of ale," for instance—literally a yard long but very slight in circumference, opening at the mouth into the form of a bell, the whole thing being somewhat in the shape of a coachman's horn, which was very appropriate since the "yard" was first devised in an effort to produce a glass long enough to reach a drink up to a stagecoach driver (a trade aristocrat of his time) without making him descend from his high seat atop the coach and perhaps thereby lose control of his horses. (There was also a half-yard for drivers less thirsty—or maybe just less illustrious.)

There are the traditional etched glasses of Bohemia and the fantasies of those old Venetians. There are drinking vessels in the shape of books, apparently for the scholar who does not wish to display his thirst as openly as his erudition. And then there are the steins, and more steins, and more steins, some of which are photographed for this book. Their invention is endless. Some date back to the 17th Century, some are quite modern. But all are fascinating.

Some of the steins are magnificent works of art, portraying in infinite and colorful detail themes such as the Fall of Man. Others are humorous or heroic, dealing with the bedroom or the battlefield. One shows Saint Florian putting out—with beer—a fire that threatened to destroy Nuremburg. Another shows the complete legend of Lohengrin.

Very popular steins were those connected with sporting clubs. There are cycling steins, bowling steins, boating steins and even card-playing steins. The medics at the Munich School for Medicine harked back to the old ghoulish custom and took their beer from skull-shaped steins. There were also special-occasion steins. One for instance, was awarded to the winner of a bowling tournament, but after it was awarded to him, it was returned to the maker so that the victor's profile might be fired right into the ceramic as an original part of it—signifying that this stein was his and only his.

The students at Heidelberg, home of the great drinking clubs, had their own steins, reminiscent of the uniformed undergraduate and his duels for honor, with the cheekbone scars forever after signifying his contempt for pain and the common people, who usually have unblemished cheekbones.

Then there were the trade steins—railroaders, tailors, carpenters, sailors or just girl-watchers. Among these the military had some of the most noteworthy. During the period of the Imperial German Empire from 1871 to 1918, all male citizens were required to serve at one time or another in the army for at least a couple of years. It became the custom to memorialize a soldier's active service time with a special stein. The reservist would pay a decorator to paint a stein with his name, the unit name and the years he served. The decoration was covered with a clear glaze, baked in an oven and the colors thus permanently affixed. Afterward an appropriate pewter lid was attached. Some of these lids were highly specialized and eye-catching. For instance, one of the regimental steins in the Falstaff collection bears the legend: "Pioneer Hofmann served with the 3rd Railroad Battalion, Munich, Germany, 1907—1909." This stein bears the scene of the construction of a bridge, and the pewter lid is a beautifully wrought miniature engine. Another: "Sergeant Johann Fritsche served with the 4th Squadron, 2d Royal Bavarian Cavalry Regiment at Dillengen, 1903—1906." This regiment was famous as a dashing and illustrious unit, and was known as the "Baron of Thurn and Taxis' Regiment." Johann's stein has the Baron's own picture on it and the pewter lid is another beautifully fashioned small figure, this one that of a cavalry charger.

Perhaps the most famous occupational stein of all is the "Fiedel," or brewer's own stein. To symbolize his masterful trade, the brewer has his own carpenter shop, filled with expert coopers and carvers-at-large, create for him a wooden stein similar to a tiny barrel and bound with characteristic bands of metal.

The German sense of humor often found an outlet in deliberately creating odd designs for steins, such as that of a fearsome crocodile or the sneering head of a devil. But more gently humorous is the device of putting at the very bottom of the beer stein a transparent shadow picture that becomes visible to the drinker with increasing clarity as he gulps his way to the bottom. At length he is rewarded by the clear image as he tilts his stein up to the light of the brauhaus. Sometimes these pictures (known as lithopanes) are merely decorative—depicting the head of a stag or a pretty forest scene, for instance. But at least one such little work of art in the Falstaff group represents the face of a woman, a typical hausfrau, her expression showing a battle in her mind between anger and concern over the celebrant who has not yet come home. With such a reminder, it would take a brave Hans indeed to order yet another stein of beer.

And a final note on lithopanes for the collector of steins: when you are considering the purchase of a regimental or trade-craft stein bearing a lithopane, beware of those depicting a nude woman. It is most likely that such a stein is a copy of an earlier original, particularly if the nude is a sleek, modern, pin-up type. Nudes just were not depicted, as far as we know, in the base of the original stein of this type.

Today you may be a stein man or you may prefer a pewter or wooden mug, but the chances are that you drink most of your beer from glassware, as a true descendant of that old Egyptian who fashioned the turquoise goblet. In such a case, experience has taught that certain types of glasses make the drinking of beer more enjoyable. They show off its golden color. They reveal its sparkling inner life of bubbles and light reflections. They bear its head proudly and easily release its delicate bouquet. And they rest lightly in the hand (the feel of a drinking vessel is important). And they deal smoothly with the lip. All honor to those Phoenician sailors!

Chapter Six

THE FINE ART OF BEER QUAFFERY AND COOKERY

For what this house affords us,
Come, praise the brewer most—
Who caught into a bottle
The barley's gentle ghost
Until our parching throttles
In silence we employ
Like geese that drink a mouthful,
Then stretch their necks with joy!

Grace Before Beer
Higgins (1580)

*B*eer needs no plaudits from me to take its position at the head of its class as the most satisfying, uplifting and downright pleasurable drink known to mortal man. That is why when you plan a party, which is essentially an act of generosity and sociability in equal quantities, a beer party is going to bring out the best in everything and everyone— and you will know in advance that them as got asked will be there.

A beer party can be quite simple or it can get rather involved, depending upon your choice in the matter, but in either instance we shall delve here into ways of enhancing your menu with beer as well as satisfying your thirst.

First, how much beer will you need? Well, among beer drinkers men drink at least twice as much of the brew as women. We are told that the exact proportion is 80 per cent to 20 per cent. So you will want to take that into consideration and work it out against your guest list. Then, how much per person? The host who stocks a little more than he believes he needs is the host who never worries. I suggest that you figure on at least five 12-ounce measures for each man and perhaps three for each woman, giving you a slight edge on the comsumption of the girls. This may horrify the gentle advisers who consider five beers a great deal, but it may also concern others of a different persuasion who might feel that five beers is only a starter for a truly festive occasion. Anyway, that's my figure, and you might try it around with friends among the circle you are going to invite to gauge where their true capacities lie.

If you are serving bottled or canned beer, the count is relatively easy, but if you plan to hold a really big beer bust, you may be considering draught beer—a quarter- or half-barrel, or even more. And there are usually economies to be realized from serving

NUMBER OF GLASSES PER ½ BARREL	SHELL	SHAM PILSNER	FOOTED PILSNER
7 oz.	330	418	
8 oz.	294	345	305
9 oz.		305	
9½ oz.	256		
10 oz.		264	248
11 oz.			
12 oz.		214	
13 oz.			
14 oz.			
15 oz.			

draught beer.

So we had better supply you with some figures here: a half-barrel of beer contains 15½ gallons, or 1,984 ounces. First check the capacity of your beer glass, then figure out your total needs on the chart.

If you serve draught beer from the half- or quarter-barrel, special dispensing equipment will be required. This is usually available and furnished where you purchase your beer, however.

The serving of draught beer is a grand gesture of which almost anyone and everyone will approve. But it is a decision one makes with some forethought. We have already appreciated what a half-barrel of draught can offer in the way of full glasses of beer, but let's look for a moment at the very practical problem

TULIP GOBLET	SCHOONER	HOUR GLASS	GLASS STEIN
315			
305			
293	330	264	
		233	
	256	209	198
		190	
	203		184
		172	

The figures in the above table are based on an allowance of a one-inch head of foam, regardless of the shape or size of the glass. Increasing or decreasing the head of foam will change the number of glasses that can be drawn from a half barrel.

At left.

Wooden full barrel of the early 1900's. This is the standard size of 31 gallons used for all brewery measurements. When full, this weighed approximately 400 pounds.

On the barrel, left & right:

A hoop driver for a hoop driving machine. Several of these, grooved at their broad end, were pushed down by machine. The groove engaged the top of the metal hoop and forced it evenly down to draw the staves together and lock them in place. (Late 1890's.)

Hoop hammer. This has a groove on its upper side which was placed on the hoop then hammered down repeatedly to seat a hoop by hand.

Below barrel:

Staves. Wooden staves from a half barrel (15.5 gal.) and a quarter barrel "keg" (7.75 gal.). The dark coating on the inside is brewer's pitch used to keep the beer from coming in contact with the wood. Most wooden barrels were replaced with stainless steel or aluminum after Prohibition.

Hammers. (upper): Stave shaver. Used by the cooper to shape the inside of a stave. The rounded edge was used like a wood chisel to gouge a concave form to the inside of the stave. (below) A wooden tapping mallet. Originally faced with rawhide, this was used to drive wooden taps into barrels for drawing out the beer.

At the bottom:

Two hand augers used for boring holes in wooden tanks and barrels. These are the tapered type for boring 3 to 5-inch holes.

The cooper was the skilled carpenter who made and repaired wooden beer barrels in the brewery. This "schnitzel bank" or shavings bench was the work bench where he shaped and notched each barrel stave with such accuracy of seam that it would form a liquid tight container.

of mere weight: a half-barrel of beer, which includes the weight of the beer and its container, averages 160 pounds! So don't send your wife—or one of the kids with his little cart—downtown to bring home the brew for you. A quarter-barrel will come to 82 pounds or so. A "Tapper" will reach 30.

Even cases of regular bottles or canned beer should be worked out in advance re their avoirdupois.

Twenty-four 12-ounce export bottles, for example, will weigh 39 pounds. Twenty-four 12's of the stylized one-way bottles will come to 31 pounds. Twelve cans of 12-ouncers will weigh 22 pounds. Twelve quarts of 32-ouncers will come to 45 pounds in the tavern tall size and 44 pounds in the steinies. Thirty-six 7-ouncers will weigh 37 pounds.

It's a challenge in logistics . . . but not an insurmountable one for a true beer lover.

And you must also figure that after your original purchase of the beer has been made, you must provide containers in which to keep your brew cold.

If you are purchasing draught beer, chances are that your retailer will be able to provide you with a tub or some kind of container sizable enough to hold your barrel-half or quarter-barrel, and enough ice besides to keep it chilled. You might ask him at the same time if he has any small bars for rent that will fancy up the service of your beer to your guests.

So you can see that it all takes a little planning beforehand.

Likewise if you are going to pick up your brew at the grocery, the delicatessen or the supermarket. In that case, plan to purchase your beer last (if you are going to buy it already chilled) among your other supplies in order to keep its temperature as constant as possible from the outset. Keep it out of the sunlight in your car and if you really want to be a perfectionist, carry along a portable cooler with a bit of ice aboard (or some of those plastic bags or cans of liquid you can freeze in advance in your refrigerator) to keep the beer cool, man.

Also, be patient and gentle with your beer. This package is not a bunch of old bowling shoes. This is a delicate, balanced work of the brewer's art. It is obvious enough that if you bounce beer bottles around, you are going to "rile" up the beer inside and destroy the wonderful equilibrium of nature that the brewer has so painstakingly brought to perfection for you. Easy does it even in the ultimate storage in your cellar or refrigerator. Standing the bottles or cans upright is the best method, but if you must put them on their sides, try not to invert them or flip them around unduly when you come to the point of opening and serving. You should even consider whether or not the beer is to be stored under conditions of unusual vibration—try to avoid anything like this.

If the beer is bottled, keep it out of the sunlight, since light can cause an "off taste." Even something less than direct sunlight does it no good, so store the bottles in a dark place.

Now, as to temperature. The recommended temperature for the best enjoyment of beer is somewhere between 38° and 45° Fahrenheit. This will correspond, happily enough, to the temperature of a normally adjusted refrigerator.

By and large, if you need to cool it quickly, don't try to chill beer by putting it in the freezer compartment of the refrigerator. To begin with, if you get the beer down around the 32° mark, you are going to find that it may begin to cloud and that what you have done is to partially destroy some of the flavor of the beer —and warming it up again is not going to restore it by any means to the fine balance of flavor and bouquet it had when it left the brewery. Rather than run the risk of forgetting you ever put your beer in the freezer, a calamitous practice, a better plan is to put whatever amount you wish to chill in a hurry into a bucket or tub and cover it with ice, preferably shaved. Then pour water over the ice until the bottles or cans are covered. The water will conduct the chill to the beer more rapidly than plain ice ever will. Shaved ice is better in this respect than just plain cubes or chunks, which have to chill the air around the beer as well as the brew itself. Never pour salt over ice to get a little faster action: the beer will freeze in no time that way and all will be ruined.

Now, just a word about pouring beer. If you have been packing it in ice, outdoors or indoors, or if you have moved it around in getting ready for the party, make sure to carefully wipe each can or bottle lip just before opening it so that by chance some speck of foreign matter isn't clinging to the outside and could possibly find its way into the drink itself. And then, absolutely do not pour the beer down the side of the tilted glass as if to avoid creating a collar or head on it. Exactly the opposite is recommended for giving the beer the best chance to produce its finest flavor and bouquet. Hold the glass or mug perfectly straight, vertically, and pour the beer boldly into it until you have formed a marvelous, foamy collar to the depth that enhances the drink but does not completely monopolize it to the extent that it is all head and no liquid. Tilt the glass then, a little, if you must, and find a nice balance between head and body. The major point behind all this is that the head is formed by the brew's carbon dioxide, which is thus released. Carbon dioxide gives beer a zippy and piquant taste, but by forming a good head, you let the bubbles perform one of their annointed tasks and enhance the actual taste of the drink while reducing the total amount of CO_2 taken into your stomach.

And while we are on the subject of the pouring of the beer, you should also make it a practice to serve your brew in glasses that are used only for beer. You may think that glasses that have been used for drinking milk or other liquids and then washed by ordinary methods are clean, but they are not insofar as beer is concerned. Glasses used for serving beer should never be washed in soap or detergents at any time. They should be washed, when the time comes, in a solution of salt or soda and then rinsed in clean, hot water. And finally they should be allowed to dry in the air; don't wipe them with a cloth.

The beer party we are suggesting is a "total" beer party, with the brew as the high point and plenty of fixin's. That means there will be enough to eat on hand to stay the appetites whetted by the brew and to give your guests interesting little taste sensations without going into the grand gestures of serving a dinner as well. This is a stand-up affair primarily, and on that basis you can afford to invite more guests than you have chairs or sofas to accommodate. If possible, of course, the party would be first rate outdoors. However, if you decide on that, figure out in advance where you are going to put all those people in case it suddenly rains or turns too chilly to stay out there. Lucky party-minded homeowners will have their basements and made-over barns or summer pavilions all ready for a horde (more or less) of guests, but apartment dwellers and those without outdoor facilities should keep in mind the capacity of their ménage to absorb gesturing and conversing groups—for too many can be worse than too few.

The host, of course, is at the service of his guests and their pleasure is his. He hustles about, functioning as bartender, butler, chef, clean-up man alerted to minor accidents, diplomatic expert in introducing people and getting the fires of lagging conversation burning again, keeping a sharp eye on the movement of supplies; and while working like the devil, he must give the appearance of having the time of his life—which he might just find himself doing!

I have been going on the assumption that your beer party will take place on your own home grounds. But perhaps the occasion will take you afield. The logistics of this are, obviously, pretty much as described heretofore, with the exception of wheels and ice. Wheels I leave up to you, but ice is an item in this campaign that is of the most extreme and imperative nature. A lot of it you can transport from home base, and you will need plenty of it in which to pack your precious ammunition. The best thing for this operation is a supply of those wonderfully light, tough and roomy foam-plastic baskets that are watertight and capacious enough to hold generous supplies of beer cans and bottles packed in ice cubes and more ice cubes.

Ice melts, but never quite as rapidly as when you need it most, and one excellent suggestion is to reconnoiter the area where you are going to be settling down for your picnic and ascertain in advance the

place in the neighborhood that can provide a sup-
plementary supply. Ice machines often lurk in the
environs of gas stations, and if such are not available, storekeepers in the area, if properly approached with plenty of advance warning and a touch
of profit, will usually bend to the task of keeping your
refrigeration problems happily cool.

The logistics of preparing for a successful outdoor
party should even include a plan to place vessels containing quantities of ice in such a position, preferably
on a slope, that drainage does not become a problem
in the area where the party is actually being held.

One of the great things about beer is that it goes
marvelously with almost any food you can think of. It
is almost *de rigeur* to have plenty of pretzels spread
around the party area, backed up by bowls of nuts and
quantities of the snack kind of small crackers that
come in what seem like endless varieties of shapes
and flavors.

But your guests are going to be looking for a bit more
than this at a bang-up party. As a starter, without at-
tempting to bankrupt you or turn you into a Bavarian
chef overnight, try a few loaves of real fresh bread,
the greatest butter you can find and a huge bowl of
scrubbed radishes.

Quarter-sized sandwiches are also popular. You
make them as you do a regular-sized sandwich, then
just cut across twice to make four squares—presto,
they're bite-sized for quick gobbles while drinking
the beer. Here are a few good combinations:

    1. *White meat of chicken on salty rye
bread that has been spread with butter
and mayonnaise and lightly salted.*

    2. *Ham and Swiss or American cheese on
rye bread.*

    3. *Ham and cream cheese on rye bread.*

    4. *Fine-chopped hard-boiled eggs and
chicken livers. Blend with salt and mayonnaise and spread on thin rye bread.*

    5. *Fresh, chopped hard-cooked eggs and
sliced stuffed olives blended with mayonnaise and salt. Spread bread thinly with*

deviled ham, then add egg and olive mixture.

6. *White-meat tuna, mixed with finely chopped celery, a little onion juice, a squeeze of lemon and mayonnaise. Blend and spread on white bread.*

7. *Swiss cheese and cooked ham (a layer of each), a spread of butter and mustard on thin rye bread.*

8. *Fresh shrimp salad. Put together chopped shrimp, one-third as much celery (also finely chopped) as shrimp, lemon juice, salt, chopped capers, blended with mayonnaise.*

Then, as I imagine you already know, there can't be a much better combination in the world than cheese and beer. Don't forget Cheddar, sharp or bland. Even rat-trap cheese has the right tang for beer. Limburger is great, so is Bel Paese. Then there are Edam, Gruyere, Swiss and Muenster, just to mention a few in case you suddenly blank out on these familiar names precisely when you come to the point of ordering them in a store.

Potato chips, about a million of them, will go big and fast at a beer party. And while you are about it, why not whip together a few tasty dips for the gang? We don't suggest that this kitchen stint get to be too big a thing, but it does convey the thought that you're putting out with the best. Try, for example:

SWISS BEER DIP

1 egg white, stiffly beaten	1½ teaspoons salt
	2 cloves garlic, mashed
1 pound (16 ounces) Swiss cheese, grated	1 teaspoon Worcestershire sauce
1 tablespoon vegetable oil	8 ounces (approx.) beer

Beat egg white until stiff. Add remaining ingredients. Add beer gradually while stirring until mixture is the consistency of whipped cream. Chill. Serves 12. Double amounts if you plan to feed a larger group.

Or, make a . . . **ZIPPY DIP**

You go about this by turning out the desired quantity of mayonnaise into a good-sized bowl (lay it in there pretty heavy because they are going to mop this up fast) and smooth it out a bit by whipping into it a couple of teaspoonfuls of milk or cream. Then add about one-half as much catsup as mayonnaise, a couple of dashes of Worchestershire sauce and just the merest drop or two of Tabasco sauce. Whip this all together rather carefully, not beating it, until the whole has achieved a creamy consistency both in color and texture.

And here's another honey of a dip:

CHEDDAR BEER DIP

This is a dip that can be extended on the spot to feed a starving regiment. It's easy to prepare, flexible to change, delicious in any form. Serve with carrot sticks or garlic rounds as cheese scoops.

16 ounces cream cheese	2 cloves garlic
1½ cups beer	24 small gherkins
16 ounces Cheddar cheese, cubed	

Put cream cheese and 1¼ cups of the beer into blender. Cover and blend on high speed for 8 seconds. Add rest of beer, Cheddar cheese and garlic. Cover and blend on high speed about 30 seconds or until smooth. Add gherkins and blend 2 or 3 seconds more, or just until chopped.

At this point there is one special aspect of beer that you should seriously consider, and that is the fact that beer offers a special and unique flavor in cooking that many Continental chefs consider far superior to that of wine. The alcoholic content is low to begin with, and virtually negligible since a good amount evaporates during the cooking process. Beer is a *blender* and not merely an additive—in other words, you do not come out at the end with merely a familiar recipe with a beer taste added, but rather you have an entirely new taste sensation.

There are even beer cookbooks that go into tremendous culinary chef d'oeuvres. But that is not the aim here. We will simply provide a few basic dishes that make the most of this wonderful cooking ingredient, and we'll wager that your guests are going to go wild over them. Here's how, starting with the easy ones first:

CAMPER BEANS 'N' BEER

Empty two 1-pound cans of chili beans in gravy into a large skillet or pot. Stir in one package of dry chili seasoning mix and one 6-ounce can of tomato paste. Fill the empty tomato can twice with beer and stir into beans. Simmer, uncovered, for about 30 to 45 minutes. Add tiny potatoes to the beans. Serves 6. Great stuff.

FRANKFURTER SAUERKRAUT CASSEROLE

1 can (29 ounces) sauerkraut
1 cup beer
¼ teaspoon caraway seeds
12 frankfurters

Drain sauerkraut; turn into a 1½-quart casserole or baking dish. Add beer and caraway seeds; toss lightly. Cover; bake in a moderate oven (375° F.) 20 minutes. Uncover. Top with frankfurters and bake 20 minutes longer. Serves 6.

HUNGERBURGERS

Patties of chopped or ground beef, laced with beer and other tongue tinglers, are called Hungerburgers, and they are guaranteed to stifle anyone's hunger.

The orange-onion combination is quite Spanish and gourmet-like. Serve with fresh fruit in a basket. (Makes 8 servings.)

2 pounds ground
  chuck
½ cup beer
1 egg
2 slices bread, broken
  into small pieces
2 tablespoons chopped
  chives

2 tablespoons chopped
  pickles
8 hamburger buns
2 navel oranges,
  peeled and sliced
1 large red onion,
  sliced

Combine chuck steak, beer, egg, bread, chives and pickles. When well blended, shape mixture into 8 hamburger patties. Broil or grill until patties are very brown on both sides. Put hamburgers on buns and top each with an orange slice and an onion slice. Add tops of buns.

HAMBURGERS HONOLULU

These are hamburgers served on fresh pineapple slices, with the added tang of peppery sauce. Serve carrot sticks or orange slices rubbed in onion flavor. All you need to do is slice a large Spanish onion and lay the slices against the orange slices or carrot sticks for five minutes. The onion flavor added to the orange is a new taste sensation.

1½ pounds ground beef
 3 tablespoons beer
 1 teaspoon salt
 ½ teaspoon pepper
 ½ cup beer
 2 tablespoons butter
 ½ cup catsup

1 teaspoon Wor-
  cestershire sauce
1 teaspoon sugar
  few drops red-
  pepper sauce
  fresh pineapple
  slices

Mix first four ingredients. Shape patties. Brown patties on both sides in melted butter in heavy skillet. Mix rest of ingredients except pineapple slices. Pour over patties. If you like them rare, cook over high heat 5 minutes. If you prefer them well done, lower heat and cook about 10 minutes longer. Serve on slices of fresh pineapple. Serves 6.

Having proved your mettle on the foregoing, you may now proceed to your *piece de resistance*. This takes a steady hand and a cool eye in the kitchen, but if you are up to it, it's a beauty!

BEER-GLAZED HAM

1 smoked or ready-to-eat half ham (6 to 8 pounds)	½ cup brown sugar
	½ cup beer or ale
2 tablespoons prepared mustard	

Place ham, fat side up, in a shallow baking pan. Bake in a slow oven (325° F.). If smoked, bake 25 minutes per pound, or until meat thermometer registers 160° F. If ready to eat, bake 14 minutes per pound, or until meat thermometer registers 130° F. Forty-five minutes before ham is done, take from oven and remove rind if necessary. Score fat surface. Mix together brown sugar and mustard; stir to a paste. Gradually add beer, stirring until blended. Brush part of mixture over ham. Continue baking, brushing frequently with remaining mixture. Serves 10-12.

Buffet Glaze:

2 envelopes unflavored gelatin	1 cup beer
	½ cup cream

Put gelatin into heavy saucepan. Add about ¼ cup beer. Let gelatin soften. Stir in rest of beer and cook, stirring constantly, until steaming hot. Let cool. Stir in cream. Chill until consistency of egg white.

To Glaze Ham:

Place chilled ham on cake rack and set in wide, flat pan. Form a collar about ½ inch high around top edge of ham with aluminum foil. Pour glaze over top of ham to about ¼ inch thickness. Return to refrigerator to set glaze. Remove foil collar. Decorate top as desired.

Finishing Glaze:

Dissolve another envelope of gelatin in 1 cup of beer. Chill until it begins to thicken and spoon thinly over decorations to give them a final glaze.

If you are still on your feet and in a fighting mood, here is a terrific combination—a beer steak, a beer potato salad, a beer slaw and a beer layer cake! This is the magic of beer-in-cookery at its very best:

STEAK GAMBRINUS

1 thick large juicy steak
  or 6 cube steaks
6 tablespoons butter
3 tablespoons minced
  onion

¼ cup beer
1 teaspoon salt
  small jar sliced
  mushrooms
  (optional)

Put half of butter and all of onion into heavy skillet. Brown steaks for 2 minutes on each side in butter. Add beer and salt. Cook 1 minute more on each side. For extra-crisp cookery, place on broiler grill for a few minutes. Put on hot platter. Add rest of butter to sauce and mushrooms, if desired. Bring to boil and pour over steaks. Serve with garnish of small potatoes and onions alternating on the platter . . . add sprigs of parsley. Serves 6.

GERMAN (HOT) POTATO SALAD

10 to 12 medium pota-
  toes (4 pounds)
6 slices bacon, cooked
  and crumbled
1 cup diced celery
2 tablespoons finely
  chopped onion
4 teaspoons salt
½ cup butter or mar-
  garine

¼ cup flour
½ teaspoon dry mus-
  tard
3 tablespoons sugar
1 cup beer
1 teaspoon Tabasco
2 tablespoons chopped
  parsley

Cook potatoes in skins until barely tender. Peel and dice into large casserole, about 3-quart size. Add bacon, celery and onion. Sprinkle with 2 teaspoons salt. Melt butter; add flour, mustard, sugar and remaining 2 teaspoons salt; stir to a smooth paste. Gradually add beer and Tabasco. Cook, stirring constantly, until mixture thickens and comes to a boil. Pour over potatoes; sprinkle with parsley. Mix lightly with a fork. Let stand for about an hour. Cover and reheat in a moderate oven (375°F.) 25 minutes. Makes 10 to 12 servings.

BEER SLAW

For 6, shred 1 medium-size head of cabbage and 1 green pepper. Add 2 tablespoons of celery seed, 1 teaspoon minced onion, 1 teaspoon salt and ¼ teaspoon pepper. Thin 1 cup of mayonnaise with ½ cup beer and add to the cabbage. Toss thoroughly and chill in the refrigerator before serving.

BEER LAYER CAKE

1 cup beer	1 teaspoon cocoa
1 teaspoon baking soda	1 teaspoon vanilla
½ cup shortening	1-ounce bottle red food
1¼ cups sugar	color
2 eggs	2½ cups sifted cake flour
1 teaspoon salt	

Mix about a tablespoon of beer with baking soda and let settle. In mixing bowl beat shortening, sugar, eggs, salt, cocoa, vanilla and red color until light. Alternately beat in flour and beer. Stir in dissolved baking soda. Pour into 2 greased 9-inch round pans. Bake at 350° F. for 30 to 35 minutes.

Cool and split layers to make 4 layers. Spread White Frosting, below, between layers, on top and sides.

Frosting:

½ cup milk	1½ cups butter
2 tablespoons flour	1 tablespoon vanilla
1½ cups sugar	

Stir milk and flour over medium heat until thick. Cool. Beat sugar, butter and vanilla until fluffy. Add cooked mixture, 1 teaspoon at a time, beating at high speed with electric mixer until smooth. Frosting should be consistency of whipped cream. After cake is frosted, keep in refrigerator.

Have a great party . . . and *prosit!*

Chapter Seven

STAND UP AND DRINK A TOAST

Ho, a song by the fire!
  (Pass the pipes, pass the bowl)
Ho, a song by the fire!
  (With a skoal, with a skoal!)
For here's four good fellows,
And the beechwood and the bellows
And the cup is at the lip,
In the pledge of fellowship.

from Hanover Winter Song

The marvelous Hanover drinking song, written almost a hundred years ago by Richard Hovey up in New Hampshire's mountains, where "the great white cold stalks abroad," has been beloved by generations of Dartmouth College men. And justly so. It catches precisely both the sentiment and the virility of the drinking when good fellows get together. And not the least of these ringing words are those of "skoal"—the traditional toast of the Norseman, spiritual ancestor of Dartmouth skiers—and "pledge," another symbol of friendship among drinkers.

The act of pledging before a drink has an heroic origin. The ancient custom at a banquet was for all to drink from the same cup, which was passed around from hand to hand. As a guarantee that the drinker was not subject to attack while he was off guard, as it were, in the act of imbibing, his special companion would raise and "pledge" him special protection, perhaps even emphasizing the point more clearly by drawing his dagger or his sword as he spoke. This was the beginning as well of the true "loving cup"—passed from hand to hand around the table. In time the loving cup was also considered the proper tribute by an inferior individual to a superior one. And thus today we present the winners in a contest with a "cup," emblematic of their superior status over those they have just bested in competition.

Drinking a toast from a lady's slipper is a rather more charming and sentimental gesture. In Hungary the groom often drank the first toast to his bride from her very own slipper and tossed the footwear to the guests as a memento of the courtly moment. The practice continued in favor well through the 19th Century, but it has faded away almost completely today, possibly because so many slippers are open-toed and it would take the magic of a Houdini to do it at all.

WHY WE CLINK GLASSES

The gesture of clinking glasses belongs to the Christian era. The thought is that some sort of noise should be made to banish the devil while drinking the brew.

The foul fiend, as everyone knows, is very allergic to sounds, particularly those that suggest a bell, and his absence from a friendly bout of drinking is thus guaranteed.

ORIGIN OF THE WORD "TOAST"

Nationalities other than the English offer toasts, but they don't call them that. "Toast" in our language means slightly burned bread, and that is how it all started. Quite often the drinking of beer took place right by the open hearth, where bread was being toasted at the same, and it was a custom to step up the nutritive value of the drink by dropping bits of toast into it.

Of course many of the old toasts were windy things that had their listeners nodding and licking their lips at the same time. But not everything that is old is a bore. For example, in 1800 there was a high-drinking health club in London, known as the "Anacreontic Society," that met at a tavern called The Crown and Anchor. The members began each meeting by drinking to the tune of their club song, "To Anacreon in Heaven." The song finished off as follows, in honor of an ancient Greek who believed in good health:

While thus we agree,
Our toast let it be.
May our club flourish happy, united and free!
And long may the sons of Anacreon entwine,
The myrtle of Venus with Bacchus' vine!

All right, so what? Well, many Americans knew that tune. And when one, Francis Scott Key, wrote a poem called "The Star Spangled Banner," he decided that it could best be sung to the tune of "Anacreon in Heaven." That's what you're singing today, lad, when the flag goes up and our national anthem rings out.

When you offer a toast, don't forget to respect it yourself. Speak slowly—sonorously if you can—and put the emphasis on certain words right where it belongs. The Scots—fighters and poets all—used to give their toasts while standing with one foot on the chair and the other on the table. Although you could do that at a fraternity banquet or a stag dinner, I don't recommend it for private parties with ladies present. But that's the spiritual stance of the proper toast—and be sure to belt it out *loud and clear!*

Here's to ye absent lords, may they
Long in a far countree stay,
Drinking at other ladies' boards,
The health of other absent lords.

Now that's a good Scottish toast. And so I commend it to you, and at least some of those that follow:

Here's hoping that the devil never learns
that you're dead until you've spent a half
hour in heaven . . . .   *(Old Irish Toast)*

Here's to a long life and a merry one,
A quick death and easy one,
A pretty girl and a true one . . .
A cold beer—and another one.

Here's to the glass that cheers,
. . . A woman's mirror.

May we look forward with pleasure,
And backward without regret.

May bad fortune follow you all your days,
and never catch up with you.

When going up the hill of success,
May you never meet a friend coming down.

To our best friends—who know the worst about us,
but refuse to believe it.

A toast to the groom—and discretion to his bachelor friends.

To the groom—may he find the power somewhere,
to forget the names of his former girl friends.

Here's to you, as good as you are—
and here's to me as bad as I am.
And as bad as I am, and as good as you are,
I'm as good as you are, bad as I am.   *(Old Scottish Toast)*

Here's to us that are here,
To you that are there,
And the rest of us everywhere.

May you live all the days of your life.

Here's to woman, who is, generally speaking,
. . . generally speaking.

To our sweethearts and wives—may they never meet.

Chapter Eight

YOUR PH. B. OF BEER—
THE FACTS OF THE CASE
A FOAM-FILLED GLOSSARY
OF THE LANGUAGE OF BEER

Beer is both Ceres,
And good Neptune too!
Beer's froth was the sea
From which Venus grew.

London Chanticleers, (1659)

There are two important psychological facts to be understood about all human beings. One is that each of us is convinced in his heart that he has a wonderful sense of humor. The guy without a speck of one is partial to what he calls "dry" humor. The guy who will laugh every time he hears the first joke ever printed in Captain Billy's *Whiz Bang* thinks of himself as a humor connoisseur. All right. I have no argument with that, since I myself have a superb sense of humor and can afford to be generous with those who have been short-changed in this rare commodity.

But the second thing that every man feels himself to be an absolute authority on is alcoholic beverages. Of course if he happens to be in one of the trades or businesses connected with brewing, let us say, he may know a great deal on the subject. Although for the most part, the average guy in the bar has a goodly smattering of lore on the subject of beer, some of it right, some of it wrong, he doesn't know where the borderline starts . . . or ends.

At any rate, the subject of any liquor, but particularly that of beer, is one that is sure to come up in a bar conversation. And it is then, Sir, that you should be prepared to be in the right.

So we have devised this special chapter as a concentrated dose of the romance of pure fact, elucidating the fantastic facts of the brewing business itself. What Ye Need To Know is here in this chapter, even with esoteric words from deep within the industry, burgeoning with meaning and hidden nuances toward perfection in the art of making beer. With this in your grasp, you are fast on the way to being An Authority, and an authority on beer is also known as A Fascinating Fellow. This, too, can lead to all sorts of happy conclusions, the least of which is that you will be able to settle all arguments on this special subject for the rest of your life, with the ensuing benefit that you might be favored by any number of treats because of your fantastic erudition on such a companionable topic.

Of course if you are still one for just looking at your image in the mirror and letting Great Thoughts surge to the top of your head as the bubbles swarm up in your brew, I am for that as well. But at least this chapter has the terminology all assembled for you when you need it. We have read deep into beer chronologies and anthologies that have kept their wisdom hidden for centuries on the shelves of the rare-book rooms in almost-forgotten libraries. This is It. This is your Beer Encyclopedia.

Our references start with certain statements of true fact concerning the world of beer and brewing, setting the record straight, I trust, for some of your discussions. This book is considered worthy of dissemination in the brewing industry itself, and so I have not hesitated to include certain words in the Glossary of Terms that get right down to the vats and kettles. That's complicated country once in a while, but perhaps your curiosity will chance the exploration. And by all means, if you're slated for a desert island and there's no dictionary handy, take along your beer book . . . and ponder.

Let's discuss beer in barrels to begin with, and in barrels of 31-gallon capacity, for that's the standard of measure in the brewing industry. A barrel contains the approximate equivalent of 55 six-packs—or 13.7

cases, each containing 24 twelve-ounce bottles or cans.

So that's how the breweries measure beer. And we Americans consume a lot of beer. While it would be sheer folly for us to set down volumes of statistics on annual tax-paid withdrawals of beer and state-by-state consumption trends, etc., we shall provide you with some industry figures that at least show trends.*

How much beer is consumed in the United States? When beer "came back" in 1933, Americans drank—from April through December of that year—20,469,641 barrels of malt beverages. By 1965 total consumption reached the 100,000,000-barrel-per-year mark, and it has shown steady increases since.

How does the United States compare with other countries in beer production? The United States is tops by far, followed by West Germany, England, Russia, Japan, Czechoslovakia, France, Canada, East Germany, Australia, Mexico, Belgium, Spain, Poland, Brazil, Colombia, Austria, Netherlands, Denmark, Yugoslavia and Italy—in that order.

What about per-capita consumption? Nationally for the past few years, and based on total United States population, per-capita consumption has been 16 to 17 gallons per person. As to the states, and using the same yardstick, Wisconsin currently is the leader at about 25 gallons, with Alabama at the bottom of the list, in the five-plus gallon category.

Is brewing big business dollarwise? You bet it is! America's brewers are responsible for more than six billion dollars of business every year. They employ directly more than 60,000 persons; consume the output of more than four million acres of farmland; and pay more than a billion and a half dollars a year in excise taxes alone.

Which are the leading United States breweries? The following list gives the order of rank at the time of writing. Such figures, of course, tend to vary from year to year, but these are the most recent available:

(see listing on page 119)

---

* If you are a real bug for figures, a wealth of such information is compiled and published annually by the United States Brewers Association, Inc.

TAPPING THE BEER KEG

There are a number of different types of draught beer kegs, and each requires its own kind of tapping equipment. With all, however, the operating principle is much the same. Either air or CO_2 gas is introduced into the keg to force the beer out to a tap, or faucet, used to control the flow.

These beer kegs, constructed of either stainless steel or aluminum, are filled with cold unpasteurized draught beer at the brewery and the opening on the side through which they were filled is sealed with a bung, usually made of hardwood. From this point on, through delivery, storage, and your use, the beer must be kept refrigerated.

The types of keg most broadly used in the industry are the Golden Gate, the Peerless, the Hoff-Stevens Peerless modification, the Kwik-Tap Peerless modification, and the Sankey System.

The Golden Gate system provides a coupling at the top of the barrel where the air or gas is introduced, and a coupling at the bottom where the beer is withdrawn. All the other systems feature a single coupling at the top of the barrel which provides for both the introduction of the propellant and for withdrawal of the beer.

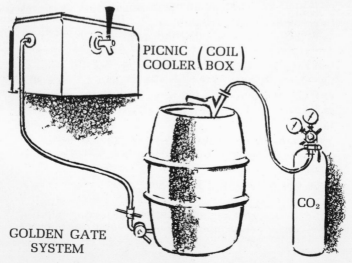

PICNIC COOLER (COIL BOX)

CO_2

GOLDEN GATE SYSTEM

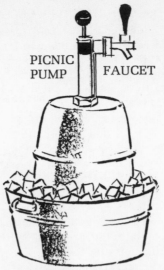

PICNIC
PUMP   FAUCET

PEERLESS SYSTEM

The systems use either a "picnic pump" which is used to pump air into the keg, or a connection for a tank of CO_2 gas which provides the pressure. At the business end of the system where the beer flows out through a hose to a faucet, a "coil box" is sometimes introduced. This is an insulated box containing a coil of copper or stainless tubing through which the beer flows, and ice is poured into the midst of the tubing to keep the beer cool as it is withdrawn.

If you are using the "direct draw" method without a coil box, be sure that your keg is kept cold in a tub of ice. If you have a coil box with its own ice, it's still advisable to cover the keg with a special jacket, or a blanket . . . and try and keep your equipment out of the sun.

Just one word of caution. You are dealing with high pressure containers, so be certain to follow directions for tapping carefully.

Of course, the Tapper draught beer container is the ultimate in convenience. It holds the equivalent of a case of beer; its CO_2 unit is self-contained; the faucet or tap is attached and ready to go, and the unit fits easily into most home refrigerators.

1.	Anheuser-Busch, Inc.	14.	Ballantine
2.	Schlitz	15.	Stroh
3.	Pabst	16.	National
4.	Coors	17.	Heileman
5.	Falstaff	18.	Pearl
6.	Carling	19.	Lucky Breweries
7.	Schaefer	20.	Genesee
8.	Miller	21.	Grain Belt
9.	Hamm	22.	Lone Star
10.	Associated	23.	Pittsburgh
11.	Rheingold	24.	Meister Brau
12.	Olympia	25.	Jackson
13.	Schmidt		

Are breweries ever modernized? The industry puts out about $130,000,000 every year for plant modernization. This is to insure top-grade grains, pure water, exact temperatures at various stages of brewing, precise timing of operations, close control of yeast action, clinic-clean apparatus and dust-free atmosphere. These things are not just claims—if you don't actually have 'em, you don't turn out quality beer.

How much beer goes into bottles and cans? Packaged pasteurized beer in cans and bottles, represents 85.2 per cent of total beer sales.

Where is beer sold? Grocery stores handle 51 per cent of the beer sales, taverns 13 per cent, liquor stores 27 per cent (some states do not sell beer in liquor stores), and there is a miscellaneous 9 per cent.

Do men or women drink the most beer? Men drink most of the beer in this country, accounting for 80 per cent of the intake.

Is income a factor? Contrary to popular belief, although beer is certainly a boon to the man who works with his muscles, providing both energy and coolth, there is little difference in the popularity of beer among income groups. Fifty-five per cent in the top-income brackets enjoy beer; 53 per cent in the middle-income brackets; and 45 per cent in the lower-income group.

Who drinks the most beer—city or country dwellers? City people drink more beer than country folk. In cities of more than 100,000 population, 53 per cent are beer drinkers; in cities of 100,000 population or less, 40 per cent; and among the rural population, it's 37 per cent. Since the country is gradually turning to urban rather than rural population clusters, things look solid for the beer business.

Do people often drink beer at home? Beer in packages continues to grow in popularity as a home beverage. In 1944 seven out of ten beer drinkers enjoyed beer at home regularly. Now the number is nine out of ten. Beer is enjoyed with friends 49 per cent of the time; consumed among the family 39 per cent of the time; and consumed by the individual (robbing the refrigerator) 12 per cent of the time.

When do people drink beer? And how much do they drink in ratio to specific activities? Beer is downed at times that might surprise you. TV watchers, for instance, consume only 35 per cent of the beer drunk in the home. Twenty-seven per cent goes down the hatch during the relaxing time before dinner. Twenty per cent is drunk as a nightcap, thanks to beer's deserved reputation as a soothing and restful potable. The balance, about 18 per cent, is consumed during meals.

The "entertaining informally" data is rather interesting. It's the moment when people just happen to stop by unexpectedly for a chat or a visit. Of everything the host offers his guests on such an occasion, it is coffee, tea or cocoa nine out of ten times; soft drinks two out of three times; beer two out of three times; fruit drinks three out of five times and wine one out of three times.

On such occasions, when the host puts out some form of food with his beverage, such as crackers, cheese or pretzels, the chances are 41 per cent that beer will go with it. With spicy foods such as pizza, the odds are 31 per cent.

How much beer is usually consumed per sitting? The usual amount of beer consumed with the meal is one bottle or can. On other occasions, social visits and the like, a couple of bottles or cans is about the average ... although for a really gala affair, I shall stick to my guns with my original estimate of five for him and three for her.

I think that the gentlemen who conduct surveys have come up with some kind of a record with the niceties of the following statistics: when consumed indoors, beer is drunk directly from the container by 29 per cent of beer drinkers, poured into a glass by 35 per cent and consumed both ways by 36 per cent. When the beer is enjoyed outdoors, it is drunk directly from the container by 65 per cent, poured into a glass by 11 per cent and consumed both ways by 24 per cent of beer drinkers.

When did bottled beer start? Don't ask me how he did it—or for that matter why he was working on this instead of counting his beads—but the first bottling of beer was in 1561, and it was accomplished by the good Dean of St. Paul's, Dr. Alexander Nowel, flourishing under the not-so-good Edward VI. However, it was actually not until 1873, when Louis Pasteur invented the heating process named after him, that bottling was possible on a commercial scale. Even after that the joys of the saloon made it difficult for the bottlers of beer. After Repeal in 1933, the bottlers came into their own, as many beer drinkers turned to the comforts of home to accompany the quaffing hour.

The first beer can came along in 1935. There was some resistance on the natural but not very logical basis that the can gave the beer a metallic taste. Then, during World War II, domestic use of metals was curtailed and the limited supply of cans was largely made available to the armed forces. These consisted of young men, and they set the habits of the future. They drank their brew straight out of the can, and when they came home after the war, they kept drinking it that way. The tab-opening end on the beer can arrived in 1962, and you know the rest.

Is beer a seasonal drink? The pace of beer consumption according to months is not exactly a startler. Americans drink more beer in hot weather than they do in cold weather, but not so much more than you

would think. Modern heating and cooling methods
smooth out the comfort index. A seasonal index of
monthly consumption against the normal average
puts March and April as the normal beer-drinking
months at 103.4 and 100.9 respectively. May moves
on to 110.8, June to 120.6 and July to a peak of 121.0. It
begins to taper off in August to 116.5, perhaps because the northern states are beginning to cool a bit
by then, with September at 98.5, October at 89.6,
November at 89.1, December at 91.4, January at 79.4,
and February at 78.8.

What is beer's future? Getting back to the future of
beer as a drink, it is robustly on the upgrade and
shows every sign of continuing its climb. From the
early 1900s to World War II, the demand advanced
steadily at about 3 per cent. After World War II, the
demand increased 3½ per cent; 4 per cent since the
Korean War; and 4+per cent during the 60s. The current outlook calls for an annual growth rate of nearly
5 per cent.

This kind of growth is closely. linked with population. In 1951, 41.6 per cent of the total population
was under 25 years of age and by 1968 this ratio had increased to 46.4 per cent, or nearly half of our whole
population.

Now, the fact is that approximately 41 per cent of
the beer consumed is consumed by persons between
the ages of 21 and 34; 28 per cent by those between 35
and 44; 18 per cent by those between 45 and 54; and 13
per cent by those 55 years of age or older.

If you put these two fact classifications together—the youth population growth and the age
groups in which beer is preferred—you can see that
the young people are moving into the prime drinking
group. It thus behooves the brewers to respect the
taste preferences of this group.

The potential customer is worth a study in depth by
any brewer, of course, and he interests us here as
well. To begin with, it is reasonably clear that a liking
for the flavor of beer is a learned experience.
Normally, sweet foods are easy for young people to
take, since little taste training is involved; hence their

plunge toward soft drinks and milkshakes. However, other flavors such as beer, coffee, strong cheeses, oysters and olives require more trials and exposure.

Young men turn to beer faster than do young girls. (Youths usually have their first drink of beer on social occasions, most often with members of their own sex and age group.) A couple in a bar will often order beer for the guy, a sweet cocktail for the girl. This may be a question of economics—he can save at least on his own drink—but just as often it is a matter of preference. Seventy-five per cent of young unmarried men are beer drinkers as compared with only 35 per cent of young single women in the same age bracket.

There is a tendency in the next age bracket for women to increase their beer intake. After marriage they take to beer by way of indicating a desire to share a pleasure their husbands enjoy, and also because by then they may have cultivated a greater preference for the brew. The proportion of women beer drinkers under age 25 increases from 35 per cent before marriage to 42 per cent after they are married and reign in their own homes.

On the single-married axis, here is how the beer drinkers, both male and female, partake:

Beer Consumed:	Single Customers	Married Customers
At home only	20%	54%
Away from home only	50%	26%
Both places	30%	20%

What is the tax on beer? Beer certainly pays its own way in terms of the taxes it turns over to the government. These taxes constitute the largest individual item in the price of beer. The federal excise tax is $9 per barrel and state taxes average approximately $3.92 a barrel. In addition, there are federal and state occupational taxes on brewers, wholesalers and retailers, as well as local taxes in some states.

A little simple arithmetic indicates that the brewing industry contributes about 1½ billion dollars in excise taxes alone, not counting the various licensing taxes and exclusive of property, income and corporation taxes in this huge industry. The federal revenue from this source goes in the general treasury, but many states allocate all or part of this income to education and public welfare. Brewers thus make indirect contributions toward the public good via these substantial taxes. It does not take much figuring to conclude that a high percentage of the cost of any unit of beer purchased by the consumer must hark back to these built-in tax costs at the very outset. Handed such a sizable problem in production economics, the brewing business actually does a superb job in pricing its product out at the other end where you come in, paying for your drink of the brew.

These facts that have been shot at you in the foregoing pages are of interest in themselves and they also have some bearing on what we shall be doing in the next and final chapter of this book, which is taking a trip through a typical brewery for a firsthand view of how the trick is turned.

It is a world in itself—a very different world—there in the brewery and you can get much more out of your trip by knowing something about what you are looking at. We won't pretend that the Glossary of Terms, which follows next, will contain absolutely every word that a brewmaster might use or know, but it will include a good many of them. By and large, it is intended equally to solve some of those barside discussions, as well as to serve as a reference to those of my readers who have a mind to look at things more technically than the next guy. You will see, as you glance through the Glossary, the way in which German words and technology have dominated the industry. There has been no attempt made whatsoever to "Anglicize" these German words, simply because they do not deserve that fate. They belong to the basic language of brewing, its generic vocabulary, and they shall traditionally designate the equipment and the arts of this craft.

THE LANGUAGE OF BEER

Adjunct . . . . Unmalted grains used in brewing.

Alcohol . . . . A colorless, volatile liquid (C_2H_5OH) that is the stimulating principle in fermented and distilled liquors.

Anlaufen . . . . To start filling wort or beer into tanks, "racking."

Anstellen . . . . The addition of yeast to wort.

Anschieber . . . . . . In Germany a brewery employee with no formal training, who works without having taken tests (see also *lehre bube*).

Aufziehen . . . . To rouse the yeast; to agitate; aerate.

Ausbrennen . . . . Removing old pitch from kegs before pitching.

Barm . . . . Same as yeast.

Bierstube . . . . A get-together featuring beer, German food, and often appropriate decorations, costumes and music, creating a festive German atmosphere.

Bung . . . . A plug used for closing the bunghole in a barrel.

Bunging . . . . To close a container with a bung or to connect a container to a pressure-regulating system.

Bung Starter . . . . . . A wooden mallet used for tapping on a bungstave to loosen a bung.

Calorie . . . . Amount of heat required to raise the temperature of one gram of water one degree Centigrade (averaged between the freezing and boiling points of water).

Carbon Dioxide . . . . A heavy, colorless gas (CO_2). Two grams of fermented wort extract will produce about one gram of alcohol and one gram of CO_2.

Cask . . . . A large barrel.

Catkin (hops) . . . . . . The hop bud. The blossom of the female hop plant.

Cone . . . . Any of several cone-like flower or fruit clusters, as in the hop.

Cooker . . . . Vessel that allows heating and boiling of mash.

Cooper . . . . One who makes or repairs barrels.

Cooperage . . . . Containers made of staves and bound together with hoops, such as barrels and kegs; also the plant in which these containers are made.

Extract . . . . The total solids contained in a liquid.

Fahrenheit Scale . Thermometer scale having 180 divisions between freezing (32° F.) and boiling (212° F.) of water. Material used for beer filtration.

Filter Mass . . . . Geniality, good nature, comfort.

Gemutlichkeit . . . . Sometimes used to describe a cheerful atmosphere in a tavern or pub.

Grant . . . . A horizontally-placed vessel between the straining tank and brewkettle to facilitate the straining of the wort.

Grits . . . . Hulled and coarsely ground grain.

Growler . . . . Quart bucket that in earlier times was filled with beer from a nearly empty barrel and sold at cut-rate. This beer usually foamed more than fresh beer, but the foam quickly disappeared, leaving much less beer than it first appeared that the customer was getting. The word describes the customer's complaint when he found he had been cheated. "Rushing the growler" means going to a bar or tavern to buy beer, usually to take out to a number of people (as in a quart bucket).

Head (of beer) . . . The foam on beer.

Hogshead . . . . A large wooden barrel or cask, usually of more than 60-gallon capacity.

Hoop . . . . A circular band of metal, wire or wood used to hold the staves of a barrel together.

Hoop-Driver . . . . . A tool used for driving the hoops on barrels to make them tighter.

Keg . . . . A small barrel (in trade practice, usually any barrel of under eight-gallon capacity).

Kellermeister . . . . (In English a "cellar master," to-day sometimes called a "cellar boss")—the brewer in charge of the cellars.

Kraeusen . . . . The foamy head on beer in fermentation. Also the stage of beer during fermentation while producing a foam head.

Kraeusening . . . . . The addition of a smaller portion of beer or wort in the early stages of fermentation to a larger portion of fermented beer in order to produce an after-fermentation.

Kuhlschiffe . . . . . . (Also called *cool schiff* or *coolship*)—a shallow vessel in which hot wort direct from the brew-kettle is placed for preliminary cooling before going to the refrigerated cooling machine.

Lager . . . . (From the German *lagern*, meaning "to store.") Most beer made in America today is lager beer. This means that it is made with yeast that settles to the bottom of the tank during fermentation (rather than rising to the top as in, say, ale) and is stored at relatively low temperatures for maturing and clarification.

Lehre bube . . . . Literally a "learning boy." An apprentice brewer.

Lupulin . . . . The fine, yellow, resinous powder on the strobile of hops.

Malting . . . . Steeping, germinating and drying grain.

Original Gravity . . Extract of the wort before the addition of yeast.

pH . . . . The pH value of any water or solution is merely a number to indicate the degree of acidity or alkalinity of the water or solution. The pH scale is divided into 14 points or values. The mid-point is 7.0, which is the neutral point where the solution is neither acid nor alkaline.

Pasteurization . . . . . The partial sterilization of a fluid at a temperature (131-158° F.) that destroys or inhibits microorganisms.

Pilsner . . . . A name sometimes applied to light beer; also a kind of tall, conical beer glass. The name derives from the city of Pilsen (Plzen) in Bohemia (western Czechoslovakia).

Poker Beer . . . . Beer heated with a red-hot poker as a winter drink. Beer heated with spices added is called "mulled beer."

Schallander . . . . Originally the living quarters of unmarried journeymen in a brewery. Now used to designate lunch and dressing rooms in a brewery.

Schauglas . . . . Insertion of glass in pipelines, etc., to facilitate inspection and control; sight glass.

Scooper . . . . Grain shovel.

Seed Yeast . . . . Yeast used to start fermentation in a brew.

Shandy . . . . A drink made of beer and lemonade, sometimes called *radlmass*. It is consumed by German bicyclists.

Shoe Pegs . . . . Small wooden pins used for plugging small holes in barrels.

Sparge . . . . To distribute water over grains or hops in order to wash out extract.

Spritz . . . . Literally "to squirt." To give the inside of a brewkettle or tank a temporary cleaning by hosing down.

Steeping . . . . To prepare grain for germination by soaking in water, usually to 45 per cent moisture.

Stein . . . . A beer mug, usually fairly large and ornate. The word in German means "stone," from which the first steins were made hundreds of years ago.

Sternewirt . . . . The brewery taproom.

Treber . . . . The spent grains.

Vat . . . . Usually a fermenting or storage vessel.

Wort . . . . Pronounced "wert." Liquid obtained from steeping malt in hot water. Wort does not become beer until yeast fermentation.

Yeast . . . . A group of unicellular organisms of the family Saccharomyceta-ceae, which ferments sugars to alcohol and carbon dioxide by virtue of its enzymes.

Yeast Crop . . . . Yeast collected from fermenters during or after the fermentation.

Yield of Extract . . . Number of pounds of extract obtained from 100 pounds of brewing material, given in per cent.

Zwickel . . . . Test petcock for sampling beer directly from the storage tank.

Chapter Nine

WE VISIT A BREWERY

How easy can the barley tree
cement the quarrel!
It's aye the cheapest lawyer's fee
to taste the barrel

Robert Burns
(1789)

Our host brewery is a modern giant: Falstaff's eastern most unit in Rhode Island.

As we approach the entrance to the great plant, we discover that the brewing business is not without soul. The driveway is spacious and well landscaped, and we are greeted by an heroic sculpture of our old friend Gambrinus, the legendary patron saint of beer. The old boy looks great—very imaginatively inspiring, very regal—and he is holding aloft a warrior's-sized flagon of the brew as if in a toast to the visitor. A very nice kind of welcome indeed.

Our visit has been honored by having as its guide the head brewmaster of the entire Falstaff operation, a gentleman who handles with utter grace the somewhat difficult task of translating his understanding of this complex art and science into terms a few wide-eyed denizens from the outer world can understand.

Within a few moments we are happily at home—sniffing appreciatively the warm and earthy smells of the brewery. The great vats and conduits talk of science and mechanization, but the brew itself keeps bubbling away at you as if to say, "Never mind them, this is your old buddy here, just as natural as on the day the world was born." These aromas waft a cleansing quality to the lungs, and the shining brewery has the aura of an enormous kitchen.

A brewery is a giant in dimension. Its proportions have a certain Gothic grandeur that is frequently heightened by the type of medieval Teutonic *brauhaus* used as a reception room for honored and thirsty guests. But a brewery is more ship than cathedral: there is a great deal of vastness here, a lot of lateral and vertical space, and this is conquered by mazes of ladders and crosswalks and small elevators; and of course the housekeeping is sparklingly shipshape.

The skipper of all this is the brewmaster, and here again the ship analogy fits. The captain of any ship is The Boss. The brewmaster's ironclad authority is that born of an enormous and comprehensive erudition. He must possess a wide background of technical training. The chances are that he is a graduate of one of the brewers' schools such as Wallerstein, Siebel, Wahl-Henius, or the United States Brewers' Academy.

In addition he must be versed in electrical, chemical and mechanical engineering on a sophisticated level; he must know chemistry and biochemistry; he must be informed on refrigeration, bottling, canning, cooperage, sanitation, storage—and of course he must have the years of experience and apprenticeship behind him that have taught him the intricate science of making beer, which also has the elements of an art. He must have a mind like a computer, but he must also be sensitive to the nuances of his trade, to the little shifts in timing and processing that long practice has indicated to him are the special ways of developing the kind of product he regards as perfect. He is, as I said, The Boss. He sees everything as he goes through the plant, and he knows the function of everything he is looking at and whether or not it is clicking with proper precision.

To the uninitiated, another of the instant analogies to the ship derives from the miles and miles of pipes coiling and winding on all sides in a gleaming world of copper and stainless steel. There are lines of pipes, refrigeration lines, steam condensate lines, hot and cold water pipes, cooling towers, wort and sanitary lines—all spiraling, curling and winding about in intricate metallic patterns.

Brewery refrigeration alone takes as much as 400 feet of 2-inch pipe for each ton of refrigeration, and there are breweries that require 1,000 tons of refrigeration, counting the building's cooling system, the water cooler, the beer cooler and the air conditioning. All this can run to more than 75 miles of pipe alone.

An interesting sidelight on the piping aspect of brewing: hygienic standards require that there be no pockets or obstructions wherein the liquid food might adhere and perhaps spoil, and so in many lines no threaded connections whatsoever are used—thereby providing an extra precaution against even a single drop clinging to the crevices of the threads and affecting the flavor and quality of the final product.

Steam lines are all over the place, carrying 400-pound, 120-pound, 30-pound or 10-pound loads, depending on their functions. The brewing process requires a lot of energy: heat energy for cooking, bottle washing, mashing, pasteurizing and space heating; mechanical and electrical energy for refrigeration, conveying, pumping, mixing and many other things.

It takes more than two miles of steam and steam condensate lines just for processing the brew, heating the building, powering the engines and providing steam for cooking, for brewkettles and for pasteurizing. Beer lines, carrying the product through its varying phases of production through filters and into storage vessels, may run an additional 10,000 feet.

A brewery such as the one we are visiting may also have cold-water lines aggregating about 12,000 feet, liquid ammonia lines of some 2,000 feet, hot-water lines of 7,000 feet and air lines running another 6,000 feet.

These are the things that create an overall impression as you walk about the brewery—the miles of winding pipes, the huge generators producing power, engines pumping relentlessly, vats as big as caves holding the liquid temporarily as it goes along its way from one process to another—until it becomes beer.

The Internal Revenue Service of the United States Treasury Department, which is so interested in the amount of beer produced in our breweries that it has a measuring device at the end of the line in every last brewery, describes a malt beverage as follows:

> Malt beverage means a beverage made by the alcoholic fermentation of an infusion or decoction, or combination of both, in potable brewing water, of malted barley with hops, or their parts, or their products and with or without other malted cereals, and with or without the addition of unmalted or prepared cereals, other carbohydrates or products prepared therefrom, and with or without other wholesome products suitable for human food consumption.

Not being one to readily contend with the IRS and its complexities of definition, I think it wise to return to the firmer ground of our tour. As the first step, we pause to inspect a display case that shows visitors the basic raw materials of beer. We reach in and experience the "handle" of malted barley and learn that other grains such as corn and rice are "adjuncts" that may also be used in the brewing process.

Our Falstaff barley is a so-called "six-row" type (as opposed to the two-row, referring to the number of rows of flowers surrounding the barley stem and ultimately developing into seeds). It has already been malted in another plant, which results—after steeping, germinating and kilning procedures—in a grain containing less moisture than the original; and the original hard, raw, flat-tasting barley has now been transformed into a mellow, crisp, aromatic malt, slightly sweet to the taste, and ready for the mysterious processes to come.

We are now at the threshold where nature departs and man takes over. We stand with the grains in our hands, about to witness a miracle of metamorphosis.

THE TOUR OF THE BREWERY BEGINS

To clarify in my own mind the brewing steps we are about to see in complicated array, I memorized in advance a sequence of what turns out to be a somewhat misleading simplicity. However, it goes like this:

First, malt is mashed with hot water, then combined with boiled corn or rice and the water solubles extracted to produce a solution known as wort.

Second, hops* are added and the boiling continued.

Third, the hops are removed and the boiling wort cooled to about 50°F.

Fourth, yeast is added and fermentation ensues.

Fifth, the yeast is removed and the beer is filtered and aged.

You, dear reader, don't have to memorize this, of course, but I urge you to tuck it away in the back of your mind and keep the page handy for future reference.

(See pp. 136-39 for a graphic tour of a brewery.)

---

*The industry is gradually moving into the use of hop extract, which eliminates the need for a hop jack to remove the spent blossoms.

The cellar of a brewery is on the roof—but there is a method to this madness for there the grains are stored in bulk and fed into the brewing process by gravity. (In addition to Gambrinus et al., we must remember a toast of gratitude to Newton.)

Now at this point our brew consists of only some grains, and these in the hands of gravity. How does it all become that ultimate glorious thirst-quencher? Where is the *water* of the golden liquid? We learn that our brewery of the moment has deep wells sunk into the ground nearby from which it draws its water. This water, pure to begin with, is scientifically balanced to bring it as close as possible to the perfect ideal.

Satisfied on this point, we go on to the next step and soon learn by looking in at the malt mill that what happens when the malt is "ground"—the technical term used in the brewery—is not that it is pulverized but that it is broken down into something resembling the oatmeal you handle when you are getting ready to cook your breakfast. We understand how important this is to the final product when we learn that for every 500 gallons of beer to be made, 550 pounds of the ground malt will be used.

While this has been happening to the malt, the adjuncts have been going through a sifting process (but not ground) and then they are weighed with the same care as was the malt. The total amount used may vary, since here is one of the steps where the judgment and taste of the brewmaster enter into the process, and we might find one brewery using more or less of these adjuncts than another. But once the proportion has been established, you may be sure that the measurements are followed with scientific dedication.

The adjuncts are now cooked separately from the malt, and agitated as they reach the boiling point, the main purpose being to gelatinize the starch in the grains through this heating process. Again at the discretion of the brewmaster, a bit of the malt may be added into the cereal cooker at this time, in order to induce a subtle taste metamorphosis which, though slight, could be very significant in terms of the final product.

HERE'S HOW BEER IS MADE (A Typical Brewery

Barley malt is crushed in the malt mill in preparation for . . .

"Mashing" in hot water, then blended with other grain adjuncts in the cereal cooker

A straining process at the "grant" removes spent grain solids, leaving amber liquid called "wort."

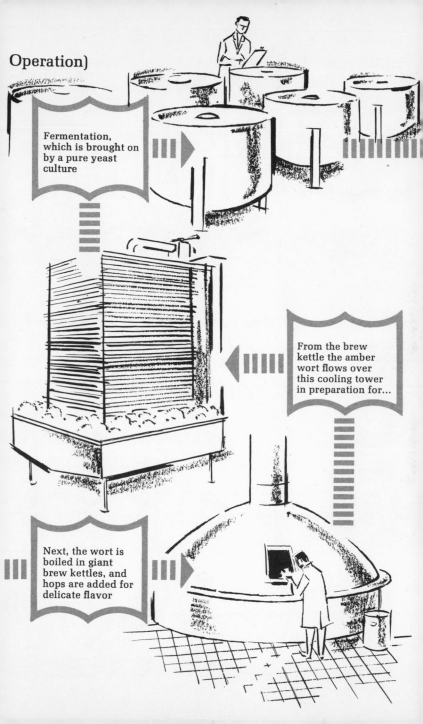

Operation)

Fermentation, which is brought on by a pure yeast culture

From the brew kettle the amber wort flows over this cooling tower in preparation for...

Next, the wort is boiled in giant brew kettles, and hops are added for delicate flavor

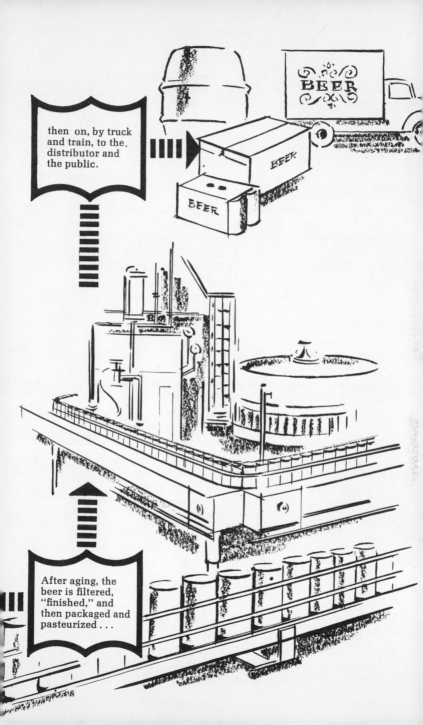

then on, by truck and train, to the distributor and the public.

BEER

BEER

BEER

After aging, the beer is filtered, "finished," and then packaged and pasteurized . . .

The malt meanwhile undergoes its own cooking treatment in one of the huge, shining mash tanks, where it is infused in warm-to-hot water. The brewmaster has his say on just how long the malt should be cooked, and then the adjuncts and malt are brought together and cooked to a temperature of about 154°F. The visitor finds himself impressed by the immensity of the equipment used in this process, but another immensity is taking place chemically now as the starch of both the malt and the grains is converted by the malt enzymes into sugar. Here is part of the "mystery" we have mentioned earlier, which struck the ancients with a veritable religious awe.

In modern terms, we now have the kind of sugar in our cooker known as dextrose. And, of course, our friend the brewmaster must make precise calculations in order to relate the amount of fermentable material he now has in his batch to what he knows it will have to do further along in the beer brewing process. We are looking at kettles big enough to boil cereal for a large part of the Russian Army, but the brewmaster sees this great output in terms of a few minute formulae in his head. We see a mash; he sees a variety of fermentable and flavorful sugars. This sheer, natural miracle of compositional change has produced myriads of sugars in precise ratios from the original starch. Yet these sugars still contain the same elements of carbon, hydrogen, and oxygen while still being different from the starch in taste, texture and other qualities. It is all the same; but all different, too. No wonder it has taken centuries of brewing to reach an understanding of the underlying chemistry.

Our next step is a straining process known as "lautering." This is accomplished in a tank known in brewing as a tun (vintners call a tun any large cask which will hold 252 gallons of wine, but brewers use the term refer to any big vat or tank). What we have here is really a large vessel with perforations at the bottom which functions like the familiar kitchen collander. We are now draining off the liquid from the barley husks and undissolved portions of the other cereals. The latter, called "spent grain," are really far from spent, in that they are cleaned (we are now technical enough to know that this is called "sparging") and then they go on in the form of livestock feed because of the rich supply of protein they have retained.

So now we have an amber colored liquid known as wort, but the thirsty visitor must refrain from saying anything yet about *beer* to avoid inflicting great mental pain on our host the brewmaster. *Beer*, to be called that, just hasn't happened yet. It is lurking around the corner, but the most you are permitted to put the possibility into words is something like the baseball announcer, watching a .300 hitter taking preliminary swings with the wood, who hopefully remarks that the tieing run is now in the on-deck box. So we beer lovers all shrug our shoulders, join the club, and call our liquid wort.

The next step is to pump the wort into huge brew kettles, where life, liberty and the pursuit of hoppiness takes place—for here is where the hops are added, a key step indeed in our brewing. These are gargantuan tanks—the two we are looking at have a combined capacity of 46,500 gallons. They dwarf a man, who must climb steps to look down into them.

The wort boils away merrily as in a giant's percolator, and here the hops are added and begin to release their tang to combine with the sweet essence of the wort. The character of the beer begins to emerge.

Quite obviously, the art of the brewmaster is given an exacting trial at this point, for here is where so many of the characteristics of the perfect beer he has in the back of his mind are dependant upon the amount of hops added, and how long they may be boiled with the wort—it is a delicate balance. You can read this recipe as many times as you may wish, but there are secrets of timing and combination which even he may not be able to put into words. It is the kind of thing one must feel rather than say; it is intuition reaching above mere logic.

What is going on in there is that the bitter substances of the hops, tanins and resins are balancing the bland sweetness of the wort to yield the marvelous tang of the beer. The journey from the original malt to this "hopped wort" has taken about six to eight hours.

Now the wort is to be cooled and we encounter a diverting little reminder of the ancient past of the brewing process, as this takes place in a tank called a "cool shiff," the word "shiff" being an old German term for "boat" (our word "skiff" has the same origin) and indeed there was a time in the old days when the cooling tank was in the actual form of a boat. The process is complete after the wort has passed through the schiff and over cooling coils, and its temperature has dropped from 212°F. to about 50°F.

Now the wort is ready for that mysterious metamorphosis into beer known as fermentation. We are at the very heart and "mystery" of brewing—the yeast itself is the agent of fermentation. What it does is to "digest" the sugars of the wort, which once were in the form of starch, and now to effect a changeover into approximately equal parts of carbon dioxide and alcohol. In discussing this part of the action with the brewmaster, one begins to realize that possibly here is where his deepest secrets of taste and quality determination are stored. It is what the industry terms its "controlled miracle."

Every brewery has its own prized strain of yeast, one as closely guarded as the vaults in a bank. Many varieties were brought to America years ago and have been passed down from one generation of brewers to another as the very foundation of their craft. For example, it is a fact that the yeast we see being used here is a special variety that has been treasured by the Falstaff family of brewers for over four generations, coming right on down to the present from the founder himself. For this reason breweries maintain costly laboratories where researchers are continually studying the yeast as well as testing the grains, mashes and wort at these various steps in the brewing process.

Yeast itself, that magic form of life, looks something like cream cheese. Actually, it is a mass of millions of one-celled plants which propogate primarily by budding. Those fermentable sugars serve as food for the yeast, and as the origin of the fermentable products, which are carbon dioxide and grain alcohol. The yeast cells grow and subdivide in the fermentation process. Usually more yeast comes out of the process than was put in.

Actually this is the same step with which we are familiar in the baking of bread. (Are we familiar with it? Well, we should be.) In the baking process the yeast acts on the starch sugar of the wheat in the flour to *leaven* it, meaning "to make light." The carbon dioxide released in the bread dough by this action of the yeast causes the loaf to "rise" in the presence of heat. Brewers are particularly aware that only a minimum of alcohol is necessary to give beer its friendly quality, so they establish the final amount of alcohol to be produced by controlling very carefully the conversion temperature which determines the ratio of fermentable (alcohol producing) sugars to non-fermentable substances.

This, in fact, may well be the moment of truth for the brewmaster. With everything else he has had to consider, the action of his yeast on the wort is a highly critical point in the entire process. For instance, he might take the same wort, and by adding different kinds of yeast, wind up with as many different kinds of beer. But, of course, he must be faithful to the standards of taste which he has set for his special brand of brew. That is probably why, when I mentioned the subject of yeast to my special brewmaster, and was evidently preparing to ask him a number of questions, he gave me the flaccid eye and started to talk about the weather. His yeast is his nuclear secret.

When the yeast has done its work, it is removed, returned to the vaults in the "yeast room" and washed to eliminate any cells which may have been used up in the fermentation process. The excess provides that very valuable by-product of brewing, "brewer's yeast," which I have mentioned previously as being rich in both protein and Vitamin-B complex, a precious dietary supplement for both animals and human beings. The more vigorous yeast cells are retained for another go at a brew yet to come.

In most breweries, the carbon dioxide which is created by the action of the yeast is drawn off and condensed into liquid form, then stored in high pressure tanks, and added to the brew later to give it that inimitable sparkle. (Some breweries carbonate the beer by another method called "krausening," which means they add a small percentage of young fermenting beer to a batch of finished beer which, however, has not yet aged. What happens then is that the beer is carbonated by natural process, as it were, being the action of the carbon dioxide resulting from the fermentation of the newly-added wort.)

You can see that the brewery is a busy place, indeed, and yet all this which is taking place is simply a matter of letting nature take its course with the minimal guidance of scientific control. Now the beer is drained off from the fermentation tanks, and the brew is drawn into the lagering or mellowing tanks—once again, a harking back to the ancient days of brewing when the beer was *stored* (or "*lagered*") in caves to cool.

The fermentation process has taken nine or ten days in all, while the brewmaster practically "thinks yeast" as a good chef must almost become a piece of steak in order to imagine what is going inside as broils it over the fire. And now the brew rests, and is aged. Again, the length of time is up to the brewmaster. This is another one of his secrets, I gather, so I do not pursue the subject too closely with our brewmaster-host. We stand thirstily by the great white tanks containing the aging beer. They hold 1,100 barrels each, and they resemble whales in both size and shape. We see whole schools of them—specifically, five floors with sixteen whales on each floor. That's a *lot* of beer!

Then the beer is released for filtering—passing it through layer after layer of tightly packed inert material under high pressure—and we see that incredibly clear and sparkling look so characteristic of our fine brew.

The U.S. government takes a very close interest in what goes on in every brewery. The final resting place of the finished beer is in what are called the "government tanks." What this really means is that the brew-master has put his OK on the product, but it yet remains to be measured out by the government before heading for the market. The beer passes through meters which give Uncle Sam an absolute check on the gallonage of the beer produced and the amount of taxes due. The government continues its avuncular curiosity in other functions of the brewery as well. Every American brewery must maintain a clear blueprint showing its floorplans and the location of every last single piece of equipment to keep the government inspectors informed. Every cellar, every room, and each piece of equipment on the premises must bear labels of identification and capacity if materials are stored in them. All construction changes contemplated in the brewery must be government approved before a hammer is raised or a blowtorch lighted. And the government looks over the brewer's shoulder even after the beer has gone out to the consumer with a variety of licensing and other controls over the areas of outside distribution and purchase.

THE BEER IS PACKAGED

The very end of the line in the brewery is the packaging plant. And here for the first time we see something in the brewery which relates to what goes on in the more conventional food packing or processing plants. For now we see the machine-gun action of automatic filling equipment which can fill and seal 1,000 units per minute. In another section of the packaging department, we see the draught beer filling barrels in the "racking room." The barrels, of stainless steel or aluminum, are first cleaned and sterilized, and then filled at a pressure of approximately 14 pounds to the square inch. The filled barrel is finally closed with a fresh plug of wood called a bung. A fellow who could knock down the defensive line of a professional football team entirely on his own, flexes his biceps and wallops the bung into the hole with one single unerring blow of a mallet that would fell a rhinoceros. The boys in the racking room are nice to have as friends.

The wonders of the bottling operation, outside of the sheer mechanical speed of the operation, were focused for me in the testing device at one point along the line. This is a machine with a brain and an eye for beauty. Not only will it automatically reject any bottle that is cracked or imperfectly sealed, but it also casts a light beam through the beer inside of the package and judges its condition thereby: anything less than perfection is ejected from the rapidly moving line.

And finally the canned and bottled beer is pasteurized—shades of the great French scientist! This is done quickly—at 140° F.—and then the beer is ready for its journey to the distributors and retailers who will pass it along to the consumer.

Our tour ends with a side trip to the laboratory, where the brewmaster immediately engages in a scholarly discussion with one of his aides. The atmosphere has suddenly changed from the noise and din of the bottling plant to the studious air of the lab. To all intents and purposes we could well be in the science department of a great university.

Our tour of the brewery is over. From now on, when I hold a glass of beer in my hand and squint at it lovingly—noting the marvelous head of foam, the sparkling bubbles within and the pure, clear color—I shall not only appreciate that it is a superb taste accomplishment and a controlled miracle of nature, but I am also going to know why, how, when and wherefore. I heartily recommend that as soon as you can, you make arrangements to follow in my footsteps and visit one of the great breweries of America, where you are sure to be welcome.

It is adventure and education and enjoyment, and a lingering sense of wonder, all in one.

And there, as we leave, looms the heroic statue of Gambrinus, once again.

Hail, great patron saint, but not farewell. For we shall return. If not here, then wherever there is a glass of the golden brew and the mystery and the art of beer ply their magic once more for the enrichment of man.

INDEX

Region	Caribbean	Population (000, 2017)	3 663 [a]
Surface area (km2)	8 868 [b]	Pop. density (per km2, 2017)	413.0 [a]
Sex ratio (m per 100 f, 2017)	92.6 [a]	Capital city	San Juan
National currency	US Dollar (USD)	Capital city pop. (000)	2 463.2 [c,b]

Economic indicators	2005	2010	2017
GDP: Gross domestic product (million current US$)	83 914	98 381	102 906 [b]
GDP growth rate (annual %, const. 2005 prices)	- 2.0	- 0.4	~-0.0 [b]
GDP per capita (current US$)	22 310.9	26 520.2	27 939.0 [b]
Economy: Agriculture (% of GVA) [d]	0.6	0.8	0.8 [b]
Economy: Industry (% of GVA) [d]	47.3	50.7	50.0 [b]
Economy: Services and other activity (% of GVA) [d]	52.1	48.4	49.1 [b]
Employment: Agriculture (% of employed) [e]	2.2	1.8	2.0
Employment: Industry (% of employed) [e]	20.1	16.9	17.5
Employment: Services (% of employed) [e]	77.7	81.3	80.5
Unemployment (% of labour force)	11.4	16.1	12.8 [e]
Labour force participation (female/male pop. %) [e]	38.1 / 61.0	35.1 / 53.7	34.4 / 51.7
CPI: Consumer Price Index (2000=100)	111	131	139 [f]
Agricultural production index (2004-2006=100)	96	106	110 [f]
Food production index (2004-2006=100)	97	107	111 [f]

Social indicators	2005	2010	2017
Population growth rate (average annual %) [g]	- 0.2	- 0.3	- 0.2 [b]
Urban population (% of total population)	94.1	93.8	93.6 [b]
Urban population growth rate (average annual %) [g]	- 0.2	- 0.3	- 0.2 [b]
Fertility rate, total (live births per woman) [g]	1.8	1.7	1.5 [b]
Life expectancy at birth (females/males, years) [g]	80.9 / 72.7	81.8 / 73.8	83.2 / 75.2 [b]
Population age distribution (0-14 and 60+ years, %)	22.3 / 16.7	20.6 / 18.1	17.9 / 20.4 [a]
International migrant stock (000/% of total pop.)	352.1 / 9.4	305.0 / 8.2	275.0 / 7.5 [b]
Infant mortality rate (per 1 000 live births) [g]	8.0	7.0	6.3 [b]
Education: Government expenditure (% of GDP)	...	...	6.4 [b]
Education: Primary gross enrol. ratio (f/m per 100 pop.)	... / ...	96.5 / 93.2	90.4 / 89.1 [f]
Education: Secondary gross enrol. ratio (f/m per 100 pop.)	... / ...	85.3 / 80.7	83.9 / 78.8 [f]
Education: Tertiary gross enrol. ratio (f/m per 100 pop.)	... / ...	103.2 / 69.9	98.8 / 70.1 [f]
Intentional homicide rate (per 100 000 pop.)	20.5	26.3	15.9 [b]

Environment and infrastructure indicators	2005	2010	2017
Mobile-cellular subscriptions (per 100 inhabitants)	53.0	79.1	87.1 [b]
Individuals using the Internet (per 100 inhabitants)	23.4 [e]	45.3 [i]	79.5 [e,b]
Research & Development expenditure (% of GDP)	...	0.5 [j]	0.4 [h]
Threatened species (number)	97 [k]	103	126
Forested area (% of land area)	52.2	54.0 [e]	55.5 [e,f]
Energy production, primary (Petajoules)	0	0	1 [f]
Energy supply per capita (Gigajoules)	6	7	16 [f]
Tourist/visitor arrivals at national borders (000) [l]	3 686	3 186	3 542 [b]
Important sites for terrestrial biodiversity protected (%)	34.0	34.0	34.0
Pop. using improved drinking water (urban/rural, %)	93.6 / 93.6 [m]	... / ...	... / ...
Pop. using improved sanitation facilities (urban/rural, %)	99.3 / 99.3	99.3 / 99.3	99.3 / 99.3 [b]

a Projected estimate (medium fertility variant). **b** 2015. **c** Refers to the Metropolitan Statistical Area. **d** At producers' prices. **e** Estimate. **f** 2014. **g** Data refers to a 5-year period preceding the reference year. **h** 2013. **i** Population aged 12 years and over. **j** 2009. **k** 2004. **l** Arrivals of non-resident tourists by air. **m** 2000.

Qatar

Region	Western Asia	UN membership date	21 September 1971	
Population (000, 2017)	2 639 [a]	Surface area (km2)	11 607 [b]	
Pop. density (per km2, 2017)	227.3 [a]	Sex ratio (m per 100 f, 2017)	301.2 [a]	
Capital city	Doha	National currency	Qatari Rial (QAR)	
Capital city pop. (000)	717.8 [b]	Exchange rate (per US$)	3.6 [c]	

Economic indicators

	2005	2010	2017
GDP: Gross domestic product (million current US$)	43 998	123 627	164 641 [b]
GDP growth rate (annual %, const. 2005 prices)	7.5	16.7	3.6 [b]
GDP per capita (current US$)	52 571.5	70 023.3	73 653.4 [b]
Economy: Agriculture (% of GVA) [d]	0.1	0.1	0.2 [b]
Economy: Industry (% of GVA) [d]	74.6	67.5	56.4 [b]
Economy: Services and other activity (% of GVA) [d]	25.3	32.4	43.5 [b]
Employment: Agriculture (% of employed) [e]	2.8	1.5	1.2
Employment: Industry (% of employed) [e]	41.4	56.8	54.1
Employment: Services (% of employed) [e]	55.8	41.8	44.7
Unemployment (% of labour force)	1.6 [e]	0.5	0.3 [e]
Labour force participation (female/male pop. %) [e]	43.5 / 94.1	51.5 / 95.7	53.1 / 93.6
CPI: Consumer Price Index (2000=100) [f]	119	162	178 [g]
Agricultural production index (2004-2006=100)	97	127	154 [g]
Food production index (2004-2006=100)	97	127	154 [g]
Index of industrial production (2005=100) [h]	100	190	226 [g]
International trade: Exports (million US$)	25 762	74 964	57 254 [c]
International trade: Imports (million US$)	10 061	23 240	32 058 [c]
International trade: Balance (million US$)	15 702	51 725	25 196 [c]
Balance of payments, current account (million US$)	...	...	13 751 [b]

Major trading partners   2016

Export partners (% of exports)	Japan	20.8	Republic of Korea	17.3	India	11.9
Import partners (% of imports)	China	11.5	United States	11.0	United Arab Emirates	8.8

Social indicators

	2005	2010	2017
Population growth rate (average annual %) [i]	7.6	14.4	6.6 [b]
Urban population (% of total population)	97.4	98.7	99.2 [b]
Urban population growth rate (average annual %) [i]	6.7	15.4	6.0 [b]
Fertility rate, total (live births per woman) [i]	3.0	2.2	2.0 [b]
Life expectancy at birth (females/males, years) [i]	78.1 / 75.6	78.6 / 75.9	79.4 / 76.8 [b]
Population age distribution (0-14 and 60+ years, %)	21.7 / 2.5	13.1 / 1.8	13.9 / 2.8 [a]
International migrant stock (000/% of total pop.) [j]	646.0 / 77.2	1 456.4 / 82.5	1 687.6 / 75.5 [b]
Refugees and others of concern to UNHCR (000)	0.1 [k]	1.3 [k]	1.5 [c]
Infant mortality rate (per 1 000 live births) [i]	9.4	7.8	7.2 [b]
Health: Total expenditure (% of GDP) [l]	3.0	2.1	2.2 [g]
Health: Physicians (per 1 000 pop.)	2.6	3.9	2.0 [g]
Education: Government expenditure (% of GDP)	4.0	4.5	3.6 [g]
Education: Primary gross enrol. ratio (f/m per 100 pop.)	103.7 / 107.1	105.9 / 104.7	103.6 / 102.4 [b]
Education: Secondary gross enrol. ratio (f/m per 100 pop.)	96.0 / 102.3	103.3 / 99.2	103.6 / 82.0 [b]
Education: Tertiary gross enrol. ratio (f/m per 100 pop.)	31.1 / 8.8 [e]	25.6 / 4.8	43.9 / 6.3 [b]
Intentional homicide rate (per 100 000 pop.)	4.9	6.9	8.1 [b]
Seats held by women in national parliaments (%)	...	0.0	0.0

Environment and infrastructure indicators

	2005	2010	2017
Mobile-cellular subscriptions (per 100 inhabitants)	87.3 [m]	125.0 [n]	153.6 [b]
Individuals using the Internet (per 100 inhabitants)	24.7	69.0	92.9 [o,b]
Research & Development expenditure (% of GDP)	...	...	0.5 [p]
Threatened species (number)	12 [q]	32	39
Forested area (% of land area) [e]	0.0	0.0	0.0 [g]
CO2 emission estimates (million tons/tons per capita)	51.0 / 62.1	72.5 / 41.1	107.9 / 49.7 [g]
Energy production, primary (Petajoules)	3 718	7 428	9 166 [g]
Energy supply per capita (Gigajoules)	886	660	846 [g]
Tourist/visitor arrivals at national borders (000)	...	...	2 930 [r,b]
Important sites for terrestrial biodiversity protected (%)	12.4	12.4	12.4
Pop. using improved drinking water (urban/rural, %)	99.7 / 99.7	100.0 / 100.0	100.0 / 100.0 [b]
Pop. using improved sanitation facilities (urban/rural, %)	98.8 / 98.8	98.3 / 98.2	98.0 / 98.0 [b]

a Projected estimate (medium fertility variant). b 2015. c 2016. d Data classified according to ISIC Rev. 4. e Estimate. f Index base: 2002=100. g 2014. h Data classified according to ISIC Rev. 3. i Data refers to a 5-year period preceding the reference year. j Refers to foreign citizens. k Data as at the end of December. l Data revision. m Includes inactive subscriptions. n Data refers to active subscriptions only. o Population aged 15 years and over. p 2012. q 2004. r Arrivals in hotels only.

Republic of Korea

Region	Eastern Asia	UN membership date	17 September 1991
Population (000, 2017)	50 982 [a]	Surface area (km2)	100 284 [b]
Pop. density (per km2, 2017)	524.3 [a]	Sex ratio (m per 100 f, 2017)	100.2 [a]
Capital city	Seoul	National currency	South Korean Won (KRW)
Capital city pop. (000)	9 773.7 [c,b]	Exchange rate (per US$)	1 208.5 [d]

Economic indicators	2005	2010	2017
GDP: Gross domestic product (million current US$)	898 137	1 094 499	1 377 873 [b]
GDP growth rate (annual %, const. 2005 prices)	3.9	6.5	2.6 [b]
GDP per capita (current US$)	18 866.1	22 295.8	27 396.7 [b]
Economy: Agriculture (% of GVA) [e]	3.1	2.5	2.3 [b]
Economy: Industry (% of GVA) [e]	37.5	38.3	38.0 [b]
Economy: Services and other activity (% of GVA) [e]	59.4	59.3	59.7 [b]
Employment: Agriculture (% of employed) [f]	7.9	6.6	5.0
Employment: Industry (% of employed) [f]	26.8	24.9	24.7
Employment: Services (% of employed) [f]	65.3	68.5	70.3
Unemployment (% of labour force)	3.7	3.7	3.6 [f]
Labour force participation (female/male pop. %) [f]	49.5 / 72.6	49.3 / 71.7	50.2 / 71.9
CPI: Consumer Price Index (2000=100) [h]	100 [g]	116	127 [i]
Agricultural production index (2004-2006=100)	100	101	104 [i]
Food production index (2004-2006=100)	100	101	104 [i]
Index of industrial production (2005=100)	100	139 [j]	151 [j,i]
International trade: Exports (million US$)	284 418	466 381	495 418 [d]
International trade: Imports (million US$)	261 236	425 208	406 182 [d]
International trade: Balance (million US$)	23 183	41 173	89 236 [d]
Balance of payments, current account (million US$)	12 655	28 850	105 871 [b]

Major trading partners					2016
Export partners (% of exports)	China	25.1	United States	13.5	China, Hong Kong SAR 6.6
Import partners (% of imports)	China	21.4	Japan	11.7	United States 10.7

Social indicators	2005	2010	2017
Population growth rate (average annual %) [k]	0.6	0.3	0.4 [b]
Urban population (% of total population)	81.3	81.9	82.5 [b]
Urban population growth rate (average annual %) [k]	0.9	0.7	0.7 [b]
Fertility rate, total (live births per woman) [k]	1.2	1.2	1.2 [b]
Life expectancy at birth (females/males, years) [k]	80.6 / 73.6	82.7 / 76.0	84.4 / 77.9 [b]
Population age distribution (0-14 and 60+ years, %)	18.8 / 12.8	16.1 / 15.3	13.5 / 20.1 [a]
International migrant stock (000/% of total pop.) [l]	485.5 / 1.0	919.3 / 1.9	1 327.3 / 2.6 [b]
Refugees and others of concern to UNHCR (000)	0.6 [m]	1.2 [m]	8.0 [d]
Infant mortality rate (per 1 000 live births) [k]	5.0	3.5	3.0 [b]
Health: Total expenditure (% of GDP)	5.3	6.8	7.4 [i]
Health: Physicians (per 1 000 pop.)	1.8	2.0	2.2 [i]
Education: Government expenditure (% of GDP)	3.9	4.7 [n]	5.1 [b]
Education: Primary gross enrol. ratio (f/m per 100 pop.)	111.2 / 112.0	101.3 / 102.5	98.7 / 99.3 [b]
Education: Secondary gross enrol. ratio (f/m per 100 pop.)	92.2 / 94.1	95.6 / 96.6	98.4 / 99.3 [b]
Education: Tertiary gross enrol. ratio (f/m per 100 pop.)	71.1 / 107.4	83.9 / 113.5	80.2 / 104.8 [b]
Intentional homicide rate (per 100 000 pop.)	...	...	0.7 [i]
Seats held by women in national parliaments (%)	13.0	14.7	17.0

Environment and infrastructure indicators	2005	2010	2017
Mobile-cellular subscriptions (per 100 inhabitants)	81.5	104.8	118.5 [b]
Individuals using the Internet (per 100 inhabitants)	73.5 [o]	83.7 [o]	89.9 [p,b]
Research & Development expenditure (% of GDP)	2.6 [q]	3.5	4.3 [i]
Threatened species (number)	55 [r]	64	111
Forested area (% of land area)	64.6	64.0 [f]	63.5 [f,i]
CO2 emission estimates (million tons/tons per capita)	462.9 / 9.8	566.7 / 11.6	587.2 / 11.7 [i]
Energy production, primary (Petajoules)	1 776	1 855	2 023 [i]
Energy supply per capita (Gigajoules)	186	213	223 [i]
Tourist/visitor arrivals at national borders (000) [s]	6 023	8 798	13 232 [b]
Important sites for terrestrial biodiversity protected (%)	27.3	36.4	36.6
Pop. using improved drinking water (urban/rural, %)	99.1 / 83.2	99.7 / 87.9	99.7 / 87.9 [b,t]
Pop. using improved sanitation facilities (urban/rural, %)	100.0 / 100.0	100.0 / 100.0	100.0 / 100.0 [b]
Net Official Development Assist. disbursed (% of GNI) [u]	0.10	0.12	0.14 [v,d]

a Projected estimate (medium fertility variant). b 2015. c Refers to Seoul Special City. d 2016. e Data classified according to ISIC Rev. 4. f Estimate. g Break in the time series. h Index base: 2005=100. i 2014. j Excluding water and waste management. k Data refers to a 5-year period preceding the reference year. l Refers to foreign citizens. m Data as at the end of December. n 2009. o Population aged 3 years and over. p Population aged 16 to 74 years. q Excluding social sciences and humanities. r 2004. s Including nationals residing abroad and crew members. t 2012. u Development Assistance Committee member (OECD) v Provisional data.

Republic of Moldova

Region	Eastern Europe	UN membership date	02 March 1992
Population (000, 2017)	4 051 [a,b]	Surface area (km2)	33 846 [c]
Pop. density (per km2, 2017)	123.3 [a,b]	Sex ratio (m per 100 f, 2017)	92.2 [a,b]
Capital city	Chisinau	National currency	Moldovan Leu (MDL)
Capital city pop. (000)	725.4 [c]	Exchange rate (per US$)	20.0 [d]

Economic indicators

	2005	2010	2017
GDP: Gross domestic product (million current US$)	2 988	5 812	6 475 [c]
GDP growth rate (annual %, const. 2005 prices)	7.5	7.1	- 0.7 [c]
GDP per capita (current US$)	718.7	1 422.9	1 591.4 [c]
Economy: Agriculture (% of GVA)	19.1	14.1	13.4 [c]
Economy: Industry (% of GVA)	22.2	19.5	20.8 [c]
Economy: Services and other activity (% of GVA)	58.7	66.4	65.8 [c]
Employment: Agriculture (% of employed) [e]	32.9	27.5	28.8
Employment: Industry (% of employed) [e]	32.5	32.2	30.9
Employment: Services (% of employed) [e]	34.6	40.3	40.3
Unemployment (% of labour force)	7.3	7.5	5.0 [e]
Labour force participation (female/male pop. %) [e]	47.9 / 50.4	38.6 / 45.3	39.1 / 46.5
CPI: Consumer Price Index (2000=100) [f]	99 [g]	152	189 [h]
Agricultural production index (2004-2006=100)	100	93	109 [h]
Food production index (2004-2006=100)	100	93	109 [h]
Index of industrial production (2005=100) [i]	100	82	94 [j]
International trade: Exports (million US$)	1 091	1 541	2 045 [d]
International trade: Imports (million US$)	2 292	3 855	4 020 [d]
International trade: Balance (million US$)	- 1 201	- 2 314	- 1 975 [d]
Balance of payments, current account (million US$)	- 248	- 534	- 415 [c]

Major trading partners

						2016
Export partners (% of exports)	Romania	25.1	Russian Federation	11.4	Italy	9.7
Import partners (% of imports)	Romania	13.7	Russian Federation	13.3	China	9.8

Social indicators

	2005	2010	2017
Population growth rate (average annual %) [b,k]	- 0.2	- 0.4	- 0.1 [c]
Urban population (% of total population) [b]	45.3	44.9	45.0 [c]
Urban population growth rate (average annual %) [b,k]	- 1.9	- 1.2	- 0.7 [c]
Fertility rate, total (live births per woman) [b,k]	1.2	1.3	1.3 [c]
Life expectancy at birth (females/males, years) [b,k]	71.6 / 63.6	72.1 / 64.4	75.2 / 66.7 [c]
Population age distribution (0-14 and 60+ years, %) [b]	18.5 / 13.6	16.5 / 14.1	15.7 / 17.6 [a]
International migrant stock (000/% of total pop.) [b]	174.0 / 4.2	157.7 / 3.9	142.9 / 3.5 [c]
Refugees and others of concern to UNHCR (000)	1.8 [l]	2.3 [l]	5.5 [d]
Infant mortality rate (per 1 000 live births) [b,k]	18.9	15.5	14.3 [c]
Health: Total expenditure (% of GDP) [m]	9.2	12.1	10.3 [h]
Health: Physicians (per 1 000 pop.)	...	2.4	2.5 [h]
Education: Government expenditure (% of GDP)	7.2	9.1	7.5 [h]
Education: Primary gross enrol. ratio (f/m per 100 pop.) [e]	97.2 / 98.6	93.3 / 93.7	91.9 / 92.9 [c]
Education: Secondary gross enrol. ratio (f/m per 100 pop.) [e]	90.0 / 86.2	89.0 / 87.0	86.5 / 85.8 [c]
Education: Tertiary gross enrol. ratio (f/m per 100 pop.) [e]	42.9 / 29.5	43.7 / 32.7	47.4 / 35.3 [c]
Intentional homicide rate (per 100 000 pop.)	7.1	6.5	3.2 [h]
Seats held by women in national parliaments (%)	15.8	23.8	22.8

Environment and infrastructure indicators

	2005	2010	2017
Mobile-cellular subscriptions (per 100 inhabitants)	28.9 [n]	71.4 [e]	108.0 [c]
Individuals using the Internet (per 100 inhabitants)	14.6	32.3 [e]	49.8 [e,c]
Research & Development expenditure (% of GDP)	0.4	0.4	0.4 [h]
Threatened species (number)	27 [o]	27	35
Forested area (% of land area) [e]	11.0	11.8	12.3 [h]
CO2 emission estimates (million tons/tons per capita)	4.9 / 1.3	4.9 / 1.2	4.9 / 1.2 [h]
Energy production, primary (Petajoules)	4	8	15 [h]
Energy supply per capita (Gigajoules)	24	22	23 [h]
Tourist/visitor arrivals at national borders (000) [p,q]	67	64	94 [c]
Important sites for terrestrial biodiversity protected (%)	23.6	23.6	23.6
Pop. using improved drinking water (urban/rural, %)	96.8 / 77.4	96.9 / 79.6	96.9 / 81.4 [c]
Pop. using improved sanitation facilities (urban/rural, %)	87.1 / 63.1	87.5 / 65.3	87.8 / 67.1 [c]
Net Official Development Assist. received (% of GNI)	5.07	7.51	4.49 [c]

a Projected estimate (medium fertility variant). b Including Transnistria. c 2015. d 2016. e Estimate. f Index base: 2005=100. g Break in the time series. h 2014. i Data classified according to ISIC Rev. 3. j 2013. k Data refers to a 5-year period preceding the reference year. l Data as at the end of December. m The health expenditure data as well as the population data after 2000 do not include Transdniestria. Data on GDP and private final consumption expenditure exclude Transdniestria from 1995. n Includes inactive subscriptions. o 2004. p Visitors who have benefited from tourism services provided by the tourism agencies and tour operators (titular of tourism licences). q Excluding the left side of the river Nistru and the municipality of Bender.

Réunion

Region	Eastern Africa	Population (000, 2017)	877 [a]
Surface area (km2)	2 513 [b]	Pop. density (per km2, 2017)	350.6 [a]
Sex ratio (m per 100 f, 2017)	93.9 [a]	Capital city	Saint-Denis
National currency	Euro (EUR)	Capital city pop. (000)	143.6 [c]
Exchange rate (per US$)	0.9 [d]		

Economic indicators	2005	2010	2017
Employment: Agriculture (% of employed) [f]	...	4.2 [e]	4.3 [g,h]
Employment: Industry (% of employed) [f]	...	14.1 [e]	12.7 [g,h]
Employment: Services (% of employed) [f]	...	67.1 [e]	81.7 [g,h]
Unemployment (% of labour force) [f]	30.1	28.9	28.9 [g,i]
Labour force participation (female/male pop. %) [f]	41.1 / 60.3	45.3 / 59.9	49.1 / 61.3 [g,i]
CPI: Consumer Price Index (2000=100)	110	121	127 [c]
Agricultural production index (2004-2006=100)	99	105	104 [c]
Food production index (2004-2006=100)	99	105	104 [c]

Social indicators	2005	2010	2017
Population growth rate (average annual %) [j]	1.4	1.0	0.8 [b]
Urban population (% of total population)	92.4	94.0	95.0 [b]
Urban population growth rate (average annual %) [j]	2.0	1.7	1.4 [b]
Fertility rate, total (live births per woman) [j]	2.4	2.4	2.4 [b]
Life expectancy at birth (females/males, years) [j]	80.6 / 73.0	81.9 / 74.5	82.9 / 76.0 [b]
Population age distribution (0-14 and 60+ years, %)	26.9 / 10.3	25.4 / 12.2	23.6 / 16.4 [a]
International migrant stock (000/% of total pop.)	115.1 / 14.5	123.0 / 14.8	127.2 / 14.8 [b]
Infant mortality rate (per 1 000 live births) [j]	7.6	5.6	4.2 [b]
Intentional homicide rate (per 100 000 pop.)	3.2	1.8 [k]	...

Environment and infrastructure indicators	2005	2010	2017
Threatened species (number)	48 [l]	104	130
Forested area (% of land area) [m]	34.0	35.2	35.1 [c]
CO2 emission estimates (million tons/tons per capita)	3.4 / 4.3	4.2 / 5.0	4.2 / 4.9 [c]
Energy production, primary (Petajoules)	7	8	8 [c]
Energy supply per capita (Gigajoules)	61	70	68 [c]
Tourist/visitor arrivals at national borders (000)	409	420	426 [b]
Important sites for terrestrial biodiversity protected (%)	3.2	90.6	90.6
Pop. using improved drinking water (urban/rural, %)	99.2 / 97.8	99.2 / 97.8	99.2 / 97.8 [b]
Pop. using improved sanitation facilities (urban/rural, %)	98.4 / 95.2	98.4 / 95.2	98.4 / 95.3 [b]

a Projected estimate (medium fertility variant). b 2015. c 2014. d 2016. e Population aged 15 to 64 years. f Excluding the institutional population. g Break in the time series. h 2012. i 2013. j Data refers to a 5-year period preceding the reference year. k 2009. l 2004. m Estimate.

Romania

Region	Eastern Europe	
Population (000, 2017)	19 679[a]	
Pop. density (per km2, 2017)	85.5[a]	
Capital city	Bucharest	
Capital city pop. (000)	1 867.7[b]	

UN membership date	14 December 1955
Surface area (km2)	238 391[b]
Sex ratio (m per 100 f, 2017)	94.0[a]
National currency	Romanian Leu (RON)
Exchange rate (per US$)	4.3[c]

Economic indicators

	2005	2010	2017
GDP: Gross domestic product (million current US$)	99 699	167 998	177 956[b]
GDP growth rate (annual %, const. 2005 prices)	4.2	- 0.8	3.7[b]
GDP per capita (current US$)	4 657.2	8 276.2	9 120.7[b]
Economy: Agriculture (% of GVA)[d]	9.5	6.3	4.8[b]
Economy: Industry (% of GVA)[d]	36.0	41.3	34.9[b]
Economy: Services and other activity (% of GVA)[d]	54.5	52.4	60.3[b]
Employment: Agriculture (% of employed)[e]	32.3	30.1	25.5
Employment: Industry (% of employed)[e]	30.5	28.6	27.7
Employment: Services (% of employed)[e]	37.3	41.3	46.8
Unemployment (% of labour force)	7.2	7.0	7.1[e]
Labour force participation (female/male pop. %)[e]	47.4 / 62.1	47.3 / 63.6	47.3 / 64.5
CPI: Consumer Price Index (2000=100)[f]	232	313	359[g]
Agricultural production index (2004-2006=100)	95	91	100[g]
Food production index (2004-2006=100)	95	91	100[g]
Index of industrial production (2005=100)	100	123[h]	155[h,g]
International trade: Exports (million US$)	27 730	49 413	63 581[c]
International trade: Imports (million US$)	40 463	62 007	74 605[c]
International trade: Balance (million US$)	- 12 733	- 12 593	- 11 024[c]
Balance of payments, current account (million US$)	- 8 541[i]	- 8 479	- 2 096[b]

Major trading partners

							2016
Export partners (% of exports)	Germany	21.5	Italy	11.6	France	7.2
Import partners (% of imports)	Germany	20.5	Italy	10.3	Hungary	7.5

Social indicators

	2005	2010	2017
Population growth rate (average annual %)[j]	- 0.6	- 0.9	- 0.6[b]
Urban population (% of total population)	53.2	53.8	54.6[b]
Urban population growth rate (average annual %)[j]	- 0.2	-0.0	-0.0[b]
Fertility rate, total (live births per woman)[j]	1.3	1.4	1.5[b]
Life expectancy at birth (females/males, years)[j]	75.2 / 67.9	76.7 / 69.5	78.4 / 71.4[b]
Population age distribution (0-14 and 60+ years, %)	15.9 / 19.6	15.8 / 21.4	15.3 / 24.9[a]
International migrant stock (000/% of total pop.)	145.2 / 0.7	156.0 / 0.8	226.9 / 1.2[b]
Refugees and others of concern to UNHCR (000)	2.7[k]	1.7[k]	3.2[c]
Infant mortality rate (per 1 000 live births)[l]	16.9	12.0	8.7[b]
Health: Total expenditure (% of GDP)	5.5	5.8	5.6[g]
Health: Physicians (per 1 000 pop.)	2.0[l]	2.5	2.7[m]
Education: Government expenditure (% of GDP)	3.5	3.5	3.1[g]
Education: Primary gross enrol. ratio (f/m per 100 pop.)	107.9 / 109.4	96.5 / 98.0	89.0 / 90.5[b]
Education: Secondary gross enrol. ratio (f/m per 100 pop.)	84.5 / 82.9	99.8 / 100.7	92.0 / 92.5[b]
Education: Tertiary gross enrol. ratio (f/m per 100 pop.)	51.1 / 40.2	78.9 / 57.4	59.0 / 47.8[b]
Intentional homicide rate (per 100 000 pop.)[n]	2.1	2.0	1.5[b]
Seats held by women in national parliaments (%)	11.4	11.4	20.7

Environment and infrastructure indicators

	2005	2010	2017
Mobile-cellular subscriptions (per 100 inhabitants)	60.4	111.4[o]	107.1[o,b]
Individuals using the Internet (per 100 inhabitants)[p]	21.5[e]	39.9	55.8[b]
Research & Development expenditure (% of GDP)	0.4	0.5	0.4[g]
Threatened species (number)	63[q]	64	104
Forested area (% of land area)	27.8	28.3	29.5[e,g]
CO2 emission estimates (million tons/tons per capita)	96.5 / 4.4	79.4 / 3.9	70.0 / 3.6[g]
Energy production, primary (Petajoules)	1 173	1 155	1 109[g]
Energy supply per capita (Gigajoules)	75	73	68[g]
Tourist/visitor arrivals at national borders (000)	5 839	7 498	9 331[b]
Important sites for terrestrial biodiversity protected (%)	14.8	65.4	77.8
Pop. using improved drinking water (urban/rural, %)	98.1 / 83.2	99.7 / 93.7	100.0 / 100.0[b]
Pop. using improved sanitation facilities (urban/rural, %)	90.7 / 58.4	91.5 / 61.1	92.2 / 63.3[b]
Net Official Development Assist. disbursed (% of GNI)	...	0.07	0.11[r,c]

a Projected estimate (medium fertility variant). b 2015. c 2016. d Data classified according to ISIC Rev. 4. e Estimate. f Annual average is weighted mean of monthly data. g 2014. h Excluding water and waste management. i Break in the time series. j Data refers to a 5-year period preceding the reference year. k Data as at the end of December. l 2002. m 2013. n Data refer to offences, not victims, of intentional homicide. o Data refers to pre-paid subscriptions active in the last 6 months (or 180 days). p Population aged 16 to 74 years. q 2004. r Provisional data.

Russian Federation

Region	Eastern Europe	UN membership date	24 October 1945
Population (000, 2017)	143 990 [a]	Surface area (km2)	17 098 246 [b]
Pop. density (per km2, 2017)	8.8 [a]	Sex ratio (m per 100 f, 2017)	86.8 [a]
Capital city	Moscow	National currency	Russian Ruble (RUB)
Capital city pop. (000)	12 165.7 [b]	Exchange rate (per US$)	60.7 [c]

Economic indicators	2005	2010	2017
GDP: Gross domestic product (million current US$)	764 016	1 524 917	1 326 016 [b]
GDP growth rate (annual %, const. 2005 prices)	6.4	4.5	- 3.7 [b]
GDP per capita (current US$)	5 319.6	10 652.0	9 243.3 [b]
Economy: Agriculture (% of GVA)	5.0	3.9	4.7 [b]
Economy: Industry (% of GVA)	38.1	34.7	31.8 [b]
Economy: Services and other activity (% of GVA)	57.0	61.4	63.5 [b]
Employment: Agriculture (% of employed) [d]	10.1	7.9	6.8
Employment: Industry (% of employed) [d]	29.8	27.7	27.1
Employment: Services (% of employed) [d]	60.1	64.4	66.1
Unemployment (% of labour force)	7.1	7.3	5.8 [d]
Labour force participation (female/male pop. %) [d]	56.2 / 68.6	56.5 / 70.7	56.3 / 71.3
CPI: Consumer Price Index (2000=100)	200	325	396 [e]
Agricultural production index (2004-2006=100)	100	94	120 [f]
Food production index (2004-2006=100)	100	94	120 [f]
Index of industrial production (2005=100) [g]	100	109	121 [f]
International trade: Exports (million US$)	241 452	397 068	285 491 [c]
International trade: Imports (million US$)	98 707	228 912	182 257 [c]
International trade: Balance (million US$)	142 744	168 156	103 234 [c]
Balance of payments, current account (million US$)	84 389	67 452	69 000 [b]

Major trading partners					2016
Export partners (% of exports)	Netherlands	10.2	China	9.8	Germany 7.4
Import partners (% of imports)	China	20.9	Germany	10.7	United States 6.1

Social indicators	2005	2010	2017
Population growth rate (average annual %) [h]	- 0.4	- 0.1	0.1 [b]
Urban population (% of total population)	73.5	73.7	74.0 [b]
Urban population growth rate (average annual %) [h]	- 0.4	-0.0	- 0.1 [b]
Fertility rate, total (live births per woman) [h]	1.3	1.4	1.7 [b]
Life expectancy at birth (females/males, years) [h]	72.0 / 58.6	73.7 / 61.0	75.9 / 64.7 [b]
Population age distribution (0-14 and 60+ years, %)	15.2 / 17.2	14.9 / 18.0	17.6 / 21.1 [a]
International migrant stock (000/% of total pop.)	11 667.8 / 8.1	11 194.7 / 7.8	11 643.3 / 8.1 [b]
Refugees and others of concern to UNHCR (000)	483.1 [i]	132.6 [i]	418.4 [c]
Infant mortality rate (per 1 000 live births) [h]	16.2	10.7	8.3 [b]
Health: Total expenditure (% of GDP)	5.2	6.8	7.1 [f]
Health: Physicians (per 1 000 pop.)	...	2.4	3.3 [f]
Education: Government expenditure (% of GDP)	3.8	4.1 [j]	3.9 [k]
Education: Primary gross enrol. ratio (f/m per 100 pop.)	95.4 / 95.2	99.4 / 99.0 [l]	100.9 / 100.1 [b]
Education: Secondary gross enrol. ratio (f/m per 100 pop.)	82.5 / 83.4	84.2 / 85.6 [l]	103.4 / 105.5 [b]
Education: Tertiary gross enrol. ratio (f/m per 100 pop.)	84.2 / 61.3	86.9 / 64.3 [j]	88.3 / 72.9 [b]
Intentional homicide rate (per 100 000 pop.)	...	16.0	11.3 [b]
Seats held by women in national parliaments (%)	9.8	14.0	15.8

Environment and infrastructure indicators	2005	2010	2017
Mobile-cellular subscriptions (per 100 inhabitants)	83.4	165.5 [m]	160.0 [b]
Individuals using the Internet (per 100 inhabitants)	15.2	43.0 [n]	73.4 [o,p,b]
Research & Development expenditure (% of GDP)	1.1	1.1	1.2 [f]
Threatened species (number)	151 [q]	126	235
Forested area (% of land area)	49.4	49.8 [d]	49.8 [d,f]
CO2 emission estimates (million tons/tons per capita)	1 615.1 / 11.2	1 670.5 / 11.7	1 705.3 / 11.9 [f]
Energy production, primary (Petajoules)	50 506	53 679	54 829 [f]
Energy supply per capita (Gigajoules)	190	202	208 [f]
Tourist/visitor arrivals at national borders (000)	22 201	22 281	33 729 [b]
Important sites for terrestrial biodiversity protected (%)	27.1	27.2	27.2
Pop. using improved drinking water (urban/rural, %)	98.5 / 87.6	98.7 / 89.6	98.9 / 91.2 [b]
Pop. using improved sanitation facilities (urban/rural, %)	77.3 / 58.6	77.1 / 58.7	77.0 / 58.7 [b]
Net Official Development Assist. disbursed (% of GNI)	...	0.03	0.08 [r,s,c]

a Projected estimate (medium fertility variant). b 2015. c 2016. d Estimate. e 2013. f 2014. g Data classified according to ISIC Rev. 3. h Data refers to a 5-year period preceding the reference year. i Data as at the end of December. j 2008. k 2012. l 2009. m Includes inactive subscriptions. n Population aged 16 to 74 years. o Population aged 15 to 72 years. p Users in the last 12 months. q 2004. r Some of the debt relief reported by Russia from 2014 onwards may correspond to the credits included in these estimates. Therefore, the statistics currently published on ODA by Russia and the estimates from the previous Chairman's reports should not be used at the same time. s Provisional data.

Rwanda

Region	Eastern Africa	UN membership date	18 September 1962
Population (000, 2017)	12 208[a]	Surface area (km2)	26 338[b]
Pop. density (per km2, 2017)	494.9[a]	Sex ratio (m per 100 f, 2017)	96.2[a]
Capital city	Kigali	National currency	Rwanda Franc (RWF)
Capital city pop. (000)	1 257.0[b]	Exchange rate (per US$)	819.8[c]

Economic indicators	2005	2010	2017
GDP: Gross domestic product (million current US$)	2 581	5 699	8 096[b]
GDP growth rate (annual %, const. 2005 prices)	9.4	7.3	6.9[b]
GDP per capita (current US$)	286.6	553.6	697.3[b]
Economy: Agriculture (% of GVA)[d]	41.3	34.7	34.6[b]
Economy: Industry (% of GVA)[d]	12.5	13.8	15.1[b]
Economy: Services and other activity (% of GVA)[d]	46.2	51.5	50.3[b]
Employment: Agriculture (% of employed)[e]	77.9	77.9	75.0
Employment: Industry (% of employed)[e]	3.8	5.5	7.2
Employment: Services (% of employed)[e]	18.3	16.5	17.8
Unemployment (% of labour force)[e]	2.4	2.7	2.4
Labour force participation (female/male pop. %)[e]	85.6 / 82.5	86.4 / 84.0	86.1 / 83.3
CPI: Consumer Price Index (2000=100)	138	100[f,g]	123[g,h,i]
Agricultural production index (2004-2006=100)	101	140	139[i]
Food production index (2004-2006=100)	101	141	139[i]
International trade: Exports (million US$)	150	242	622[c]
International trade: Imports (million US$)	374	1 405	1 778[c]
International trade: Balance (million US$)	- 224	- 1 163	- 1 157[c]
Balance of payments, current account (million US$)	- 98	- 412	- 1 099[b]

Major trading partners						2016
Export partners (% of exports)	Dem. Rep. of Congo	31.8	Kenya	16.0	United Arab Emirates	14.0
Import partners (% of imports)	China	21.2	Uganda	11.2	Kenya	7.8

Social indicators	2005	2010	2017
Population growth rate (average annual %)[j]	2.3	2.6	2.5[b]
Urban population (% of total population)	19.3	24.0	28.8[b]
Urban population growth rate (average annual %)[j]	7.4	7.1	6.4[b]
Fertility rate, total (live births per woman)[j]	5.4	4.8	4.2[b]
Life expectancy at birth (females/males, years)[j]	51.5 / 49.6	61.5 / 58.6	67.1 / 63.1[b]
Population age distribution (0-14 and 60+ years, %)	41.7 / 4.1	41.8 / 4.1	40.1 / 4.9[a]
International migrant stock (000/% of total pop.)[k]	432.8 / 4.8	436.8 / 4.2	441.5 / 3.8[b]
Refugees and others of concern to UNHCR (000)	64.4[l]	55.7[l]	155.1[c]
Infant mortality rate (per 1 000 live births)	90.7	59.8	44.0[b]
Health: Total expenditure (% of GDP)	6.8	7.9	7.5[i]
Health: Physicians (per 1 000 pop.)	~0.0[m]	0.1	...
Education: Government expenditure (% of GDP)	5.7[n]	4.9	3.6[e,c]
Education: Primary gross enrol. ratio (f/m per 100 pop.)	137.1 / 136.1	144.1 / 140.5	133.4 / 131.7[b]
Education: Secondary gross enrol. ratio (f/m per 100 pop.)	15.1 / 16.9	32.6 / 32.9	38.2 / 35.2[b]
Education: Tertiary gross enrol. ratio (f/m per 100 pop.)	2.0 / 3.5[m]	4.9 / 6.3	6.9 / 9.1[c]
Intentional homicide rate (per 100 000 pop.)	...	4.9	4.5[o]
Seats held by women in national parliaments (%)	48.8	56.3	61.3

Environment and infrastructure indicators	2005	2010	2017
Mobile-cellular subscriptions (per 100 inhabitants)	2.4	32.8	70.5[b]
Individuals using the Internet (per 100 inhabitants)[e]	0.6	8.0	18.0[b]
Threatened species (number)	37[m]	55	62
Forested area (% of land area)[e]	15.6	18.1	19.2[i]
CO2 emission estimates (million tons/tons per capita)	0.5 / 0.1	0.6 / 0.1	0.8 / 0.1[i]
Energy production, primary (Petajoules)	63	76	84[e,i]
Energy supply per capita (Gigajoules)	8	8	8[e,i]
Tourist/visitor arrivals at national borders (000)	...	504	987[b]
Important sites for terrestrial biodiversity protected (%)	45.7	45.7	45.7
Pop. using improved drinking water (urban/rural, %)	85.9 / 65.9	86.2 / 68.9	86.6 / 71.9[b]
Pop. using improved sanitation facilities (urban/rural, %)	59.6 / 50.4	59.1 / 56.7	58.5 / 62.9[b]
Net Official Development Assist. received (% of GNI)	22.42	18.27	13.67[b]

a Projected estimate (medium fertility variant). b 2015. c 2016. d Data classified according to ISIC Rev. 4. e Estimate. f Break in the time series. g Index base: 2010=100. h Series linked to former series. i 2014. j Data refers to a 5-year period preceding the reference year. k Including refugees. l Data as at the end of December. m 2004. n 2001. o 2013.

Saint Helena

Region	Western Africa	Population (000, 2017)	4[a,b]
Surface area (km2)	308[a,c]	Pop. density (per km2, 2017)	10.4[a,b]
Capital city	Jamestown	National currency	Saint Helena Pound (SHP)
Capital city pop. (000)	0.6[d]	Exchange rate (per US$)	0.8[e]

Economic indicators	2005	2010	2017
Employment: Agriculture (% of employed)	...	7.3[f,g,h]	...
Employment: Industry (% of employed)	...	20.0[f,g,h]	...
Employment: Services (% of employed)	...	72.7[f,g,h]	...
Unemployment (% of labour force)	5.2	2.0	...
CPI: Consumer Price Index (2000=100)	116	155[i]	180[d]
International trade: Exports (million US$)[j]	1	~0	~0[e]
International trade: Imports (million US$)[j]	12	20	48[e]
International trade: Balance (million US$)[j]	- 12	- 20	- 48[e]

Major trading partners						2016
Export partners (% of exports)	United States	57.1	Japan	15.8	Australia	7.0
Import partners (% of imports)	United Kingdom	45.3	South Africa	32.1	Austria	6.4

Social indicators	2005	2010	2017
Population growth rate (average annual %)[a,k]	- 3.6	- 0.5	- 0.7[c]
Urban population (% of total population)[a]	39.9	39.5	39.4[c]
Urban population growth rate (average annual %)[a,k]	- 2.0	- 2.2	- 0.6[c]
International migrant stock (000/% of total pop.)[a]	0.5 / 11.4	0.6 / 13.6	0.6 / 15.2[c]

Environment and infrastructure indicators	2005	2010	2017
Mobile-cellular subscriptions (per 100 inhabitants)	0.0	0.0	30.7[c]
Individuals using the Internet (per 100 inhabitants)	15.9	24.9	37.6[l,m]
Threatened species (number)[a]	60[n]	60	100
Forested area (% of land area)[a,l]	5.1	5.1	5.1[d]
CO2 emission estimates (million tons/tons per capita)	~0.0 / 2.0	~0.0 / 2.9	~0.0 / 3.1[d]
Energy production, primary (Petajoules)	0	0	0[l,d]
Energy supply per capita (Gigajoules)	33	38	41[l,d]
Important sites for terrestrial biodiversity protected (%)	16.7	16.7	54.8

a Including Ascension and Tristan da Cunha. **b** Projected estimate (medium fertility variant). **c** 2015. **d** 2014. **e** 2016. **f** Population aged 15 to 69 years. **g** Data classified according to ISIC Rev. 3. **h** 2008. **i** Series linked to former series. **j** Year ending 31 March of the following year. **k** Data refers to a 5-year period preceding the reference year. **l** Estimate. **m** 2012. **n** 2004.

Saint Kitts and Nevis

Region	Caribbean	UN membership date	23 September 1983
Population (000, 2017)	55[a]	Surface area (km2)	261[b]
Pop. density (per km2, 2017)	212.9[a]	Sex ratio (m per 100 f, 2017)	97.0[c,d]
Capital city	Basseterre	National currency	E. Caribbean Dollar (XCD)[e]
Capital city pop. (000)	14.1[f]	Exchange rate (per US$)	2.7[g]

Economic indicators	2005	2010	2017
GDP: Gross domestic product (million current US$)	543	705	876[b]
GDP growth rate (annual %, const. 2005 prices)	8.8	- 2.2	3.8[b]
GDP per capita (current US$)	11 053.7	13 466.8	15 771.9[b]
Economy: Agriculture (% of GVA)	1.9	1.6	1.2[b]
Economy: Industry (% of GVA)	25.4	28.1	28.1[b]
Economy: Services and other activity (% of GVA)	72.7	70.3	70.7[b]
Employment: Agriculture (% of employed)	0.2[h,i,j]	...	...
Employment: Industry (% of employed)	48.8[h,i,j]	...	...
Employment: Services (% of employed)	42.1[h,i,j]	...	...
Unemployment (% of labour force)	5.1[j]	...	...
Labour force participation (female/male pop. %)	74.9 / 62.8[i,j]	... / ...	... / ...
CPI: Consumer Price Index (2000=100)[k]	111[i]	136	149[f]
Agricultural production index (2004-2006=100)	91	35	39[f]
Food production index (2004-2006=100)	91	35	39[f]
International trade: Exports (million US$)	34	32	51[g]
International trade: Imports (million US$)	210	270	332[g]
International trade: Balance (million US$)	- 176	- 238	- 280[g]
Balance of payments, current account (million US$)	- 65	- 139	- 63[l]

Major trading partners						2016
Export partners (% of exports)	United States	75.6	Trinidad and Tobago	3.9	Saint Lucia	3.4
Import partners (% of imports)	United States	63.8	Trinidad and Tobago	3.5	Japan	3.0

Social indicators	2005	2010	2017
Population growth rate (average annual %)[m]	1.4	1.1	1.1[b]
Urban population (% of total population)	32.0	31.8	32.0[b]
Urban population growth rate (average annual %)[m]	1.1	1.1	1.3[b]
Population age distribution (0-14 and 60+ years, %)	28.0 / 9.9[n]	... / ...	... / ...
International migrant stock (000/% of total pop.)	6.7 / 13.6	7.2 / 13.8	7.4 / 13.4[b]
Refugees and others of concern to UNHCR (000)	...	...	-0.0[b]
Health: Total expenditure (% of GDP)[o]	4.8	5.5	5.1[f]
Health: Physicians (per 1 000 pop.)	1.1[i]	...	...
Education: Government expenditure (% of GDP)	3.9	4.3[p]	2.8[b]
Education: Primary gross enrol. ratio (f/m per 100 pop.)	100.1 / 98.2	93.5 / 93.4	83.4 / 81.7[b]
Education: Secondary gross enrol. ratio (f/m per 100 pop.)	89.9 / 84.1[q]	97.1 / 97.9[q]	92.8 / 88.0[b]
Education: Tertiary gross enrol. ratio (f/m per 100 pop.)	... / ...	24.7 / 11.8[r]	107.2 / 52.6[b]
Intentional homicide rate (per 100 000 pop.)	16.3	40.1	33.6[s]
Seats held by women in national parliaments (%)	0.0	6.7	13.3

Environment and infrastructure indicators	2005	2010	2017
Mobile-cellular subscriptions (per 100 inhabitants)	103.8[t]	152.8	131.8[b]
Individuals using the Internet (per 100 inhabitants)	34.0[q]	63.0	75.7[q,b]
Threatened species (number)	19[u]	36	52
Forested area (% of land area)	42.3	42.3	42.3[q,f]
CO2 emission estimates (million tons/tons per capita)	0.2 / 4.0	0.2 / 4.2	0.2 / 4.2[f]
Energy production, primary (Petajoules)	1	0	0[q,f]
Energy supply per capita (Gigajoules)	67[q]	61	59[q,f]
Tourist/visitor arrivals at national borders (000)[v]	141	98	122[b]
Important sites for terrestrial biodiversity protected (%)	29.2	29.2	29.2
Pop. using improved drinking water (urban/rural, %)	98.3 / 98.3	98.3 / 98.3	98.3 / 98.3[b]
Pop. using improved sanitation facilities (urban/rural, %)	87.3 / 87.3	... / ...	... / ...
Net Official Development Assist. received (% of GNI)	0.51	1.73	3.93[l]

a Projected estimate (medium fertility variant). **b** 2015. **c** Provisional data. **d** 2011. **e** East Caribbean Dollar. **f** 2014. **g** 2016. **h** Data classified according to ISIC Rev. 2. **i** Break in the time series. **j** 2001. **k** Index base: 2001=100. **l** 2013. **m** Data refers to a 5-year period preceding the reference year. **n** 2000. **o** Data revision. **p** 2007. **q** Estimate. **r** 2008. **s** 2012. **t** Data as at the end of December. **u** 2004. **v** Arrivals of non-resident tourists by air.

Saint Lucia

Region	Caribbean	UN membership date	18 September 1979
Population (000, 2017)	179 [a]	Surface area (km2)	539 [b,c]
Pop. density (per km2, 2017)	293.2 [a]	Sex ratio (m per 100 f, 2017)	95.9 [a]
Capital city	Castries	National currency	E. Caribbean Dollar (XCD) [d]
Capital city pop. (000)	22.2 [e]	Exchange rate (per US$)	2.7 [f]

Economic indicators	2005	2010	2017
GDP: Gross domestic product (million current US$)	935	1 244	1 450 [c]
GDP growth rate (annual %, const. 2005 prices)	- 1.7	- 1.0	1.9 [c]
GDP per capita (current US$)	5 655.5	7 014.2	7 839.4 [c]
Economy: Agriculture (% of GVA)	3.5	2.9	2.7 [c]
Economy: Industry (% of GVA)	18.7	15.5	12.9 [c]
Economy: Services and other activity (% of GVA)	77.8	81.6	84.4 [c]
Employment: Agriculture (% of employed) [g]	13.8	14.7	14.8
Employment: Industry (% of employed) [g]	20.3	18.7	17.6
Employment: Services (% of employed) [g]	65.9	66.6	67.6
Unemployment (% of labour force)	18.7	20.6	19.0 [g]
Labour force participation (female/male pop. %) [g]	63.1 / 77.6	61.9 / 75.5	63.1 / 76.6
CPI: Consumer Price Index (2000=100)	112	128	144 [e]
Agricultural production index (2004-2006=100)	91	89	69 [e]
Food production index (2004-2006=100)	91	89	69 [e]
International trade: Exports (million US$)	64	215	120 [f]
International trade: Imports (million US$)	486	647	654 [f]
International trade: Balance (million US$)	- 422	- 432	- 535 [f]
Balance of payments, current account (million US$)	- 129	- 203	- 100 [h]

Major trading partners					2016
Export partners (% of exports)	United States	47.5	United Kingdom	15.8	Areas nes [i] 8.5
Import partners (% of imports)	United States	44.4	Trinidad and Tobago	19.7	United Kingdom 4.5

Social indicators	2005	2010	2017
Population growth rate (average annual %) [j]	0.8	1.1	0.5 [c]
Urban population (% of total population)	23.1	18.5	18.5 [c]
Urban population growth rate (average annual %) [j]	- 2.6	- 3.1	0.9 [c]
Fertility rate, total (live births per woman) [j]	1.8	1.6	1.5 [c]
Life expectancy at birth (females/males, years) [j]	74.0 / 70.1	76.6 / 71.4	77.6 / 72.2 [c]
Population age distribution (0-14 and 60+ years, %)	27.7 / 9.8	23.2 / 12.1	18.9 / 13.7 [a]
International migrant stock (000/% of total pop.)	11.5 / 6.9	12.1 / 6.8	12.8 / 6.9 [c]
Refugees and others of concern to UNHCR (000)	...	~0.0 [k]	~0.0 [f]
Infant mortality rate (per 1 000 live births) [j]	14.2	11.8	10.9 [c]
Health: Total expenditure (% of GDP)	6.2	8.1	6.7 [e]
Health: Physicians (per 1 000 pop.)	0.5	0.1 [l]	...
Education: Government expenditure (% of GDP)	5.1	4.1 [g]	4.9 [c]
Education: Primary gross enrol. ratio (f/m per 100 pop.)	100.7 / 105.4	97.7 / 102.9 [m]	... / ...
Education: Secondary gross enrol. ratio (f/m per 100 pop.)	84.0 / 71.4	94.7 / 95.8	84.8 / 85.5 [c]
Education: Tertiary gross enrol. ratio (f/m per 100 pop.)	19.0 / 7.0	18.0 / 7.0	22.0 / 11.6 [c]
Intentional homicide rate (per 100 000 pop.)	24.8	24.8	21.6 [n]
Seats held by women in national parliaments (%)	11.1	11.1	16.7

Environment and infrastructure indicators	2005	2010	2017
Mobile-cellular subscriptions (per 100 inhabitants)	63.9 [g]	111.7	101.5 [c]
Individuals using the Internet (per 100 inhabitants)	21.6	43.3	52.4 [g,c]
Threatened species (number)	29 [o]	46	62
Forested area (% of land area) [g]	34.3	33.8	33.4 [e]
CO2 emission estimates (million tons/tons per capita)	0.4 / 2.2	0.4 / 2.3	0.4 / 2.2 [e]
Energy production, primary (Petajoules)	0	0	0 [e]
Energy supply per capita (Gigajoules)	33 [g]	33	33 [e]
Tourist/visitor arrivals at national borders (000) [p]	318	306	345 [c]
Important sites for terrestrial biodiversity protected (%)	40.3	46.0	46.0
Pop. using improved drinking water (urban/rural, %)	98.0 / 94.0	98.8 / 94.9	99.5 / 95.6 [c]
Pop. using improved sanitation facilities (urban/rural, %)	82.8 / 86.6	83.9 / 89.5	84.7 / 91.9 [c]
Net Official Development Assist. received (% of GNI)	1.22	3.40	0.97 [c]

a Projected estimate (medium fertility variant). **b** Refers to habitable area. Excludes St. Lucia's Forest Reserve. **c** 2015. **d** East Caribbean Dollar. **e** 2014. **f** 2016. **g** Estimate. **h** 2013. **i** Areas not elsewhere specified. **j** Data refers to a 5-year period preceding the reference year. **k** Data as at the end of December. **l** 2009. **m** 2007. **n** 2012. **o** 2004. **p** Excluding nationals residing abroad.

Saint Pierre and Miquelon

Region	Northern America	Population (000, 2017)	6[a]	
Surface area (km2)	242[b]	Pop. density (per km2, 2017)	27.5[a]	
Sex ratio (m per 100 f, 2017)	98.2[c]	Capital city	Saint-Pierre	
National currency	Euro (EUR)	Capital city pop. (000)	5.5[d]	
Exchange rate (per US$)	0.9[e]			

Economic indicators

	2005	2010	2017
CPI: Consumer Price Index (2000=100)	114[f]	...	...
Agricultural production index (2004-2006=100)	94	110	112[d]
Food production index (2004-2006=100)	94	110	112[d]
International trade: Exports (million US$)	31	137	653[e]
International trade: Imports (million US$)	216	747	2 629[e]
International trade: Balance (million US$)	- 185	- 610	- 1 976[e]

Major trading partners

							2016
Export partners (% of exports)	Canada	33.8	Portugal	19.9	Slovakia	19.6
Import partners (% of imports)	France	52.6	Canada	42.1	Belgium	2.0

Social indicators

	2005	2010	2017
Population growth rate (average annual %)[g]	--0.0	--0.0	~0.0[b]
Urban population (% of total population)	89.5	89.9	90.4[b]
Urban population growth rate (average annual %)[g]	- 0.3	- 0.2	0.1[b]
Population age distribution (0-14 and 60+ years, %)	... / ...	19.1 / 17.8[c]	... / ...
International migrant stock (000/% of total pop.)	1.1 / 18.3	1.0 / 16.2	1.0 / 15.7[b]
Intentional homicide rate (per 100 000 pop.)	...	15.9[h]	...

Environment and infrastructure indicators

	2005	2010	2017
Threatened species (number)	2[i]	4	12
Forested area (% of land area)[j]	13.0	12.6	12.3[d]
CO2 emission estimates (million tons/tons per capita)	0.1 / 10.5	0.1 / 11.3	0.1 / 12.2[d]
Energy production, primary (Petajoules)	0[j]	0	0[j,d]
Energy supply per capita (Gigajoules)[j]	148	159	174[d]

a Projected estimate (medium fertility variant). b 2015. c 2006. d 2014. e 2016. f Break in the time series. g Data refers to a 5-year period preceding the reference year. h 2009. i 2004. j Estimate.

Saint Vincent and the Grenadines

Region	Caribbean	UN membership date	16 September 1980
Population (000, 2017)	110[a]	Surface area (km2)	389[b]
Pop. density (per km2, 2017)	281.8[a]	Sex ratio (m per 100 f, 2017)	101.7[a]
Capital city	Kingstown	National currency	E. Caribbean Dollar (XCD)[c]
Capital city pop. (000)	27.3[d]	Exchange rate (per US$)	2.7[e]

Economic indicators	2005	2010	2017
GDP: Gross domestic product (million current US$)	551	681	738[b]
GDP growth rate (annual %, const. 2005 prices)	2.5	- 3.4	1.6[b]
GDP per capita (current US$)	5 064.2	6 231.7	6 739.2[b]
Economy: Agriculture (% of GVA)	6.2	7.1	7.5[b]
Economy: Industry (% of GVA)	18.6	19.2	17.2[b]
Economy: Services and other activity (% of GVA)	75.1	73.7	75.3[b]
Employment: Agriculture (% of employed)[f]	19.3	23.7	22.1
Employment: Industry (% of employed)[f]	18.1	17.1	16.1
Employment: Services (% of employed)[f]	62.7	59.2	61.8
Unemployment (% of labour force)[f]	19.4	18.9	19.1
Labour force participation (female/male pop. %)[f]	53.3 / 78.0	55.4 / 77.9	56.4 / 76.9
CPI: Consumer Price Index (2000=100)[g]	109	135	156[d]
Agricultural production index (2004-2006=100)	104	119	115[d]
Food production index (2004-2006=100)	104	119	115[d]
International trade: Exports (million US$)	40	42	47[e]
International trade: Imports (million US$)	240	379	335[e]
International trade: Balance (million US$)	- 201	- 338	- 288[e]
Balance of payments, current account (million US$)	- 102	- 208	- 210[h]

Major trading partners					2016
Export partners (% of exports)	Barbados	17.8	Saint Lucia	17.2	Antigua and Barbuda 14.5
Import partners (% of imports)	United States	38.2	Trinidad and Tobago	17.6	United Kingdom 7.2

Social indicators	2005	2010	2017
Population growth rate (average annual %)[i]	0.2	0.1	~0.0[b]
Urban population (% of total population)	47.0	48.8	50.6[b]
Urban population growth rate (average annual %)[i]	0.9	0.9	0.7[b]
Fertility rate, total (live births per woman)[i]	2.2	2.1	2.0[b]
Life expectancy at birth (females/males, years)[i]	73.3 / 68.3	74.0 / 69.8	74.9 / 70.7[b]
Population age distribution (0-14 and 60+ years, %)	28.5 / 9.4	26.5 / 9.5	23.8 / 11.7[a]
International migrant stock (000/% of total pop.)	4.4 / 4.0	4.5 / 4.1	4.6 / 4.2[b]
Infant mortality rate (per 1 000 live births)[i]	21.2	18.5	16.5[b]
Health: Total expenditure (% of GDP)	3.7	4.7	8.6[d]
Health: Physicians (per 1 000 pop.)	0.6[i]	...	...
Education: Government expenditure (% of GDP)	6.4	5.1	
Education: Primary gross enrol. ratio (f/m per 100 pop.)	112.3 / 123.9	101.2 / 108.8	103.2 / 105.8[b]
Education: Secondary gross enrol. ratio (f/m per 100 pop.)	99.5 / 79.6	108.8 / 106.3	105.0 / 107.9[b]
Intentional homicide rate (per 100 000 pop.)	21.2	22.9	25.6[k]
Seats held by women in national parliaments (%)	22.7	21.7	13.0

Environment and infrastructure indicators	2005	2010	2017
Mobile-cellular subscriptions (per 100 inhabitants)	64.9	120.6	103.6[b]
Individuals using the Internet (per 100 inhabitants)[f]	9.2	33.7	51.8[b]
Research & Development expenditure (% of GDP)	0.1[l]	...	...
Threatened species (number)	24[m]	38	58
Forested area (% of land area)[f]	66.7	69.2	69.2[d]
CO2 emission estimates (million tons/tons per capita)	0.2 / 2.0	0.2 / 2.0	0.2 / 1.9[d]
Energy production, primary (Petajoules)	0	0[f]	0[f,d]
Energy supply per capita (Gigajoules)	31[f]	31	29[f,d]
Tourist/visitor arrivals at national borders (000)[n]	96	72	75[b]
Important sites for terrestrial biodiversity protected (%)	42.7	42.7	42.7
Pop. using improved drinking water (urban/rural, %)	95.1 / 95.1	95.1 / 95.1	95.1 / 95.1[b]
Pop. using improved sanitation facilities (urban/rural, %)	76.1 / 76.1	... / ...	... / ...
Net Official Development Assist. received (% of GNI)	1.51	2.52	1.80[b]

a Projected estimate (medium fertility variant). b 2015. c East Caribbean Dollar. d 2014. e 2016. f Estimate. g Saint Vincent h 2013. i Data refers to a 5-year period preceding the reference year. j 2001. k 2012. l 2002. m 2004. n Arrivals of non-resident tourists by air.

Samoa

Region	Polynesia	UN membership date	15 December 1976
Population (000, 2017)	196[a]	Surface area (km2)	2 842[b]
Pop. density (per km2, 2017)	69.4[a]	Sex ratio (m per 100 f, 2017)	106.6[a]
Capital city	Apia	National currency	Tala (WST)
Capital city pop. (000)	36.9[c]	Exchange rate (per US$)	2.6[d]

Economic indicators	2005	2010	2017
GDP: Gross domestic product (million current US$)	434	679	774[b]
GDP growth rate (annual %, const. 2005 prices)	5.1	4.3	2.8[b]
GDP per capita (current US$)	2 413.5	3 651.3	4 006.0[b]
Economy: Agriculture (% of GVA)[e]	12.3	9.1	9.3[b]
Economy: Industry (% of GVA)[e]	30.6	25.8	24.2[b]
Economy: Services and other activity (% of GVA)[e]	57.2	65.1	66.6[b]
Employment: Agriculture (% of employed)[f]	29.4	38.6	5.3
Employment: Industry (% of employed)[f]	35.5	13.5	14.8
Employment: Services (% of employed)[f]	35.0	47.9	79.8
Unemployment (% of labour force)[f]	4.8	8.8	6.5
Labour force participation (female/male pop. %)[f]	28.3 / 69.2	24.1 / 60.5	23.3 / 58.2
CPI: Consumer Price Index (2000=100)[g]	133	174	189[h]
Agricultural production index (2004-2006=100)	101	107	107[c]
Food production index (2004-2006=100)	101	107	107[c]
International trade: Exports (million US$)	87	70	56[d]
International trade: Imports (million US$)	239	310	350[d]
International trade: Balance (million US$)	- 151	- 240	- 294[d]
Balance of payments, current account (million US$)	- 48[i]	- 44	- 44[b]

Major trading partners						2016
Export partners (% of exports)	Australia	35.9	American Samoa	25.8	New Zealand	12.0
Import partners (% of imports)	New Zealand	23.9	Singapore	14.6	China	14.1

Social indicators	2005	2010	2017
Population growth rate (average annual %)[j]	0.6	0.7	0.8[b]
Urban population (% of total population)	21.2	20.1	19.1[b]
Urban population growth rate (average annual %)[j]	- 0.1	- 0.4	- 0.2[b]
Fertility rate, total (live births per woman)[j]	4.4	4.5	4.2[b]
Life expectancy at birth (females/males, years)[j]	73.6 / 67.2	75.4 / 69.1	77.4 / 71.1[b]
Population age distribution (0-14 and 60+ years, %)	39.6 / 6.9	38.3 / 7.2	36.6 / 8.5[a]
International migrant stock (000/% of total pop.)	5.7 / 3.2	5.1 / 2.8	4.9 / 2.6[b]
Refugees and others of concern to UNHCR (000)	...	...	~0.0[d]
Infant mortality rate (per 1 000 live births)[j]	25.7	21.3	18.0[b]
Health: Total expenditure (% of GDP)	4.5	5.7	7.2[c]
Health: Physicians (per 1 000 pop.)	0.3	0.5[k]	...
Education: Government expenditure (% of GDP)	3.8[f,l]	5.1[k]	...
Education: Primary gross enrol. ratio (f/m per 100 pop.)	109.8 / 109.0	109.9 / 111.5	106.7 / 106.7[b]
Education: Secondary gross enrol. ratio (f/m per 100 pop.)	88.2 / 78.2	93.6 / 82.3	89.5 / 80.7[b]
Education: Tertiary gross enrol. ratio (f/m per 100 pop.)	7.2 / 7.8[m]	... / ...	... / ...
Intentional homicide rate (per 100 000 pop.)	...	8.6	3.2[h]
Seats held by women in national parliaments (%)	6.1	8.2	10.0

Environment and infrastructure indicators	2005	2010	2017
Mobile-cellular subscriptions (per 100 inhabitants)	13.3	48.4[f]	58.5[b]
Individuals using the Internet (per 100 inhabitants)	3.4	7.0[f]	25.4[f,b]
Threatened species (number)	18[n]	78	93
Forested area (% of land area)[f]	60.4	60.4	60.4[c]
CO$_2$ emission estimates (million tons/tons per capita)	0.2 / 0.9	0.2 / 1.0	0.2 / 1.0[c]
Energy production, primary (Petajoules)	2	2[f]	2[f,c]
Energy supply per capita (Gigajoules)[f]	21	24	24[c]
Tourist/visitor arrivals at national borders (000)	102	122	128[b]
Important sites for terrestrial biodiversity protected (%)	17.5	17.5	17.5
Pop. using improved drinking water (urban/rural, %)	97.2 / 95.0	97.4 / 97.7	97.5 / 99.3[b]
Pop. using improved sanitation facilities (urban/rural, %)	93.6 / 91.5	93.4 / 91.2	93.3 / 91.1[b]
Net Official Development Assist. received (% of GNI)	9.91	23.23	12.75[b]

a Projected estimate (medium fertility variant). b. 2015. c 2014. d 2016. e At producers' prices. f Estimate. g Excluding "Rent". h 2013. i Break in the time series. j Data refers to a 5-year period preceding the reference year. k 2008. l 2002. m 2000. n 2004.

San Marino

Region	Southern Europe	UN membership date	02 March 1992
Population (000, 2017)	33[a]	Surface area (km2)	61[b]
Pop. density (per km2, 2017)	556.7[a]	Sex ratio (m per 100 f, 2017)	94.9[c,b]
Capital city	San Marino	National currency	Euro (EUR)
Capital city pop. (000)	4.2[d]	Exchange rate (per US$)	0.9[e]

Economic indicators	2005	2010	2017
GDP: Gross domestic product (million current US$)	2 027	2 139	1 565[b]
GDP growth rate (annual %, const. 2005 prices)	2.3	- 4.6	1.0[b]
GDP per capita (current US$)	69 332.8	69 708.1	49 240.2[b]
Economy: Agriculture (% of GVA)[f]	0.1	0.1	0.1[b]
Economy: Industry (% of GVA)[f]	38.2	35.6	33.3[b]
Economy: Services and other activity (% of GVA)[f]	61.7	64.4	66.6[b]
Employment: Agriculture (% of employed)	0.5[g]	0.3[h]	...
Employment: Industry (% of employed)	39.3[g]	34.3[h]	...
Employment: Services (% of employed)	60.2[g]	65.4[h]	...
Unemployment (% of labour force)	...	4.4	6.6[h,i,d]
Labour force participation (female/male pop. %)	53.8 / 79.2[j]	... / ...	... / ...
CPI: Consumer Price Index (2000=100)[k]	103[h]	118	128[d]

Social indicators	2005	2010	2017
Population growth rate (average annual %)[l]	1.3	1.2	1.2[b]
Urban population (% of total population)	94.0	94.1	94.2[b]
Urban population growth rate (average annual %)[l]	2.1	0.7	0.6[b]
Fertility rate, total (live births per woman)	1.3[m]	...	...
Life expectancy at birth (females/males, years)	84.0 / 77.4[n]	... / ...	86.4 / 81.7[o]
Population age distribution (0-14 and 60+ years, %)	15.2 / 21.5[c,m]	20.9 / 21.6[p,q,r]	15.0 / 24.1[c,b]
International migrant stock (000/% of total pop.)	4.2 / 14.4	4.4 / 14.3	4.7 / 14.8[b]
Health: Total expenditure (% of GDP)	4.1	5.0	6.1[d]
Health: Physicians (per 1 000 pop.)	...	...	6.4[d]
Education: Government expenditure (% of GDP)	...	2.3	2.4[s]
Education: Primary gross enrol. ratio (f/m per 100 pop.)[t]	... / ...	100.6 / 88.8	92.6 / 93.9[u]
Education: Secondary gross enrol. ratio (f/m per 100 pop.)[t]	... / ...	98.2 / 96.3	95.9 / 93.5[u]
Education: Tertiary gross enrol. ratio (f/m per 100 pop.)[t]	... / ...	77.3 / 53.0	69.9 / 50.5[u]
Seats held by women in national parliaments (%)	16.7	16.7	26.7

Environment and infrastructure indicators	2005	2010	2017
Mobile-cellular subscriptions (per 100 inhabitants)	57.6	99.1	115.2[b]
Individuals using the Internet (per 100 inhabitants)	50.3	54.2[v]	49.6[s]
Threatened species (number)	...	0	1
Forested area (% of land area)[t]	0.0	0.0	0.0[d]
Tourist/visitor arrivals at national borders (000)[w]	50	120	54[b]

a Projected estimate (medium fertility variant). b 2015. c Population statistics are compiled from registers. d 2014. e 2016. f Data classified according to ISIC Rev. 4. g Data classified according to ISIC Rev. 3. h Break in the time series. i Population aged 14 years and over. j 2003. k Index base: 2003=100. l Data refers to a 5-year period preceding the reference year. m 2004. n 2000. o 2013. p Provisional data. q Population aged 0 to 20 years. r Population aged 61 years and over. s 2011. t Estimate. u 2012. v 2009. w Including Italian tourists.

Sao Tome and Principe

Region	Middle Africa	UN membership date	16 September 1975
Population (000, 2017)	204 [a]	Surface area (km2)	964 [b]
Pop. density (per km2, 2017)	212.8 [a]	Sex ratio (m per 100 f, 2017)	99.2 [a]
Capital city	Sao Tome	National currency	Dobra (STD)
Capital city pop. (000)	71.3 [c]	Exchange rate (per US$)	23 242.6 [d]

Economic indicators

	2005	2010	2017
GDP: Gross domestic product (million current US$)	126	206	334 [b]
GDP growth rate (annual %, const. 2005 prices)	7.1	6.6	4.0 [b]
GDP per capita (current US$)	824.0	1 205.6	1 752.8 [b]
Economy: Agriculture (% of GVA)	18.3	11.8	12.3 [b]
Economy: Industry (% of GVA)	14.9	18.2	14.7 [b]
Economy: Services and other activity (% of GVA)	66.8	70.1	73.0 [b]
Employment: Agriculture (% of employed) [e]	27.9	25.8	22.2
Employment: Industry (% of employed) [e]	17.2	15.8	13.5
Employment: Services (% of employed) [e]	54.9	58.5	64.3
Unemployment (% of labour force)	16.5	14.3 [e]	13.6 [e]
Labour force participation (female/male pop. %) [e]	43.4 / 72.9	44.6 / 75.2	45.4 / 76.2
CPI: Consumer Price Index (2000=100) [f]	561	1 432	2 095 [c]
Agricultural production index (2004-2006=100)	101	107	119 [c]
Food production index (2004-2006=100)	101	107	119 [c]
International trade: Exports (million US$)	3	6	10 [d]
International trade: Imports (million US$)	50	112	139 [d]
International trade: Balance (million US$)	- 46	- 106	- 129 [d]
Balance of payments, current account (million US$)	- 36	- 88	- 69 [b]

Major trading partners

							2016
Export partners (% of exports)	Poland	31.9	Belgium	20.1	Spain	16.0
Import partners (% of imports)	Portugal	59.1	Angola	15.2	China	5.4

Social indicators

	2005	2010	2017
Population growth rate (average annual %) [g]	2.3	2.3	2.2 [b]
Urban population (% of total population)	58.0	61.9	65.1 [b]
Urban population growth rate (average annual %) [g]	3.7	4.1	3.6 [b]
Fertility rate, total (live births per woman) [g]	5.1	4.9	4.7 [b]
Life expectancy at birth (females/males, years) [g]	65.6 / 62.0	67.4 / 63.6	68.2 / 64.0 [b]
Population age distribution (0-14 and 60+ years, %)	44.1 / 5.6	44.1 / 4.7	42.8 / 4.3 [a]
International migrant stock (000/% of total pop.) [h]	3.4 / 2.2	2.7 / 1.6	2.4 / 1.3 [b]
Infant mortality rate (per 1 000 live births) [g]	51.8	46.0	43.8 [b]
Health: Total expenditure (% of GDP)	9.9	5.3	8.1 [i]
Health: Physicians (per 1 000 pop.)	0.5 [j]	...	...
Education: Government expenditure (% of GDP)	5.3	9.7	3.8 [c]
Education: Primary gross enrol. ratio (f/m per 100 pop.)	127.2 / 132.3	121.4 / 122.6	112.2 / 117.7 [d]
Education: Secondary gross enrol. ratio (f/m per 100 pop.)	44.4 / 41.9	53.4 / 52.5	91.7 / 80.8 [d]
Education: Tertiary gross enrol. ratio (f/m per 100 pop.)	... / ...	4.2 / 4.4	13.6 / 13.2 [b]
Intentional homicide rate (per 100 000 pop.)	...	3.5	3.4 [k]
Seats held by women in national parliaments (%)	9.1	7.3	18.2

Environment and infrastructure indicators

	2005	2010	2017
Mobile-cellular subscriptions (per 100 inhabitants)	7.7	57.6	65.1 [e,b]
Individuals using the Internet (per 100 inhabitants)	13.8 [e]	18.8	25.8 [e,b]
Threatened species (number)	61 [j]	70	94
Forested area (% of land area) [e]	58.3	55.8	55.8 [c]
CO2 emission estimates (million tons/tons per capita)	0.1 / 0.5	0.1 / 0.6	0.1 / 0.6 [c]
Energy production, primary (Petajoules)	1	1	1 [c]
Energy supply per capita (Gigajoules)	13 [e]	14	14 [e,c]
Tourist/visitor arrivals at national borders (000)	16	8	...
Important sites for terrestrial biodiversity protected (%)	0.0	54.4	54.4
Pop. using improved drinking water (urban/rural, %)	91.6 / 80.6	97.7 / 91.5	98.9 / 93.6 [b]
Pop. using improved sanitation facilities (urban/rural, %)	33.1 / 18.4	39.5 / 22.5	40.8 / 23.3 [b]
Net Official Development Assist. received (% of GNI)	26.58	25.76	12.39 [c]

a Projected estimate (medium fertility variant). **b** 2015. **c** 2014. **d** 2016. **e** Estimate. **f** Index base: 1996=100. **g** Data refers to a 5-year period preceding the reference year. **h** Refers to foreign citizens. **i** 2013. **j** 2004. **k** 2011.

Saudi Arabia

Region	Western Asia	UN membership date	24 October 1945
Population (000, 2017)	32 938[a]	Surface area (km2)	2 206 714[b]
Pop. density (per km2, 2017)	15.3[a]	Sex ratio (m per 100 f, 2017)	132.9[a]
Capital city	Riyadh	National currency	Saudi Riyal (SAR)
Capital city pop. (000)	6 369.7[b]	Exchange rate (per US$)	3.8[c]

Economic indicators	2005	2010	2017
GDP: Gross domestic product (million current US$)	328 461	526 811	653 219[b]
GDP growth rate (annual %, const. 2005 prices)	5.6	4.8	3.4[b]
GDP per capita (current US$)	13 273.7	18 754.0	20 710.6[b]
Economy: Agriculture (% of GVA)	3.2	2.4	2.3[b]
Economy: Industry (% of GVA)	62.1	58.7	46.0[b]
Economy: Services and other activity (% of GVA)	34.7	38.9	51.8[b]
Employment: Agriculture (% of employed)[d]	4.1	4.3	5.9
Employment: Industry (% of employed)[d]	20.3	21.7	22.7
Employment: Services (% of employed)[d]	75.6	74.0	71.4
Unemployment (% of labour force)	6.1	5.6	5.5[d]
Labour force participation (female/male pop. %)[d]	17.5 / 75.4	18.3 / 75.8	20.0 / 78.5
CPI: Consumer Price Index (2000=100)[e]	100	130	139[f]
Agricultural production index (2004-2006=100)	100	103	96[f]
Food production index (2004-2006=100)	100	103	96[f]
Index of industrial production (2005=100)[g]	100	112	135[f]
International trade: Exports (million US$)	180 278	250 577	182 329[c]
International trade: Imports (million US$)	57 233	103 622	135 904[c]
International trade: Balance (million US$)	123 045	146 955	46 426[c]
Balance of payments, current account (million US$)	90 060[h]	66 751	- 56 724[b]

Major trading partners						2016
Export partners (% of exports)	Asia nes[i]	48.1	N & C Ame nes[j]	10.5	Other Europe nes[k]	9.5
Import partners (% of imports)	China	14.6	United States	13.4	Germany	7.2

Social indicators	2005	2010	2017
Population growth rate (average annual %)[l]	2.8	2.7	2.8[b]
Urban population (% of total population)	81.0	82.1	83.1[b]
Urban population growth rate (average annual %)[l]	4.4	2.3	2.1[b]
Fertility rate, total (live births per woman)[l]	3.6	3.2	2.7[b]
Life expectancy at birth (females/males, years)[l]	74.6 / 71.5	74.8 / 71.9	75.6 / 72.7[b]
Population age distribution (0-14 and 60+ years, %)	33.8 / 4.4	29.8 / 4.5	25.2 / 5.6[a]
International migrant stock (000/% of total pop.)[m,n]	6 501.8 / 26.3	8 430.0 / 30.0	10 185.9 / 32.3[b]
Refugees and others of concern to UNHCR (000)	311.0[o]	70.7[o]	70.2[c]
Infant mortality rate (per 1 000 live births)[l]	17.5	14.7	13.0[b]
Health: Total expenditure (% of GDP)[p]	3.4	3.5	4.7[f]
Health: Physicians (per 1 000 pop.)	0.7[q]	2.4	2.6[f]
Education: Government expenditure (% of GDP)	5.4	5.1[r]	...
Education: Primary gross enrol. ratio (f/m per 100 pop.)	92.3 / 93.7[d]	99.1 / 99.2	111.1 / 107.9[b]
Education: Secondary gross enrol. ratio (f/m per 100 pop.)[d]	83.8 / 88.4	89.4 / 101.8[s]	93.7 / 122.6[f]
Education: Tertiary gross enrol. ratio (f/m per 100 pop.)	33.9 / 25.2	39.6 / 33.7	61.8 / 64.4[b]
Intentional homicide rate (per 100 000 pop.)	...	...	1.5[i]
Seats held by women in national parliaments (%)	0.0	0.0	19.9

Environment and infrastructure indicators	2005	2010	2017
Mobile-cellular subscriptions (per 100 inhabitants)	57.4	189.2	176.6[b]
Individuals using the Internet (per 100 inhabitants)	12.7	41.0	69.6[t,b]
Research & Development expenditure (% of GDP)[u]	~0.0[v]	0.1[s]	...
Threatened species (number)	41[w]	103	131
Forested area (% of land area)[d]	0.5	0.5	0.5[f]
CO2 emission estimates (million tons/tons per capita)	397.6 / 16.5	518.5 / 18.4	601.0 / 19.5[f]
Energy production, primary (Petajoules)[x]	24 162	22 115	25 904[f]
Energy supply per capita (Gigajoules)[x]	252	274	287[f]
Tourist/visitor arrivals at national borders (000)	8 037	10 850	17 994[b]
Important sites for terrestrial biodiversity protected (%)	15.1	15.1	15.1
Pop. using improved drinking water (urban/rural, %)	96.7 / 96.7	97.0 / 97.0	97.0 / 97.0[b]
Pop. using improved sanitation facilities (urban/rural, %)	99.7 / 99.7	100.0 / 100.0	100.0 / 100.0[b]
Net Official Development Assist. received (% of GNI)	0.01		

a Projected estimate (medium fertility variant). b 2015. c 2016. d Estimate. e All cities. f 2014. g Data classified according to ISIC Rev. 3. h Break in the time series. i Asia not elsewhere specified. j North and Central America not elsewhere specified. k Other Europe, not elsewhere specified. l Data refers to a 5-year period preceding the reference year. m Including refugees. n Refers to foreign citizens. o Data as at the end of December. p Data revision. q 2001. r 2008. s 2009. t Population aged 12 to 65 years. u Partial data. v R&D budget instead of R&D expenditure or based on R&D budget. w 2004. x The data for crude oil production include 50 per cent of the output of the Neutral Zone.

Senegal

Region	Western Africa	UN membership date	28 September 1960
Population (000, 2017)	15 851 [a]	Surface area (km2)	196 712 [b,c]
Pop. density (per km2, 2017)	82.3 [a]	Sex ratio (m per 100 f, 2017)	96.6 [a]
Capital city	Dakar	National currency	CFA Franc (XOF)
Capital city pop. (000)	3 520.2 [c]	Exchange rate (per US$)	622.3 [d]

Economic indicators

	2005	2010	2017
GDP: Gross domestic product (million current US$)	8 708	12 926	13 633 [c]
GDP growth rate (annual %, const. 2005 prices)	5.6	4.2	6.5 [c]
GDP per capita (current US$)	772.7	997.6	901.1 [c]
Economy: Agriculture (% of GVA)	16.8	17.5	15.5 [c]
Economy: Industry (% of GVA)	23.6	23.4	24.1 [c]
Economy: Services and other activity (% of GVA)	59.6	59.2	60.4 [c]
Employment: Agriculture (% of employed) [e]	41.0	55.5	51.4
Employment: Industry (% of employed) [e]	16.8	21.0	20.7
Employment: Services (% of employed) [e]	42.1	23.5	27.9
Unemployment (% of labour force) [e]	8.5	9.2	9.3
Labour force participation (female/male pop. %) [e]	35.6 / 71.2	42.4 / 69.6	45.3 / 70.5
CPI: Consumer Price Index (2000=100)	108 [f]	99 [g,h]	104 [h,i]
Agricultural production index (2004-2006=100)	110	151	126 [i]
Food production index (2004-2006=100)	110	153	127 [i]
Index of industrial production (2005=100) [j]	100 [k]	104	102 [i]
International trade: Exports (million US$)	1 471	2 088	2 640 [d]
International trade: Imports (million US$)	3 498	4 782	5 478 [d]
International trade: Balance (million US$)	- 2 027	- 2 694	- 2 838 [d]
Balance of payments, current account (million US$)	- 676 [g]	- 589	- 1 348 [i]

Major trading partners

						2016
Export partners (% of exports)	Mali	17.5	Switzerland	10.2	India	7.9
Import partners (% of imports)	France	15.9	China	10.3	Nigeria	7.8

Social indicators

	2005	2010	2017
Population growth rate (average annual %) [l]	2.6	2.8	3.0 [c]
Urban population (% of total population)	41.1	42.2	43.7 [c]
Urban population growth rate (average annual %) [l]	3.1	3.3	3.6 [c]
Fertility rate, total (live births per woman) [l]	5.3	5.1	5.0 [c]
Life expectancy at birth (females/males, years) [l]	60.6 / 57.3	63.8 / 61.0	67.5 / 63.8 [c]
Population age distribution (0-14 and 60+ years, %)	43.7 / 4.9	43.2 / 4.7	42.9 / 4.7 [a]
International migrant stock (000/% of total pop.) [m]	238.3 / 2.1	256.1 / 2.0	263.2 / 1.7 [c]
Refugees and others of concern to UNHCR (000)	23.4 [n]	24.2 [n]	17.6 [d]
Infant mortality rate (per 1 000 live births) [l]	61.1	51.1	43.9 [c]
Health: Total expenditure (% of GDP)	5.4	4.6	4.7 [i]
Health: Physicians (per 1 000 pop.)	0.1 [o]	0.1 [p]	...
Education: Government expenditure (% of GDP)	5.1	6.5	7.4 [i]
Education: Primary gross enrol. ratio (f/m per 100 pop.)	77.2 / 80.2	84.2 / 79.7	86.9 / 77.6 [c]
Education: Secondary gross enrol. ratio (f/m per 100 pop.)	18.8 / 25.2	33.1 / 38.0	49.1 / 50.2 [c]
Education: Tertiary gross enrol. ratio (f/m per 100 pop.)	... / ...	5.5 / 9.3 [e]	7.8 / 12.9 [c]
Intentional homicide rate (per 100 000 pop.)	9.3	8.5	7.3 [c]
Seats held by women in national parliaments (%)	19.2	22.7	42.7

Environment and infrastructure indicators

	2005	2010	2017
Mobile-cellular subscriptions (per 100 inhabitants)	15.4	64.4	100.0 [c]
Individuals using the Internet (per 100 inhabitants)	4.8	8.0 [e]	21.7 [e,c]
Research & Development expenditure (% of GDP)	...	0.5	...
Threatened species (number)	47 [o]	82	123
Forested area (% of land area) [e]	45.0	44.0	43.2 [i]
CO2 emission estimates (million tons/tons per capita)	5.8 / 0.6	7.7 / 0.6	8.9 / 0.6 [i]
Energy production, primary (Petajoules)	52	86	77 [i]
Energy supply per capita (Gigajoules)	11	13	11 [i]
Tourist/visitor arrivals at national borders (000)	769	900 [e]	1 007 [e,c]
Important sites for terrestrial biodiversity protected (%)	41.1	41.1	41.2
Pop. using improved drinking water (urban/rural, %)	91.4 / 56.9	92.2 / 62.1	92.9 / 67.3 [c]
Pop. using improved sanitation facilities (urban/rural, %)	62.5 / 28.7	63.9 / 31.2	65.4 / 33.8 [c]
Net Official Development Assist. received (% of GNI)	8.20	7.32	6.49 [c]

a Projected estimate (medium fertility variant). **b** Surface area is based on the 2002 population and housing census. **c** 2015. **d** 2016. **e** Estimate. **f** Dakar **g** Break in the time series. **h** Index base: 2008=100. **i** 2014. **j** Data classified according to ISIC Rev. 3. **k** Country data supplemented with data from the Observatoire Economique et Statistique d'Afrique Subsaharienne (Afristat). **l** Data refers to a 5-year period preceding the reference year. **m** Including refugees. **n** Data as at the end of December. **o** 2004. **p** 2008.

Serbia

Region	Southern Europe	UN membership date	01 November 2000
Population (000, 2017)	8 791 a,b	Surface area (km2)	88 499 c,d
Pop. density (per km2, 2017)	100.5 a,b	Sex ratio (m per 100 f, 2017)	95.6 a,b
Capital city	Belgrade	National currency	Serbian Dinar (RSD)
Capital city pop. (000)	1 181.8 e,d	Exchange rate (per US$)	117.1 f

Economic indicators	2005	2010	2017
GDP: Gross domestic product (million current US$)g	26 252	39 460	37 160 d
GDP growth rate (annual %, const. 2005 prices)g	5.5	0.6	0.8 d
GDP per capita (current US$)g	3 528.1	5 411.9	5 238.6 d
Economy: Agriculture (% of GVA)g,h	12.0	10.2	8.2 d
Economy: Industry (% of GVA)g,h	29.3	28.4	31.4 d
Economy: Services and other activity (% of GVA)g,h	58.7	61.4	60.5 d
Employment: Agriculture (% of employed)i	23.3	22.2	19.4
Employment: Industry (% of employed)i	27.6	26.0	24.5
Employment: Services (% of employed)i	49.1	51.8	56.1
Unemployment (% of labour force)	20.9	19.2	15.5 i
Labour force participation (female/male pop. %)i	44.9 / 63.9	42.6 / 59.1	43.4 / 59.9
CPI: Consumer Price Index (2000=100)	330	137 j,k	153 k,l
Agricultural production index (2004-2006=100)	...	103	102 m
Food production index (2004-2006=100)	...	103	102 m
Index of industrial production (2005=100)	100	97 n	96 n,m
International trade: Exports (million US$)	...	9 795	14 852 f
International trade: Imports (million US$)	...	16 735	19 231 f
International trade: Balance (million US$)	...	- 6 940	- 4 379 f
Balance of payments, current account (million US$)	...	- 2 692	- 1 751 d

Major trading partners						2016
Export partners (% of exports)	Italy	14.6	Germany	13.1	Bosnia-Herzegovina	8.3
Import partners (% of imports)	Germany	12.9	Italy	10.3	China	8.3

Social indicators	2005	2010	2017
Population growth rate (average annual %)b,o	- 0.6	- 0.4	- 0.4 d
Urban population (% of total population)b	54.5	55.2	55.6 d
Urban population growth rate (average annual %)b,o	- 0.1	- 0.4	- 0.3 d
Fertility rate, total (live births per woman)b,o	1.7	1.6	1.6 d
Life expectancy at birth (females/males, years)b,o	75.4 / 69.4	76.1 / 70.6	77.5 / 71.8 d
Population age distribution (0-14 and 60+ years, %)b	18.6 / 19.0	17.3 / 21.0	16.5 / 24.5 a
International migrant stock (000/% of total pop.)b	845.1 / 9.2	826.1 / 9.1	807.4 / 9.1 d
Refugees and others of concern to UNHCR (000)	486.9 b,p	312.6 b,p	254.1 f
Infant mortality rate (per 1 000 live births)b,o	14.1	12.4	9.8 d
Health: Total expenditure (% of GDP)g	8.7	10.1	10.4 m
Health: Physicians (per 1 000 pop.)	...	2.5	2.5 m
Education: Government expenditure (% of GDP)	...	4.6	4.2 m
Education: Primary gross enrol. ratio (f/m per 100 pop.)i	103.0 / 102.5	95.6 / 96.1	101.2 / 101.5 d
Education: Secondary gross enrol. ratio (f/m per 100 pop.)i	90.0 / 87.3	92.4 / 90.5	97.4 / 96.0 d
Education: Tertiary gross enrol. ratio (f/m per 100 pop.)i	50.1 / 38.6	55.6 / 42.8	66.9 / 50.2 d
Intentional homicide rate (per 100 000 pop.)	1.6	1.4	1.1 d
Seats held by women in national parliaments (%)	...	21.6	34.4

Environment and infrastructure indicators	2005	2010	2017
Mobile-cellular subscriptions (per 100 inhabitants)	67.0 q	125.3 q	120.5 d
Individuals using the Internet (per 100 inhabitants)	26.3 i,r	40.9	65.3 r,d
Research & Development expenditure (% of GDP)s	0.4 t	0.7	0.8 m
Threatened species (number)	...	46	71
Forested area (% of land area)l	...	31.0	31.1 m
CO2 emission estimates (million tons/tons per capita)	... / ...	46.0 / 5.1	37.7 / 4.3 m
Energy production, primary (Petajoules)u	431	440	393 m
Energy supply per capita (Gigajoules)u	68	72	62 m
Tourist/visitor arrivals at national borders (000)	453	683	1 132 d
Important sites for terrestrial biodiversity protected (%)	23.3	25.5	26.1
Pop. using improved drinking water (urban/rural, %)	99.5 / 99.1	99.4 / 99.0	99.4 / 98.9 d
Pop. using improved sanitation facilities (urban/rural, %)	97.9 / 95.4	98.1 / 94.8	98.2 / 94.2 d
Net Official Development Assist. received (% of GNI)	4.12	1.71	0.90 d

a Projected estimate (medium fertility variant). b Including Kosovo. c Changes in total area per year are the result of new measuring and correcting of the administrative borders between former Yugoslavian countries. d 2015. e Refers to Belgrade settlement. f 2016. g Excluding Kosovo and Metohija. h Data classified according to ISIC Rev. 4. i Estimate. j Break in the time series. k Index base: 2006=100. l 2011. m 2014. n Excluding water and waste management. o Data refers to a 5-year period preceding the reference year. p Data as at the end of December. q Includes inactive pre-paid subscriptions. r Population aged 16 to 74 years. s Excluding data from some regions, provinces or states. t Do not correspond exactly to Frascati Manual recommendations. u Excluding Kosovo.

Seychelles

Region	Eastern Africa	UN membership date	21 September 1976
Population (000, 2017)	95 [a]	Surface area (km2)	457 [b]
Pop. density (per km2, 2017)	206.0 [a]	Sex ratio (m per 100 f, 2017)	97.2 [a]
Capital city	Victoria	National currency	Seychelles Rupee (SCR)
Capital city pop. (000)	26.1 [c]	Exchange rate (per US$)	13.5 [d]

Economic indicators

	2005	2010	2017
GDP: Gross domestic product (million current US$)	919	970	1 363 [b]
GDP growth rate (annual %, const. 2005 prices)	9.0	5.9	6.8 [b]
GDP per capita (current US$)	10 356.5	10 420.7	14 133.2 [b]
Economy: Agriculture (% of GVA) [e]	3.8	2.7	2.7 [b]
Economy: Industry (% of GVA) [e]	19.4	16.5	13.6 [b]
Economy: Services and other activity (% of GVA) [e]	76.8	80.8	83.8 [b]
Employment: Agriculture (% of employed)	...	...	3.6 [f,g,h]
Employment: Industry (% of employed)	...	...	17.9 [f,g,h]
Employment: Services (% of employed)	...	...	78.2 [f,g,h]
Unemployment (% of labour force)	5.5	...	4.1 [f,g,i,h]
Labour force participation (female/male pop. %)	... / ...	... / ...	61.9 / 68.3 [f,g,i,h]
CPI: Consumer Price Index (2000=100)	115	215	250 [c]
Agricultural production index (2004-2006=100)	99	92	105 [c]
Food production index (2004-2006=100)	98	96	109 [c]
International trade: Exports (million US$)	340	418	335 [d]
International trade: Imports (million US$)	675	1 180	833 [d]
International trade: Balance (million US$)	- 335	- 763	- 498 [d]
Balance of payments, current account (million US$)	- 188	- 214	- 256 [d]

Major trading partners

						2016
Export partners (% of exports)	United Arab Emirates	30.3	France	19.7	United Kingdom	17.8
Import partners (% of imports)	United Arab Emirates	26.1	Spain	8.2	France	7.9

Social indicators

	2005	2010	2017
Population growth rate (average annual %) [j]	1.8	0.6	0.5 [b]
Urban population (% of total population)	51.1	52.3	53.9 [b]
Urban population growth rate (average annual %) [j]	2.1	1.4	1.1 [b]
Fertility rate, total (live births per woman) [j]	2.2	2.3	2.4 [b]
Life expectancy at birth (females/males, years) [j]	76.8 / 67.9	77.3 / 68.0	77.9 / 68.7 [b]
Population age distribution (0-14 and 60+ years, %)	24.9 / 9.2	22.8 / 10.0	22.2 / 13.3 [a]
International migrant stock (000/% of total pop.)	9.0 / 10.1	11.4 / 12.3	12.8 / 13.3 [b]
Infant mortality rate (per 1 000 live births) [j]	10.6	10.2	10.2 [b]
Health: Total expenditure (% of GDP)	3.9	3.6	3.4 [c]
Health: Physicians (per 1 000 pop.)	1.2	1.1	1.0 [k]
Education: Government expenditure (% of GDP)	5.4 [l]	4.8 [m]	3.6 [b]
Education: Primary gross enrol. ratio (f/m per 100 pop.)	108.0 / 110.1	112.5 / 108.9	103.6 / 101.1 [b]
Education: Secondary gross enrol. ratio (f/m per 100 pop.)	84.8 / 79.0	75.9 / 72.4 [n]	84.5 / 78.8 [b]
Education: Tertiary gross enrol. ratio (f/m per 100 pop.)	... / ...	... / ...	19.6 / 9.3 [b]
Intentional homicide rate (per 100 000 pop.)	3.4	2.2	...
Seats held by women in national parliaments (%)	29.4	23.5	21.2

Environment and infrastructure indicators

	2005	2010	2017
Mobile-cellular subscriptions (per 100 inhabitants)	67.5	128.9 [o]	158.1 [b]
Individuals using the Internet (per 100 inhabitants)	25.4	41.0 [n]	58.1 [n,b]
Research & Development expenditure (% of GDP)	0.3	...	...
Threatened species (number)	84 [p]	190	439
Forested area (% of land area)	88.4	88.4 [n]	88.4 [n,c]
CO2 emission estimates (million tons/tons per capita)	0.7 / 8.3	0.4 / 4.8	0.5 / 5.2 [c]
Energy production, primary (Petajoules)	0	0	0 [c]
Energy supply per capita (Gigajoules)	115	66	72 [c]
Tourist/visitor arrivals at national borders (000)	129	175	276 [b]
Important sites for terrestrial biodiversity protected (%)	21.9	21.9	21.9
Pop. using improved drinking water (urban/rural, %)	95.7 / 95.7	95.7 / 95.7	95.7 / 95.7 [b]
Pop. using improved sanitation facilities (urban/rural, %)	98.4 / 98.4	98.4 / 98.4	98.4 / 98.4 [b]
Net Official Development Assist. received (% of GNI)	1.85	5.89	0.50 [b]

a Projected estimate (medium fertility variant). b 2015. c 2014. d 2016. e Data classified according to ISIC Rev. 4. f Excluding some areas. g Excluding the institutional population. h 2011. i Break in the time series. j Data refers to a 5-year period preceding the reference year. k 2012. l 2003. m 2006. n Estimate. o Data as at end of January of the following year. p 2004.

Sierra Leone

Region	Western Africa	UN membership date	27 September 1961
Population (000, 2017)	7 557 [a]	Surface area (km2)	72 300 [b]
Pop. density (per km2, 2017)	104.7 [a]	Sex ratio (m per 100 f, 2017)	98.1 [a]
Capital city	Freetown	National currency	Leone (SLL)
Capital city pop. (000)	1 007.1 [b]	Exchange rate (per US$)	5 639.1 [b]

Economic indicators	2005	2010	2017
GDP: Gross domestic product (million current US$)	1 650	2 578	4 483 [b]
GDP growth rate (annual %, const. 2005 prices)	4.5	5.3	- 20.3 [b]
GDP per capita (current US$)	325.5	446.3	694.8 [b]
Economy: Agriculture (% of GVA)	51.0	55.2	51.4 [b]
Economy: Industry (% of GVA)	11.6	8.1	17.6 [b]
Economy: Services and other activity (% of GVA)	37.4	36.7	31.1 [b]
Employment: Agriculture (% of employed) [c]	68.4	68.7	68.0
Employment: Industry (% of employed) [c]	6.4	6.4	6.5
Employment: Services (% of employed) [c]	25.2	25.0	25.5
Unemployment (% of labour force) [c]	3.3	3.0	3.1
Labour force participation (female/male pop. %) [c]	65.1 / 66.7	65.1 / 67.9	65.1 / 68.8
CPI: Consumer Price Index (2000=100) [d]	132 [e]	239 [f]	370 [g]
Agricultural production index (2004-2006=100)	93	146	168 [g]
Food production index (2004-2006=100)	93	147	168 [g]
International trade: Exports (million US$)	154	342	466 [h]
International trade: Imports (million US$)	341	776	958 [h]
International trade: Balance (million US$)	- 187	- 434	- 492 [h]
Balance of payments, current account (million US$)	- 171	- 746	- 1 317 [g]

Major trading partners						2016
Export partners (% of exports)	Côte d'Ivoire	34.7	United States	31.0	Belgium	19.3
Import partners (% of imports)	China	12.6	United States	9.8	India	7.8

Social indicators	2005	2010	2017
Population growth rate (average annual %) [i]	4.3	2.6	2.3 [b]
Urban population (% of total population)	36.8	38.2	39.9 [b]
Urban population growth rate (average annual %) [i]	4.9	3.1	2.7 [b]
Fertility rate, total (live births per woman) [i]	6.1	5.6	4.8 [b]
Life expectancy at birth (females/males, years) [i]	42.6 / 40.1	46.7 / 45.0	50.7 / 49.6 [b]
Population age distribution (0-14 and 60+ years, %)	44.4 / 4.1	44.0 / 4.1	42.1 / 4.2 [a]
International migrant stock (000/% of total pop.) [j]	149.6 / 3.0	97.5 / 1.7	91.2 / 1.4 [b]
Refugees and others of concern to UNHCR (000)	66.3 [k]	8.6 [k]	0.8 [h]
Infant mortality rate (per 1 000 live births) [i]	134.9	116.9	94.4 [b]
Health: Total expenditure (% of GDP) [l]	12.2	10.3	11.1 [g]
Health: Physicians (per 1 000 pop.)	~0.0 [m]	~0.0	...
Education: Government expenditure (% of GDP)	2.8 [c]	2.6	2.7 [g]
Education: Primary gross enrol. ratio (f/m per 100 pop.)	68.6 / 98.3 [n]	... / ...	128.2 / 127.0 [b]
Education: Secondary gross enrol. ratio (f/m per 100 pop.)	22.5 / 31.8 [c,n]	... / ...	40.1 / 46.5 [b]
Education: Tertiary gross enrol. ratio (f/m per 100 pop.)	1.2 / 3.1 [c,o]	... / ...	... / ...
Intentional homicide rate (per 100 000 pop.)	2.0	2.8	1.9 [b]
Seats held by women in national parliaments (%)	14.5	13.2	12.4

Environment and infrastructure indicators	2005	2010	2017
Mobile-cellular subscriptions (per 100 inhabitants)	0.3 [p]	34.8	89.5 [c,b]
Individuals using the Internet (per 100 inhabitants)	0.2	0.6 [c]	2.5 [c,b]
Threatened species (number)	86 [m]	131	177
Forested area (% of land area) [c]	39.1	37.8	41.3 [g]
CO2 emission estimates (million tons/tons per capita)	0.5 / 0.1	0.7 / 0.1	1.3 / 0.2 [g]
Energy production, primary (Petajoules)	50	52	53 [g]
Energy supply per capita (Gigajoules)	11	10	11 [g]
Tourist/visitor arrivals at national borders (000) [q]	40	39	24 [b]
Important sites for terrestrial biodiversity protected (%)	54.6	69.0	80.3
Pop. using improved drinking water (urban/rural, %)	78.8 / 36.8	81.9 / 42.3	84.9 / 47.8 [b]
Pop. using improved sanitation facilities (urban/rural, %)	22.3 / 5.9	22.5 / 6.4	22.8 / 6.9 [b]
Net Official Development Assist. received (% of GNI)	21.38	17.33	21.56 [b]

a Projected estimate (medium fertility variant). **b** 2015. **c** Estimate. **d** Index base: 2003=100. **e** Break in the time series. **f** Series linked to former series. **g** 2014. **h** 2016. **i** Data refers to a 5-year period preceding the reference year. **j** Including refugees. **k** Data as at the end of December. **l** Data revision. **m** 2004. **n** 2001. **o** 2002. **p** 2000. **q** Arrivals by air.

Singapore

Region	South-eastern Asia	UN membership date	21 September 1965
Population (000, 2017)	5 709[a]	Surface area (km2)	719[b,c]
Pop. density (per km2, 2017)	8 155.5[a]	Sex ratio (m per 100 f, 2017)	97.7[a]
Capital city	Singapore	National currency	Singapore Dollar (SGD)
Capital city pop. (000)	5 618.9[c]	Exchange rate (per US$)	1.4[d]

Economic indicators	2005	2010	2017
GDP: Gross domestic product (million current US$)	127 418	236 420	292 734[c]
GDP growth rate (annual %, const. 2005 prices)	7.5	15.2	2.0[c]
GDP per capita (current US$)	28 343.2	46 549.0	52 239.0[c]
Economy: Agriculture (% of GVA)[e,f]	0.1	~0.0	~0.0[c]
Economy: Industry (% of GVA)[e,g]	32.4	27.6	26.4[c]
Economy: Services and other activity (% of GVA)[e]	67.6	72.3	73.6[c]
Employment: Agriculture (% of employed)[h]	0.4	0.3	0.3
Employment: Industry (% of employed)[h]	22.1	21.4	17.0
Employment: Services (% of employed)[h]	77.6	78.3	82.6
Unemployment (% of labour force)	5.6	3.1	2.0[h]
Labour force participation (female/male pop. %)[h]	53.5 / 76.7	57.3 / 77.5	57.8 / 76.1
CPI: Consumer Price Index (2000=100)	103	117	132[i]
Agricultural production index (2004-2006=100)	90	92	112[j]
Food production index (2004-2006=100)	90	92	112[j]
International trade: Exports (million US$)	229 652	351 867	329 871[d]
International trade: Imports (million US$)	200 050	310 791	283 009[d]
International trade: Balance (million US$)	29 602	41 076	46 862[d]
Balance of payments, current account (million US$)	28 133	56 292	57 922[c]

Major trading partners						2016
Export partners (% of exports)	China	13.0	China, Hong Kong SAR	12.6	Malaysia	10.6
Import partners (% of imports)	China	14.3	Malaysia	11.4	United States	10.9

Social indicators	2005	2010	2017
Population growth rate (average annual %)[k]	2.8	2.4	1.7[c]
Urban population (% of total population)	100.0	100.0	100.0[c]
Urban population growth rate (average annual %)[k]	2.7	2.4	2.0[c]
Fertility rate, total (live births per woman)[k]	1.3	1.3	1.2[c]
Life expectancy at birth (females/males, years)[k]	81.8 / 76.7	83.7 / 78.7	84.5 / 80.1[c]
Population age distribution (0-14 and 60+ years, %)	19.1 / 12.6	17.3 / 14.1	15.0 / 19.5[a]
International migrant stock (000/% of total pop.)	1 710.6 / 38.1	2 164.8 / 42.6	2 543.6 / 45.4[c]
Refugees and others of concern to UNHCR (000)	~0.0[l]	~0.0[l]	~0.0[d]
Infant mortality rate (per 1 000 live births)[k]	2.5	2.2	2.1[c]
Health: Total expenditure (% of GDP)	3.7	4.0	4.9[j]
Health: Physicians (per 1 000 pop.)	1.5	1.7	1.9[i]
Education: Government expenditure (% of GDP)	3.2	3.1	2.9[i]
Intentional homicide rate (per 100 000 pop.)	0.5	0.4	0.2[c]
Seats held by women in national parliaments (%)	16.0	23.4	23.8

Environment and infrastructure indicators	2005	2010	2017
Mobile-cellular subscriptions (per 100 inhabitants)	97.5	145.4[m]	146.1[l,h,c]
Individuals using the Internet (per 100 inhabitants)	61.0[n]	71.0[h,o]	82.1[h,c]
Research & Development expenditure (% of GDP)	2.2	2.0	2.2[j]
Threatened species (number)	85[p]	277	293
Forested area (% of land area)[h]	23.7	23.3	23.1[i]
CO2 emission estimates (million tons/tons per capita)	30.4 / 7.1	55.6 / 11.0	56.4 / 10.2[i]
Energy production, primary (Petajoules)	...	25	27[i]
Energy supply per capita (Gigajoules)	189	212	209[i]
Tourist/visitor arrivals at national borders (000)	7 079	9 161	12 051[c]
Important sites for terrestrial biodiversity protected (%)	21.1	21.1	21.1
Pop. using improved drinking water (urban/rural, %)	100.0 / ...	100.0 / ...	100.0 / ...[c]
Pop. using improved sanitation facilities (urban/rural, %)	100.0 / ...	100.0 / ...	100.0 / ...[c]

a Projected estimate (medium fertility variant). **b** The land area of Singapore comprises the mainland and other islands. **c** 2015. **d** 2016. **e** Data classified according to ISIC Rev. 4. **f** Includes mining and quarrying. **g** Excludes mining and quarrying. **h** Estimate. **i** 2013. **j** 2014. **k** Data refers to a 5-year period preceding the reference year. **l** Data as at the end of December. **m** Includes inactive subscriptions. **n** Population aged 15 years and over. **o** Population aged 7 years and over. **p** 2004.

Sint Maarten (Dutch part)

Region	Caribbean	Population (000, 2017)	40 [a]
Surface area (km2)	34 [b]	Pop. density (per km2, 2017)	1 180.0 [a]
Sex ratio (m per 100 f, 2017)	95.7 [c,d]	Capital city	Philipsburg
National currency	Neth. Ant. Guilder (ANG) [e]	Capital city pop. (000)	1.2 [f]
Exchange rate (per US$)	1.8 [g]		

Economic indicators	2005	2010	2017
GDP: Gross domestic product (million current US$)	708	896	1 094 [b]
GDP growth rate (annual %, const. 2005 prices)	...	1.1	0.5 [b]
GDP per capita (current US$)	21 764.5	27 063.9	28 241.7 [b]
Economy: Agriculture (% of GVA)	0.3	0.1	0.1 [b]
Economy: Industry (% of GVA)	16.4	13.4	12.3 [b]
Economy: Services and other activity (% of GVA)	83.3	86.5	87.6 [b]
Balance of payments, current account (million US$)	...	...	23 [b]

Social indicators	2005	2010	2017
Population growth rate (average annual %) [h]	0.4	0.4	3.1 [b]
Urban population (% of total population)	100.0	100.0	100.0 [b]
Urban population growth rate (average annual %) [h]	3.5	2.6	2.0 [b]
Life expectancy at birth (females/males, years)	... / ...	77.2 / 72.0 [i]	77.1 / 69.2 [i,k]
Population age distribution (0-14 and 60+ years, %)	... / ...	... / ...	21.0 / 10.4 [c,k]
International migrant stock (000/% of total pop.)	13.1 / 40.3	26.2 / 79.1	27.3 / 70.4 [b]
Refugees and others of concern to UNHCR (000)	...	~0.0 [l]	~0.0 [g]

Environment and infrastructure indicators	2005	2010	2017
Threatened species (number)	...	...	51
CO2 emission estimates (million tons/tons per capita)	... / ...	... / ...	0.7 / 19.5 [d]
Energy supply per capita (Gigajoules)	...	...	303 [m,d]
Tourist/visitor arrivals at national borders (000) [n]	468	443	505 [b]
Important sites for terrestrial biodiversity protected (%)	0.0	0.0	0.0

a Projected estimate (medium fertility variant). **b** 2015. **c** De jure population. **d** 2014. **e** Netherlands Antillean Guilder. **f** 2001. **g** 2016. **h** Data refers to a 5-year period preceding the reference year. **i** Data refers to a 3-year period up to and including the reference year. **j** Data refers to a 2-year period up to and including the reference year. **k** 2013. **l** Data as at the end of December. **m** Estimate. **n** Arrivals by air. Including arrivals to Saint Martin (French part).

Slovakia

Region	Eastern Europe	UN membership date	19 January 1993
Population (000, 2017)	5 448[a]	Surface area (km2)	49 035[b,c]
Pop. density (per km2, 2017)	113.3[a]	Sex ratio (m per 100 f, 2017)	94.6[a]
Capital city	Bratislava	National currency	Euro (EUR)
Capital city pop. (000)	400.7[c]	Exchange rate (per US$)	0.9[d]

Economic indicators

	2005	2010	2017
GDP: Gross domestic product (million current US$)	48 965	89 501	87 268[c]
GDP growth rate (annual %, const. 2005 prices)	6.8	5.0	3.8[c]
GDP per capita (current US$)	9 092.5	16 553.1	16 082.5[c]
Economy: Agriculture (% of GVA)[e]	3.6	2.8	3.7[c]
Economy: Industry (% of GVA)[e]	36.1	35.2	34.8[c]
Economy: Services and other activity (% of GVA)[e]	60.3	62.0	61.5[c]
Employment: Agriculture (% of employed)[f]	4.8	3.2	3.3
Employment: Industry (% of employed)[f]	38.8	37.0	34.5
Employment: Services (% of employed)[f]	56.4	59.8	62.2
Unemployment (% of labour force)	16.3	14.4	9.9[f]
Labour force participation (female/male pop. %)[f]	51.2 / 68.5	50.8 / 67.8	51.4 / 68.0
CPI: Consumer Price Index (2000=100)	133	153	167[g]
Agricultural production index (2004-2006=100)	102	82	97[g]
Food production index (2004-2006=100)	102	82	97[g]
Index of industrial production (2005=100)	100	127[h]	158[h,g]
International trade: Exports (million US$)	32 210	63 999	77 565[d]
International trade: Imports (million US$)	34 226	64 382	75 156[d]
International trade: Balance (million US$)	- 2 016	- 383	2 409[d]
Balance of payments, current account (million US$)	- 5 125	- 4 211	193[c]

Major trading partners

						2016
Export partners (% of exports)	Germany	21.9	Czechia	11.8	Poland	7.6
Import partners (% of imports)	Germany	17.0	Czechia	10.7	Other Europe nes[i]	9.1

Social indicators

	2005	2010	2017
Population growth rate (average annual %)[j]	~0.0	~0.0	0.1[c]
Urban population (% of total population)	55.6	54.7	53.6[c]
Urban population growth rate (average annual %)[j]	- 0.2	- 0.2	- 0.3[c]
Fertility rate, total (live births per woman)[j]	1.2	1.3	1.4[c]
Life expectancy at birth (females/males, years)[j]	77.8 / 69.8	78.6 / 70.8	79.8 / 72.6[c]
Population age distribution (0-14 and 60+ years, %)	16.8 / 16.1	15.3 / 17.8	15.4 / 21.8[a]
International migrant stock (000/% of total pop.)	130.5 / 2.4	146.3 / 2.7	177.2 / 3.3[c]
Refugees and others of concern to UNHCR (000)	3.1[k]	1.6[k]	2.7[d]
Infant mortality rate (per 1 000 live births)[j]	7.3	6.2	5.7[c]
Health: Total expenditure (% of GDP)	7.0	8.5	8.1[g]
Health: Physicians (per 1 000 pop.)	...	3.3[l]	3.4[m]
Education: Government expenditure (% of GDP)	3.8	4.1	4.2[g]
Education: Primary gross enrol. ratio (f/m per 100 pop.)	98.1 / 99.2	101.8 / 102.9	99.2 / 100.2[c]
Education: Secondary gross enrol. ratio (f/m per 100 pop.)	94.2 / 93.3	93.1 / 92.2	92.8 / 92.1[c]
Education: Tertiary gross enrol. ratio (f/m per 100 pop.)	45.7 / 35.4	69.3 / 44.9	64.6 / 41.8[g]
Intentional homicide rate (per 100 000 pop.)	2.0	1.6	0.9[c]
Seats held by women in national parliaments (%)	16.7	18.0	20.0

Environment and infrastructure indicators

	2005	2010	2017
Mobile-cellular subscriptions (per 100 inhabitants)	84.2[n]	109.0	122.3[c]
Individuals using the Internet (per 100 inhabitants)	55.2[o]	75.7[o,p]	85.0[f,c]
Research & Development expenditure (% of GDP)	0.5	0.6	0.9[g]
Threatened species (number)	48[q]	34	54
Forested area (% of land area)	40.2	40.3	40.3[f,g]
CO2 emission estimates (million tons/tons per capita)	39.4 / 7.3	36.2 / 6.7	30.7 / 5.6[g]
Energy production, primary (Petajoules)	265	250	264[g]
Energy supply per capita (Gigajoules)	144	136	121[g]
Tourist/visitor arrivals at national borders (000)	1 515[r]	1 327	1 721[c]
Important sites for terrestrial biodiversity protected (%)	73.0	76.2	83.6
Pop. using improved drinking water (urban/rural, %)	100.0 / 99.8	100.0 / 100.0	100.0 / 100.0[c]
Pop. using improved sanitation facilities (urban/rural, %)	99.4 / 98.2	99.4 / 98.2	99.4 / 98.2[c]
Net Official Development Assist. disbursed (% of GNI)[s]	...	0.09	0.12[t,d]

a Projected estimate (medium fertility variant). **b** Excluding inland water. **c** 2015. **d** 2016. **e** Data classified according to ISIC Rev. 4. **f** Estimate. **g** 2014. **h** Excluding water and waste management. **i** Other Europe, not elsewhere specified. **j** Data refers to a 5-year period preceding the reference year. **k** Data as at the end of December. **l** 2009. **m** 2013. **n** Includes inactive subscriptions. **o** Population aged 16 to 74 years. **p** Users in the last 3 months. **q** 2004. **r** Break in the time series. **s** Development Assistance Committee member (OECD) **t** Provisional data.

Slovenia

Region	Southern Europe	UN membership date	22 May 1992
Population (000, 2017)	2 080 [a]	Surface area (km2)	20 273 [b]
Pop. density (per km2, 2017)	103.3 [a]	Sex ratio (m per 100 f, 2017)	98.6 [a]
Capital city	Ljubljana	National currency	Euro (EUR)
Capital city pop. (000)	278.9 [c]	Exchange rate (per US$)	0.9 [d]

Economic indicators	2005	2010	2017
GDP: Gross domestic product (million current US$)	36 345	48 014	42 777 [b]
GDP growth rate (annual %, const. 2005 prices)	4.0	1.2	2.3 [b]
GDP per capita (current US$)	18 204.1	23 393.0	20 689.8 [b]
Economy: Agriculture (% of GVA) [e]	2.6	2.0	2.4 [b]
Economy: Industry (% of GVA) [e]	34.1	30.6	32.7 [b]
Economy: Services and other activity (% of GVA) [e]	63.3	67.4	64.9 [b]
Employment: Agriculture (% of employed) [f]	9.1	8.8	8.9
Employment: Industry (% of employed) [f]	37.1	32.5	29.6
Employment: Services (% of employed) [f]	53.8	58.7	61.5
Unemployment (% of labour force)	6.5	7.2	8.1 [f]
Labour force participation (female/male pop. %) [f]	52.8 / 66.0	53.2 / 65.5	51.8 / 62.2
CPI: Consumer Price Index (2000=100)	131	150	160 [c]
Agricultural production index (2004-2006=100)	99	92	89 [c]
Food production index (2004-2006=100)	99	92	89 [c]
Index of industrial production (2005=100)	100	103 [g]	104 [g,c]
International trade: Exports (million US$)	17 896	24 435	27 585 [d]
International trade: Imports (million US$)	19 626	26 592	26 646 [d]
International trade: Balance (million US$)	- 1 730	- 2 157	939 [d]
Balance of payments, current account (million US$)	- 680	- 55	2 216 [b]

Major trading partners						2016
Export partners (% of exports)	Germany	20.9	Italy	11.2	Austria	8.3
Import partners (% of imports)	Germany	17.4	Italy	14.7	Austria	8.6

Social indicators	2005	2010	2017
Population growth rate (average annual %) [h]	0.1	0.5	0.3 [b]
Urban population (% of total population)	50.5	50.0	49.7 [b]
Urban population growth rate (average annual %) [h]	~0.0	0.3	0.1 [b]
Fertility rate, total (live births per woman) [h]	1.2	1.4	1.6 [b]
Life expectancy at birth (females/males, years) [h]	80.4 / 72.8	82.0 / 75.0	83.2 / 77.2 [b]
Population age distribution (0-14 and 60+ years, %)	14.0 / 20.8	14.1 / 22.2	15.0 / 26.3 [a]
International migrant stock (000/% of total pop.)	197.3 / 9.9	253.8 / 12.4	236.0 / 11.4 [b]
Refugees and others of concern to UNHCR (000)	1.2 [i]	4.6 [i]	0.6 [d]
Infant mortality rate (per 1 000 live births) [h]	4.0	3.2	2.5 [b]
Health: Total expenditure (% of GDP)	8.5	9.1	9.2 [c]
Health: Physicians (per 1 000 pop.)	...	2.4	2.8 [c]
Education: Government expenditure (% of GDP)	5.6	5.6	5.5 [i]
Education: Primary gross enrol. ratio (f/m per 100 pop.)	99.3 / 101.0	98.0 / 98.5	99.4 / 99.2 [c]
Education: Secondary gross enrol. ratio (f/m per 100 pop.)	96.8 / 97.4	97.4 / 98.3	110.5 / 110.8 [c]
Education: Tertiary gross enrol. ratio (f/m per 100 pop.)	93.4 / 65.6	107.0 / 71.2	98.5 / 68.2 [c]
Intentional homicide rate (per 100 000 pop.)	1.0	0.7	1.2 [b]
Seats held by women in national parliaments (%)	12.2	14.4	36.7

Environment and infrastructure indicators	2005	2010	2017
Mobile-cellular subscriptions (per 100 inhabitants)	88.0 [k]	103.3	113.2 [b]
Individuals using the Internet (per 100 inhabitants)	46.8 [l]	70.0 [m]	73.1 [m,b]
Research & Development expenditure (% of GDP)	1.4	2.1	2.4 [c]
Threatened species (number)	74 [n]	95	143
Forested area (% of land area)	61.7	61.9	62.0 [f,c]
CO2 emission estimates (million tons/tons per capita)	15.9 / 7.9	15.3 / 7.5	12.8 / 6.2 [c]
Energy production, primary (Petajoules)	146	157	154 [c]
Energy supply per capita (Gigajoules)	153	149	135 [c]
Tourist/visitor arrivals at national borders (000)	1 555	1 869	2 707 [b]
Important sites for terrestrial biodiversity protected (%)	83.0	83.0	85.5
Pop. using improved drinking water (urban/rural, %)	99.8 / 99.4	99.7 / 99.4	99.7 / 99.4 [b]
Pop. using improved sanitation facilities (urban/rural, %)	99.1 / 99.1	99.1 / 99.1	99.1 / 99.1 [b]
Net Official Development Assist. disbursed (% of GNI) [o]	0.11	0.13	0.18 [p,d]

a Projected estimate (medium fertility variant). b 2015. c 2014. d 2016. e Data classified according to ISIC Rev. 4. f Estimate. g Excluding water and waste management. h Data refers to a 5-year period preceding the reference year. i Data as at the end of December. j 2013. k Data refers to active subscriptions only. l Users in the last 3 months. m Population aged 16 to 74 years. n 2004. o Development Assistance Committee member (OECD) p Provisional data.

Solomon Islands

Region	Melanesia	UN membership date	19 September 1978
Population (000, 2017)	611[a]	Surface area (km2)	28 896[b]
Pop. density (per km2, 2017)	21.8[a]	Sex ratio (m per 100 f, 2017)	103.4[a]
Capital city	Honiara	National currency	Solomon Is. Dollar (SBD)[c]
Capital city pop. (000)	73.3[d]	Exchange rate (per US$)	8.1[b]

Economic indicators	2005	2010	2017
GDP: Gross domestic product (million current US$)	429	720	1 075[b]
GDP growth rate (annual %, const. 2005 prices)	12.8	10.6	3.2[b]
GDP per capita (current US$)	915.1	1 367.6	1 841.6[b]
Economy: Agriculture (% of GVA)	30.4	28.7	28.2[b]
Economy: Industry (% of GVA)	7.5	13.3	15.6[b]
Economy: Services and other activity (% of GVA)	62.1	57.9	56.3[b]
Employment: Agriculture (% of employed)[e]	52.9	51.8	48.1
Employment: Industry (% of employed)[e]	2.1	2.5	2.4
Employment: Services (% of employed)[e]	45.0	45.7	49.5
Unemployment (% of labour force)[e]	31.3	31.1	31.4
Labour force participation (female/male pop. %)[e]	61.3 / 74.3	61.2 / 74.2	61.1 / 73.5
CPI: Consumer Price Index (2000=100)[f]	149	226	271[g]
Agricultural production index (2004-2006=100)	103	111	118[d]
Food production index (2004-2006=100)	103	111	118[d]
International trade: Exports (million US$)	70	215	437[h]
International trade: Imports (million US$)	139	328	454[h]
International trade: Balance (million US$)	- 68	- 112	- 17[h]
Balance of payments, current account (million US$)	- 90	- 144	- 36[b]

Major trading partners						2016
Export partners (% of exports)	China	62.5	Italy	7.0	United Kingdom	4.4
Import partners (% of imports)	Australia	20.4	Singapore	15.5	China	14.8

Social indicators	2005	2010	2017
Population growth rate (average annual %)[i]	2.6	2.3	2.1[b]
Urban population (% of total population)	17.8	20.0	22.3[b]
Urban population growth rate (average annual %)[i]	5.0	4.6	4.2[b]
Fertility rate, total (live births per woman)[i]	4.6	4.4	4.1[b]
Life expectancy at birth (females/males, years)[i]	66.0 / 63.5	68.8 / 66.1	71.1 / 68.3[b]
Population age distribution (0-14 and 60+ years, %)	41.3 / 4.8	40.8 / 5.1	38.8 / 5.4[a]
International migrant stock (000/% of total pop.)	3.3 / 0.7	2.8 / 0.5	2.6 / 0.4[b]
Refugees and others of concern to UNHCR (000)	...	...	~0.0[h]
Infant mortality rate (per 1 000 live births)[i]	49.9	38.7	30.0[b]
Health: Total expenditure (% of GDP)	7.8	7.5	5.1[d]
Health: Physicians (per 1 000 pop.)	0.2	0.2[i]	0.2[k]
Education: Government expenditure (% of GDP)	...	10.0	...
Education: Primary gross enrol. ratio (f/m per 100 pop.)	97.8 / 103.6	113.3 / 116.6	113.6 / 115.0[b]
Education: Secondary gross enrol. ratio (f/m per 100 pop.)	27.4 / 33.2	44.9 / 52.1	47.0 / 49.8[l]
Intentional homicide rate (per 100 000 pop.)	5.5	3.8[m]	...
Seats held by women in national parliaments (%)	0.0	0.0	2.0

Environment and infrastructure indicators	2005	2010	2017
Mobile-cellular subscriptions (per 100 inhabitants)	1.3	21.9	72.7[b]
Individuals using the Internet (per 100 inhabitants)	0.8	5.0[e]	10.0[e,b]
Threatened species (number)	74[n]	220	245
Forested area (% of land area)[e]	80.1	79.1	78.3[d]
CO2 emission estimates (million tons/tons per capita)	0.2 / 0.3	0.2 / 0.4	0.2 / 0.4[d]
Energy production, primary (Petajoules)[e]	3	3	3[d]
Energy supply per capita (Gigajoules)[e]	12	11	11[d]
Tourist/visitor arrivals at national borders (000)	9[o]	20	22[b]
Important sites for terrestrial biodiversity protected (%)	7.1	9.5	9.5
Pop. using improved drinking water (urban/rural, %)	93.2 / 77.2	93.2 / 77.2	93.2 / 77.2[b]
Pop. using improved sanitation facilities (urban/rural, %)	81.4 / 15.0	81.4 / 15.0	81.4 / 15.0[b]
Net Official Development Assist. received (% of GNI)	47.69	68.51	16.47[b]

a Projected estimate (medium fertility variant). **b** 2015. **c** Solomon Islands Dollar. **d** 2014. **e** Estimate. **f** Honiara **g** 2013. **h** 2016. **i** Data refers to a 5-year period preceding the reference year. **j** 2009. **k** 2011. **l** 2012. **m** 2008. **n** 2004. **o** Without first quarter.

Somalia

Region	Eastern Africa	UN membership date	20 September 1960
Population (000, 2017)	14 742[a]	Surface area (km2)	637 657[b]
Pop. density (per km2, 2017)	23.5[a]	Sex ratio (m per 100 f, 2017)	99.3[a]
Capital city	Mogadishu	National currency	Somali Shilling (SOS)
Capital city pop. (000)	2 137.8[b]	Exchange rate (per US$)	2 300.0[c,d]

Economic indicators	2005	2010	2017
GDP: Gross domestic product (million current US$)	2 316	1 071	1 559[b]
GDP growth rate (annual %, const. 2005 prices)	3.0	2.6	2.7[b]
GDP per capita (current US$)	273.5	111.8	144.5[b]
Economy: Agriculture (% of GVA)	60.1	60.2	60.2[b]
Economy: Industry (% of GVA)	7.4	7.4	7.4[b]
Economy: Services and other activity (% of GVA)	32.6	32.5	32.5[b]
Employment: Agriculture (% of employed)[e]	72.6	72.4	72.0
Employment: Industry (% of employed)[e]	4.6	4.7	4.8
Employment: Services (% of employed)[e]	22.7	22.8	23.2
Unemployment (% of labour force)[e]	6.7	6.7	6.6
Labour force participation (female/male pop. %)[e]	32.4 / 76.8	32.4 / 76.3	33.3 / 75.9
Agricultural production index (2004-2006=100)	102	105	112[f]
Food production index (2004-2006=100)	102	105	112[f]
International trade: Exports (million US$)	379	568	925[d]
International trade: Imports (million US$)	469	496	530[d]
International trade: Balance (million US$)	- 90	72	394[d]

Major trading partners					2016
Export partners (% of exports)	Saudi Arabia	41.1	Oman	23.5	United Arab Emirates 13.4
Import partners (% of imports)	India	23.9	China	19.0	United Arab Emirates 15.3

Social indicators	2005	2010	2017
Population growth rate (average annual %)[g]	2.9	2.9	2.9[b]
Urban population (% of total population)	35.2	37.3	39.6[b]
Urban population growth rate (average annual %)[g]	3.8	3.7	4.1[b]
Fertility rate, total (live births per woman)[g]	7.5	7.1	6.6[b]
Life expectancy at birth (females/males, years)[g]	53.1 / 50.0	54.8 / 51.6	56.5 / 53.3[b]
Population age distribution (0-14 and 60+ years, %)	47.9 / 4.3	47.7 / 4.3	46.4 / 4.4[a]
International migrant stock (000/% of total pop.)[e,h]	20.7 / 0.2	24.0 / 0.3	25.3 / 0.2[b]
Refugees and others of concern to UNHCR (000)	400.6[i]	1 489.8[i]	1 168.4[d]
Infant mortality rate (per 1 000 live births)[g]	97.0	89.8	79.5[b]
Health: Physicians (per 1 000 pop.)	...	~0.0[j]	~0.0[f]
Education: Primary gross enrol. ratio (f/m per 100 pop.)	... / ...	20.8 / 37.6[k]	... / ...
Education: Secondary gross enrol. ratio (f/m per 100 pop.)	... / ...	4.6 / 10.1[k]	... / ...
Intentional homicide rate (per 100 000 pop.)	6.1	6.6	5.6[b]
Seats held by women in national parliaments (%)	...	6.9	24.2

Environment and infrastructure indicators	2005	2010	2017
Mobile-cellular subscriptions (per 100 inhabitants)	5.9	6.7[e]	52.5[e,b]
Individuals using the Internet (per 100 inhabitants)[e]	1.1	1.2[l]	1.8[b]
Threatened species (number)	64[m]	128	175
Forested area (% of land area)[e]	11.4	10.8	10.3[f]
CO2 emission estimates (million tons/tons per capita)	0.6 / 0.1	0.6 / 0.1	0.6 / 0.1[f]
Energy production, primary (Petajoules)	103	124	129[f]
Energy supply per capita (Gigajoules)	13	13	12[f]
Important sites for terrestrial biodiversity protected (%)	0.0	0.0	0.0
Pop. using improved drinking water (urban/rural, %)	60.5 / 11.0	69.6 / 8.8	69.6 / 8.8[n]
Pop. using improved sanitation facilities (urban/rural, %)	50.0 / 7.4	52.0 / 6.3	52.0 / 6.3[n]
Net Official Development Assist. received (% of GNI)	...	...	22.85[b]

a Projected estimate (medium fertility variant). **b** 2015. **c** UN operational exchange rate. **d** 2016. **e** Estimate. **f** 2014. **g** Data refers to a 5-year period preceding the reference year. **h** Including refugees. **i** Data as at the end of December. **j** 2006. **k** 2007. **l** 2009. **m** 2004. **n** 2011.

South Africa

Region	Southern Africa	UN membership date	07 November 1945
Population (000, 2017)	56 717 [a]	Surface area (km2)	1 221 037 [b]
Pop. density (per km2, 2017)	46.8 [a]	Sex ratio (m per 100 f, 2017)	96.4 [a]
Capital city	Pretoria [c]	National currency	Rand (ZAR)
Capital city pop. (000)	2 058.8 [b]	Exchange rate (per US$)	13.7 [d]

Economic indicators	2005	2010	2017
GDP: Gross domestic product (million current US$)	257 772	375 348	314 571 [b]
GDP growth rate (annual %, const. 2005 prices)	5.3	3.0	1.3 [b]
GDP per capita (current US$)	5 331.0	7 271.1	5 773.0 [b]
Economy: Agriculture (% of GVA)	2.7	2.6	2.4 [b]
Economy: Industry (% of GVA)	30.3	30.2	28.9 [b]
Economy: Services and other activity (% of GVA)	67.1	67.2	68.7 [b]
Employment: Agriculture (% of employed) [e]	7.1	4.6	6.1
Employment: Industry (% of employed) [e]	24.4	23.1	26.2
Employment: Services (% of employed) [e]	68.5	72.3	67.7
Unemployment (% of labour force)	23.8	24.7	26.0 [e]
Labour force participation (female/male pop. %) [e]	46.7 / 61.5	43.8 / 59.4	46.4 / 61.1
CPI: Consumer Price Index (2000=100)	128	142	176 [f]
Agricultural production index (2004-2006=100)	102	118	125 [f]
Food production index (2004-2006=100)	102	118	126 [f]
International trade: Exports (million US$) [g,h]	46 991	82 626	74 111 [d]
International trade: Imports (million US$) [g,h]	55 033	82 949	74 744 [d]
International trade: Balance (million US$) [g,h]	- 8 042	- 323	- 633 [d]
Balance of payments, current account (million US$)	- 8 015	- 5 492	- 13 644 [b]

Major trading partners						2016
Export partners (% of exports)	China	9.9	United States	7.5	Germany	7.1
Import partners (% of imports)	China	18.1	Germany	11.8	United States	6.7

Social indicators	2005	2010	2017
Population growth rate (average annual %) [i]	1.3	1.1	1.4 [b]
Urban population (% of total population)	59.5	62.2	64.8 [b]
Urban population growth rate (average annual %) [i]	2.4	2.2	1.6 [b]
Fertility rate, total (live births per woman) [i]	2.8	2.6	2.6 [b]
Life expectancy at birth (females/males, years) [i]	56.7 / 51.2	55.6 / 50.6	63.0 / 56.1 [b]
Population age distribution (0-14 and 60+ years, %)	31.7 / 6.7	30.4 / 7.2	29.0 / 8.4 [a]
International migrant stock (000/% of total pop.) [i]	1 210.9 / 2.5	1 943.1 / 3.8	3 142.5 / 5.8 [b]
Refugees and others of concern to UNHCR (000)	169.9 [k]	229.7 [k]	1 201.9 [d]
Infant mortality rate (per 1 000 live births) [i]	60.5	52.7	36.5 [b]
Health: Total expenditure (% of GDP)	7.8	8.5	8.8 [f]
Health: Physicians (per 1 000 pop.)	0.7 [l]	0.7	0.8 [b]
Education: Government expenditure (% of GDP)	5.1	5.7	6.0 [f]
Education: Primary gross enrol. ratio (f/m per 100 pop.)	103.0 / 96.5	99.3 / 93.6	97.3 / 102.2 [f]
Education: Secondary gross enrol. ratio (f/m per 100 pop.)	93.7 / 84.3	96.7 / 84.4	111.5 / 88.0 [f]
Education: Tertiary gross enrol. ratio (f/m per 100 pop.)	... / ...	... / ...	23.3 / 15.7 [f]
Intentional homicide rate (per 100 000 pop.)	38.9	30.9	34.3 [b]
Seats held by women in national parliaments (%)	32.8	44.5	42.2

Environment and infrastructure indicators	2005	2010	2017
Mobile-cellular subscriptions (per 100 inhabitants)	70.4	97.9	159.3 [b]
Individuals using the Internet (per 100 inhabitants)	7.5	24.0 [e]	51.9 [e,b]
Research & Development expenditure (% of GDP)	0.9	0.7	0.7 [m]
Threatened species (number)	357 [l]	441	581
Forested area (% of land area)	7.6	7.6	7.6 [e,f]
CO2 emission estimates (million tons/tons per capita)	416.9 / 8.7	474.1 / 9.2	489.8 / 9.1 [f]
Energy production, primary (Petajoules)	6 648	6 909	7 102 [f]
Energy supply per capita (Gigajoules)	114	122	122 [f]
Tourist/visitor arrivals at national borders (000)	7 369 [n]	8 074 [o]	8 904 [b]
Important sites for terrestrial biodiversity protected (%)	47.7	50.3	54.5
Pop. using improved drinking water (urban/rural, %)	98.9 / 74.2	99.2 / 77.8	99.6 / 81.4 [b]
Pop. using improved sanitation facilities (urban/rural, %)	67.2 / 50.6	68.4 / 55.5	69.6 / 60.5 [b]
Net Official Development Assist. received (% of GNI)	0.27	0.28	0.47 [b]

a Projected estimate (medium fertility variant). **b** 2015. **c** Pretoria is the administrative capital, Cape Town is the legislative capital and Bloemfontein is the judiciary capital. **d** 2016. **e** Estimate. **f** 2014. **g** Exports include gold. **h** Imports FOB. **i** Data refers to a 5-year period preceding the reference year. **j** Including refugees. **k** Data as at the end of December. **l** 2004. **m** 2012. **n** Excluding arrivals for work and contract workers. **o** Break in the time series.

South Sudan

Region	Eastern Africa	UN membership date	14 July 2011
Population (000, 2017)	12 576[a]	Surface area (km2)	658 841[b]
Pop. density (per km2, 2017)	20.6[a]	Sex ratio (m per 100 f, 2017)	100.4[a]
Capital city	Juba	National currency	S. Sudanese Pound (SSP)[c]
Capital city pop. (000)	321.1[b]	Exchange rate (per US$)	83.9[d]

Economic indicators	2005	2010	2017
GDP: Gross domestic product (million current US$)	...	15 720	13 167[b]
GDP growth rate (annual %, const. 2005 prices)	...	5.5	2.0[b]
GDP per capita (current US$)	...	1 563.2	1 067.0[b]
Economy: Agriculture (% of GVA)	...	5.1	4.6[b]
Economy: Industry (% of GVA)	...	55.4	58.0[b]
Economy: Services and other activity (% of GVA)	...	39.4	37.4[b]
Unemployment (% of labour force)	...	13.7[e,f]	
Labour force participation (female/male pop. %)	... / ...	71.6 / 76.7[e,f]	... / ...
International trade: Exports (million US$)	...	...	2 389[d]
International trade: Imports (million US$)	...	...	750[d]
International trade: Balance (million US$)	...	...	1 640[d]
Balance of payments, current account (million US$)	...	...	- 935[g,h]

Major trading partners						2016
Export partners (% of exports)	China	98.8	Pakistan	0.5	Algeria	0.5
Import partners (% of imports)	Uganda	60.6	China	8.6	Pakistan	7.2

Social indicators	2005	2010	2017
Population growth rate (average annual %)[i]	3.8	4.3	3.3[b]
Urban population (% of total population)	17.2	17.9	18.8[b]
Urban population growth rate (average annual %)[i]	4.6	5.0	5.1[b]
Fertility rate, total (live births per woman)[i]	6.0	5.6	5.2[b]
Life expectancy at birth (females/males, years)[i]	51.3 / 49.1	53.3 / 51.3	56.0 / 54.1[b]
Population age distribution (0-14 and 60+ years, %)	44.3 / 5.1	43.3 / 5.3	41.7 / 5.1[a]
International migrant stock (000/% of total pop.)[j]	... / ...	257.9 / 2.6	824.1 / 6.7[b]
Refugees and others of concern to UNHCR (000)	...	...	2 231.2[d]
Infant mortality rate (per 1 000 live births)[i]	101.4	89.1	77.7[b]
Health: Total expenditure (% of GDP)	...	...	2.7[k,h]
Education: Government expenditure (% of GDP)	...	...	1.8[d]
Education: Primary gross enrol. ratio (f/m per 100 pop.)	... / ...	... / ...	53.1 / 74.9[b]
Education: Secondary gross enrol. ratio (f/m per 100 pop.)	... / ...	... / ...	6.6 / 12.3[b]
Intentional homicide rate (per 100 000 pop.)	...	...	13.7[l]
Seats held by women in national parliaments (%)	...	...	28.5

Environment and infrastructure indicators	2005	2010	2017
Mobile-cellular subscriptions (per 100 inhabitants)	...	14.4[m]	23.9[n,b]
Individuals using the Internet (per 100 inhabitants)[n]	...	7.0	17.9[b]
Threatened species (number)	...	...	49
CO2 emission estimates (million tons/tons per capita)	... / ...	... / ...	1.5 / 0.1[h]
Energy production, primary (Petajoules)	...	...	337[h]
Energy supply per capita (Gigajoules)	...	...	2[h]
Important sites for terrestrial biodiversity protected (%)	30.3	33.6	33.6
Pop. using improved drinking water (urban/rural, %)	... / ...	... / ...	66.7 / 56.9[b]
Pop. using improved sanitation facilities (urban/rural, %)	... / ...	... / ...	16.4 / 4.5[b]
Net Official Development Assist. received (% of GNI)	...	...	21.07[b]

a Projected estimate (medium fertility variant). **b** 2015. **c** South Sudanese Pound. **d** 2016. **e** Population aged 10 years and over. **f** 2008. **g** Break in the time series. **h** 2014. **i** Data refers to a 5-year period preceding the reference year. **j** Including refugees. **k** Estimates should be viewed with caution as these are derived from scarce data. **l** 2012. **m** Data obtained from five mobile operators. **n** Estimate.

Spain

Region	Southern Europe	UN membership date	14 December 1955
Population (000, 2017)	46 354 [a,b]	Surface area (km2)	505 944 [c]
Pop. density (per km2, 2017)	92.9 [a,b]	Sex ratio (m per 100 f, 2017)	96.2 [a,b]
Capital city	Madrid	National currency	Euro (EUR)
Capital city pop. (000)	6 199.3 [c]	Exchange rate (per US$)	0.9 [d]

Economic indicators

	2005	2010	2017
GDP: Gross domestic product (million current US$)	1 157 248	1 431 588	1 192 955 [c]
GDP growth rate (annual %, const. 2005 prices)	3.7	-0.0	3.2 [c]
GDP per capita (current US$)	26 388.2	30 719.8	25 865.4 [c]
Economy: Agriculture (% of GVA) [e]	3.0	2.6	2.6 [c]
Economy: Industry (% of GVA) [e]	30.4	26.0	23.6 [c]
Economy: Services and other activity (% of GVA) [e]	66.4	71.4	73.7 [c]
Employment: Agriculture (% of employed) [f]	5.3	4.3	3.9
Employment: Industry (% of employed) [f]	29.6	22.9	19.2
Employment: Services (% of employed) [f]	65.1	72.7	76.8
Unemployment (% of labour force)	9.1	19.9	18.3 [f]
Labour force participation (female/male pop. %) [f]	45.9 / 68.3	51.4 / 67.5	52.1 / 64.2
CPI: Consumer Price Index (2000=100) [g]	114 [h]	128	137 [i]
Agricultural production index (2004-2006=100)	95	103	102 [i]
Food production index (2004-2006=100)	94	104	102 [i]
Index of industrial production (2005=100)	100	83 [i]	76 [i,j]
International trade: Exports (million US$)	192 798	246 265	281 777 [d]
International trade: Imports (million US$)	289 611	315 547	302 539 [d]
International trade: Balance (million US$)	- 96 812	- 69 282	- 20 762 [d]
Balance of payments, current account (million US$)	- 87 006	- 56 363	16 208 [c]

Major trading partners

						2016
Export partners (% of exports)	France	15.1	Germany	12.6	Italy	8.1
Import partners (% of imports)	Germany	13.5	France	11.1	China	8.7

Social indicators

	2005	2010	2017
Population growth rate (average annual %) [a,k]	1.5	1.2	- 0.2 [c]
Urban population (% of total population) [a]	77.3	78.4	79.6 [c]
Urban population growth rate (average annual %) [a,k]	1.7	1.6	0.7 [c]
Fertility rate, total (live births per woman) [a,k]	1.3	1.4	1.3 [c]
Life expectancy at birth (females/males, years) [a,k]	83.3 / 76.5	84.3 / 78.1	85.3 / 79.6 [c]
Population age distribution (0-14 and 60+ years, %) [a]	14.3 / 21.6	14.6 / 22.4	14.7 / 25.3 [b]
International migrant stock (000/% of total pop.) [a]	4 107.2 / 9.4	6 280.1 / 13.5	5 853.0 / 12.7 [c]
Refugees and others of concern to UNHCR (000)	5.4 [l]	6.6 [l]	28.8 [d]
Infant mortality rate (per 1 000 live births) [a,k]	4.0	3.4	2.9 [c]
Health: Total expenditure (% of GDP)	8.1	9.6	9.0 [i]
Health: Physicians (per 1 000 pop.)	4.5	3.8	3.8 [i]
Education: Government expenditure (% of GDP)	4.1	4.8	4.3 [i]
Education: Primary gross enrol. ratio (f/m per 100 pop.)	102.4 / 103.8	105.5 / 106.0	105.6 / 104.5 [c]
Education: Secondary gross enrol. ratio (f/m per 100 pop.)	121.3 / 113.9	125.8 / 123.0	129.6 / 130.0 [c]
Education: Tertiary gross enrol. ratio (f/m per 100 pop.)	74.4 / 60.6	87.4 / 70.5	97.1 / 82.5 [c]
Intentional homicide rate (per 100 000 pop.)	1.2	0.9	0.7 [c]
Seats held by women in national parliaments (%)	36.0	36.6	39.1

Environment and infrastructure indicators

	2005	2010	2017
Mobile-cellular subscriptions (per 100 inhabitants)	98.4	111.3	107.9 [c]
Individuals using the Internet (per 100 inhabitants)	47.9 [m,n]	65.8 [o]	78.7 [n,c]
Research & Development expenditure (% of GDP)	1.1	1.3	1.2 [i]
Threatened species (number)	153 [p]	240	617
Forested area (% of land area)	34.6	36.5	36.8 [f,i]
CO2 emission estimates (million tons/tons per capita)	353.5 / 8.1	270.9 / 5.8	234.0 / 5.1 [i]
Energy production, primary (Petajoules) [q]	1 256	1 419	1 432 [i]
Energy supply per capita (Gigajoules) [q]	136	115	102 [i]
Tourist/visitor arrivals at national borders (000)	55 914 [h]	52 677	68 215 [c]
Important sites for terrestrial biodiversity protected (%)	57.8	59.5	61.0
Pop. using improved drinking water (urban/rural, %)	100.0 / 100.0	100.0 / 100.0	100.0 / 100.0 [c]
Pop. using improved sanitation facilities (urban/rural, %)	99.9 / 100.0	99.8 / 100.0	99.8 / 100.0 [c]
Net Official Development Assist. disbursed (% of GNI) [r]	0.27	0.43	0.33 [s,d]

a Including Canary Islands, Ceuta and Melilla. b Projected estimate (medium fertility variant). c 2015. d 2016. e Data classified according to ISIC Rev. 4. f Estimate. g Index base: 2001=100. h Break in the time series. i 2014. j Excluding water and waste management. k Data refers to a 5-year period preceding the reference year. l Data as at the end of December. m Users in the last 12 months. n Population aged 16 to 74 years. o Population aged 10 years and over. p 2004. q Data include the Canary Islands. r Development Assistance Committee member (OECD) s Provisional data.

Sri Lanka

Region	Southern Asia	UN membership date	14 December 1955
Population (000, 2017)	20 877[a]	Surface area (km2)	65 610[b]
Pop. density (per km2, 2017)	332.9[a]	Sex ratio (m per 100 f, 2017)	92.5[a]
Capital city	Colombo[c]	National currency	Sri Lanka Rupee (LKR)
Capital city pop. (000)	706.6[b]	Exchange rate (per US$)	149.8[d]

Economic indicators	2005	2010	2017
GDP: Gross domestic product (million current US$)	27 932	56 726	82 316[b]
GDP growth rate (annual %, const. 2005 prices)	6.2	8.0	4.8[b]
GDP per capita (current US$)	1 430.5	2 808.0	3 973.7[b]
Economy: Agriculture (% of GVA)[e]	9.1	9.5	8.7[b]
Economy: Industry (% of GVA)[e]	28.5	29.7	30.7[b]
Economy: Services and other activity (% of GVA)[e]	62.4	60.9	60.6[b]
Employment: Agriculture (% of employed)[f]	38.5	36.6	27.4
Employment: Industry (% of employed)[f]	22.1	20.2	25.9
Employment: Services (% of employed)[f]	39.4	43.2	46.6
Unemployment (% of labour force)	7.7	4.9	5.2[f]
Labour force participation (female/male pop. %)[f]	34.4 / 76.2	34.6 / 76.6	30.4 / 75.0
CPI: Consumer Price Index (2000=100)[g]	160	219[h,i]	278[i,j]
Agricultural production index (2004-2006=100)	102	123	120[j]
Food production index (2004-2006=100)	102	125	122[j]
International trade: Exports (million US$)	6 160	8 304	10 546[d]
International trade: Imports (million US$)	8 307	12 354	19 501[d]
International trade: Balance (million US$)	- 2 147	- 4 050	- 8 955[d]
Balance of payments, current account (million US$)	- 743	- 1 127	- 2 009[b]

Major trading partners						2016
Export partners (% of exports)	United States	26.6	United Kingdom	9.9	India	7.6
Import partners (% of imports)	China	21.9	India	19.6	United Arab Emirates	5.5

Social indicators	2005	2010	2017
Population growth rate (average annual %)[k]	0.8	0.7	0.5[b]
Urban population (% of total population)	18.4	18.3	18.4[b]
Urban population growth rate (average annual %)[k]	1.1	0.7	0.8[b]
Fertility rate, total (live births per woman)[k]	2.3	2.3	2.1[b]
Life expectancy at birth (females/males, years)[k]	77.1 / 69.6	77.7 / 70.6	78.0 / 71.2[b]
Population age distribution (0-14 and 60+ years, %)	25.6 / 10.4	25.4 / 11.8	24.0 / 14.9[a]
International migrant stock (000/% of total pop.)[l]	39.5 / 0.2	39.0 / 0.2	38.7 / 0.2[b]
Refugees and others of concern to UNHCR (000)	352.1[m]	435.3[m]	44.2[d]
Infant mortality rate (per 1 000 live births)[k]	13.1	10.1	8.2[b]
Health: Total expenditure (% of GDP)	4.1	3.4	3.5[h,j]
Health: Physicians (per 1 000 pop.)	0.5	0.7	...
Education: Government expenditure (% of GDP)	...	1.7	2.2[b]
Education: Primary gross enrol. ratio (f/m per 100 pop.)	99.3 / 99.9	98.4 / 101.0	100.6 / 102.7[b]
Education: Secondary gross enrol. ratio (f/m per 100 pop.)	... / ...	97.5 / 96.3	102.0 / 97.5[n]
Education: Tertiary gross enrol. ratio (f/m per 100 pop.)	... / ...	20.9 / 11.7	24.0 / 15.6[b]
Intentional homicide rate (per 100 000 pop.)[h]	6.2	3.8	2.9[n]
Seats held by women in national parliaments (%)	4.9	5.8	5.8

Environment and infrastructure indicators	2005	2010	2017
Mobile-cellular subscriptions (per 100 inhabitants)	16.8	83.6	112.8[b]
Individuals using the Internet (per 100 inhabitants)	1.8[f]	12.0	30.0[f,b]
Research & Development expenditure (% of GDP)	0.2[h,o]	0.1	0.1[n]
Threatened species (number)	394[o]	552	587
Forested area (% of land area)	33.8	33.5	33.1[f,j]
CO2 emission estimates (million tons/tons per capita)	12.1 / 0.6	13.3 / 0.7	18.4 / 0.9[j]
Energy production, primary (Petajoules)	163	184	179[j]
Energy supply per capita (Gigajoules)	16	18	20[j]
Tourist/visitor arrivals at national borders (000)[p]	549	654	1 798[b]
Important sites for terrestrial biodiversity protected (%)	41.8	47.5	49.8
Pop. using improved drinking water (urban/rural, %)	96.2 / 82.9	97.5 / 89.6	98.5 / 95.0[b]
Pop. using improved sanitation facilities (urban/rural, %)	86.2 / 86.5	87.2 / 92.7	88.1 / 96.7[b]
Net Official Development Assist. received (% of GNI)	4.83	1.03	0.53[b]

a Projected estimate (medium fertility variant). b 2015. c Colombo is the capital and Sri Jayewardenepura Kotte is the legislative capital. d 2016. e Data classified according to ISIC Rev. 4. f Estimate. g Colombo h Break in the time series. i Index base: 2002=100. j 2014. k Data refers to a 5-year period preceding the reference year. l Including refugees. m Data as at the end of December. n 2013. o 2004. p Excluding nationals residing abroad.

State of Palestine

Region	Western Asia	Population (000, 2017)	4 921 [a,b]
Surface area (km2)	6 020 [c]	Pop. density (per km2, 2017)	817.4 [a,b]
Sex ratio (m per 100 f, 2017)	102.9 [a,b]	Capital city	East Jerusalem [d]
Capital city pop. (000)	255.7 [e]		

Economic indicators

	2005	2010	2017
GDP: Gross domestic product (million current US$)	4 832	8 913	12 677 [c]
GDP growth rate (annual %, const. 2005 prices)	10.8	8.1	3.5 [c]
GDP per capita (current US$)	1 349.9	2 190.6	2 715.5 [c]
Economy: Agriculture (% of GVA) [f]	5.8	6.4	4.8 [c]
Economy: Industry (% of GVA) [f]	25.8	23.3	23.4 [c]
Economy: Services and other activity (% of GVA) [f]	68.3	70.2	71.9 [c]
Employment: Agriculture (% of employed) [g]	14.6	11.7	8.7
Employment: Industry (% of employed) [g]	26.3	26.4	29.8
Employment: Services (% of employed) [g]	59.1	61.9	61.5
Unemployment (% of labour force)	23.5	23.7	24.2 [g]
Labour force participation (female/male pop. %) [g]	14.1 / 66.8	14.8 / 66.2	18.4 / 69.7
CPI: Consumer Price Index (2000=100)	119	148	162 [h,e]
Agricultural production index (2004-2006=100)	107	77	90 [e]
Food production index (2004-2006=100)	107	77	90 [e]
Index of industrial production (2005=100)	100	115	130 [e]
International trade: Exports (million US$)	335	576	929 [i]
International trade: Imports (million US$)	2 668	3 959	5 058 [i]
International trade: Balance (million US$)	- 2 332	- 3 383	- 4 128 [i]
Balance of payments, current account (million US$)	- 1 365	- 1 307	- 1 713 [c]

Major trading partners

						2016
Export partners (% of exports)	Areas nes [j]	86.1	Israel	11.7	Jordan	0.9
Import partners (% of imports)	Areas nes [j]	93.5	Israel	3.8	Turkey	0.5

Social indicators

	2005	2010	2017
Population growth rate (average annual %) [b,k]	2.1	2.6	2.7 [c]
Urban population (% of total population) [b]	73.1	74.1	75.3 [c]
Urban population growth rate (average annual %) [b,k]	2.4	2.7	2.8 [c]
Fertility rate, total (live births per woman) [b,k]	5.0	4.6	4.2 [c]
Life expectancy at birth (females/males, years) [b,k]	72.9 / 69.5	73.9 / 70.2	74.8 / 71.1 [c]
Population age distribution (0-14 and 60+ years, %) [b]	45.6 / 4.0	42.4 / 4.3	39.6 / 4.6 [a]
International migrant stock (000/% of total pop.) [b,l]	266.6 / 7.4	258.0 / 6.3	255.5 / 5.5 [c]
Refugees and others of concern to UNHCR (000)	...	...	~0.0 [c]
Infant mortality rate (per 1 000 live births) [b,k]	24.9	22.3	20.0 [c]
Education: Government expenditure (% of GDP)	...	1.8	1.3 [c]
Education: Primary gross enrol. ratio (f/m per 100 pop.)	87.9 / 88.5	89.8 / 91.6	94.3 / 94.4 [c]
Education: Secondary gross enrol. ratio (f/m per 100 pop.)	91.7 / 87.7	89.0 / 82.4	87.0 / 79.2 [c]
Education: Tertiary gross enrol. ratio (f/m per 100 pop.)	41.2 / 40.6	54.9 / 41.1	54.4 / 34.5 [c]
Intentional homicide rate (per 100 000 pop.)	4.0	0.7	0.6 [m]

Environment and infrastructure indicators

	2005	2010	2017
Mobile-cellular subscriptions (per 100 inhabitants)	15.9	64.9	77.6 [c]
Individuals using the Internet (per 100 inhabitants) [g]	16.0 [n]	37.4	57.4 [c]
Threatened species (number)	4 [o]	18	31
Forested area (% of land area) [g]	1.5	1.5	1.5 [e]
CO2 emission estimates (million tons/tons per capita)	2.7 / 0.8	2.0 / 0.5	2.8 / 0.6 [e]
Energy production, primary (Petajoules)	8	9	9 [e]
Energy supply per capita (Gigajoules)	16	13	15 [e]
Tourist/visitor arrivals at national borders (000)	88 [p]	522 [p]	432 [q,c]
Important sites for terrestrial biodiversity protected (%)	0.0	0.0	0.0
Pop. using improved drinking water (urban/rural, %)	78.9 / 84.1	64.8 / 82.8	50.7 / 81.5 [c]
Pop. using improved sanitation facilities (urban/rural, %)	91.6 / 86.2	92.5 / 89.1	93.0 / 90.2 [c]
Net Official Development Assist. received (% of GNI)	19.61	26.41	17.52 [e]

a Projected estimate (medium fertility variant). **b** Including East Jerusalem. **c** 2015. **d** Designation and data provided by the State of Palestine. The position of the United Nations on Jerusalem is stated in A/RES/181 (II) and subsequent General Assembly and Security Council resolutions. **e** 2014. **f** Data classified according to ISIC Rev. 4. **g** Estimate. **h** Series linked to former series. **i** 2016. **j** Areas not elsewhere specified. **k** Data refers to a 5-year period preceding the reference year. **l** Refugees are not part of the foreign-born migrant stock in the State of Palestine. **m** 2012. **n** Population aged 10 years and over. **o** 2004. **p** West Bank and Gaza. **q** West Bank only.

Sudan

Region	Northern Africa	UN membership date	12 November 1956
Population (000, 2017)	40 533 [a]	Pop. density (per km2, 2017)	23.0 [a]
Sex ratio (m per 100 f, 2017)	99.9 [a]	Capital city	Khartoum
National currency	Sudanese Pound (SDG)	Capital city pop. (000)	5 129.4 [b]
Exchange rate (per US$)	6.1 [b]		

Economic indicators	2005	2010	2017
GDP: Gross domestic product (million current US$)	...	53 944	79 546 [b]
GDP growth rate (annual %, const. 2005 prices)	...	6.9	4.9 [b]
GDP per capita (current US$)	...	1 493.7	1 977.0 [b]
Economy: Agriculture (% of GVA)	...	42.9	32.4 [b]
Economy: Industry (% of GVA)	...	13.7	20.1 [b]
Economy: Services and other activity (% of GVA)	...	43.4	47.6 [b]
Employment: Agriculture (% of employed) [c]	38.3	34.3	32.9
Employment: Industry (% of employed) [c]	19.9	20.2	20.4
Employment: Services (% of employed) [c]	41.9	45.4	46.7
Unemployment (% of labour force) [c]	14.1	13.0	13.4
Labour force participation (female/male pop. %) [c]	24.5 / 73.9	23.2 / 72.9	24.4 / 72.2
International trade: Exports (million US$)	...	...	1 797 [d]
International trade: Imports (million US$)	...	...	7 658 [d]
International trade: Balance (million US$)	...	...	- 5 861 [d]
Balance of payments, current account (million US$)	- 2 473	- 1 725 [e]	- 5 933 [b]

Major trading partners						2016
Export partners (% of exports)	China	56.4	United Arab Emirates	14.4	Saudi Arabia	14.4
Import partners (% of imports)	China	22.8	Jordan	8.6	India	8.5

Social indicators	2005	2010	2017
Population growth rate (average annual %) [f]	2.5	2.1	2.3 [b]
Urban population (% of total population)	32.8	33.1	33.8 [b]
Urban population growth rate (average annual %) [f]	2.8	2.6	2.5 [b]
Fertility rate, total (live births per woman) [f]	5.3	5.0	4.8 [b]
Life expectancy at birth (females/males, years) [f]	61.3 / 57.5	63.2 / 59.8	65.1 / 62.1 [b]
Population age distribution (0-14 and 60+ years, %)	43.5 / 4.9	43.0 / 5.1	40.8 / 5.5 [a]
International migrant stock (000/% of total pop.) [g]	542.0 / 1.7 [h]	578.4 / 1.6	503.5 / 1.3 [b]
Refugees and others of concern to UNHCR (000)	1 029.7 [i]	1 951.5 [i]	3 619.6 [d]
Infant mortality rate (per 1 000 live births) [f]	61.8	53.7	48.7 [b]
Health: Total expenditure (% of GDP) [j,k]	3.2	8.0	8.4 [l]
Health: Physicians (per 1 000 pop.)	0.2 [m]	0.3 [n]	3.1 [l]
Education: Government expenditure (% of GDP)	1.6	2.2 [o]	...
Education: Primary gross enrol. ratio (f/m per 100 pop.)	57.8 / 66.0	66.1 / 73.6	66.6 / 74.1 [p]
Education: Secondary gross enrol. ratio (f/m per 100 pop.)	36.1 / 38.9	38.2 / 44.1	41.5 / 43.9 [p]
Education: Tertiary gross enrol. ratio (f/m per 100 pop.)	12.4 / 11.0	16.2 / 13.8	16.8 / 15.8 [l]
Intentional homicide rate (per 100 000 pop.)	7.5	6.8	6.4 [b]
Seats held by women in national parliaments (%)	...	...	30.5

Environment and infrastructure indicators	2005	2010	2017
Mobile-cellular subscriptions (per 100 inhabitants)	4.8 [c,q]	41.5	70.5 [b]
Individuals using the Internet (per 100 inhabitants)	1.3	16.7 [c]	26.6 [c,b]
Research & Development expenditure (% of GDP)	0.3 [r]	...	...
Threatened species (number)	55 [m]	112	133
CO2 emission estimates (million tons/tons per capita)	... / ...	... / ...	15.4 / 0.4 [l]
Energy production, primary (Petajoules)	...	...	682 [l]
Energy supply per capita (Gigajoules)	...	...	16 [l]
Tourist/visitor arrivals at national borders (000) [s]	246	495	741 [b]
Important sites for terrestrial biodiversity protected (%)	9.1	18.6	25.0
Net Official Development Assist. received (% of GNI)	7.43	3.35	1.09 [b]

a Projected estimate (medium fertility variant). b 2015. c Estimate. d 2016. e Break in the time series. f Data refers to a 5-year period preceding the reference year. g Including refugees. h The estimates for 2005 refer to Sudan and South Sudan. i Data as at the end of December. j Data revision. k Estimates should be viewed with caution as these are derived from scarce data. l 2014. m 2004. n 2008. o 2009. p 2013. q Canar counted as fixed line. r Overestimated or based on overestimated data. s Including nationals residing abroad.

Suriname

Region	South America	UN membership date	04 December 1975
Population (000, 2017)	563[a]	Surface area (km2)	163 820[b]
Pop. density (per km2, 2017)	3.6[a]	Sex ratio (m per 100 f, 2017)	100.7[a]
Capital city	Paramaribo	National currency	Surinam Dollar (SRD)
Capital city pop. (000)	234.5[c,d]	Exchange rate (per US$)	7.4[e]

Economic indicators

	2005	2010	2017
GDP: Gross domestic product (million current US$)	2 193	4 368	4 879[b]
GDP growth rate (annual %, const. 2005 prices)	3.9	5.2	- 2.7[b]
GDP per capita (current US$)	4 457.4	8 430.9	8 985.3[b]
Economy: Agriculture (% of GVA)	11.3	10.2	11.4[b]
Economy: Industry (% of GVA)	37.4	37.9	27.4[b]
Economy: Services and other activity (% of GVA)	51.3	51.9	61.1[b]
Employment: Agriculture (% of employed)[f]	7.3	4.3	3.4
Employment: Industry (% of employed)[f]	24.4	24.5	22.3
Employment: Services (% of employed)[f]	68.3	71.2	74.3
Unemployment (% of labour force)	8.7[f]	7.6	9.9[f]
Labour force participation (female/male pop. %)[f]	37.6 / 67.2	39.9 / 68.4	40.5 / 68.6
CPI: Consumer Price Index (2000=100)[g,h]	171	249	324[d]
Agricultural production index (2004-2006=100)	99	137	152[d]
Food production index (2004-2006=100)	99	137	152[d]
International trade: Exports (million US$)	997	2 026	1 437[e]
International trade: Imports (million US$)	1 050	1 397	1 244[e]
International trade: Balance (million US$)	- 53	628	193[e]
Balance of payments, current account (million US$)	- 144	651	- 808[b]

Major trading partners
						2016
Export partners (% of exports)	United States	24.3	United Arab Emirates	22.0	Switzerland	13.6
Import partners (% of imports)	United States	27.5	Netherlands	14.4	Trinidad and Tobago	10.6

Social indicators

	2005	2010	2017
Population growth rate (average annual %)[i]	1.1	1.1	1.0[b]
Urban population (% of total population)	66.7	66.3	66.0[b]
Urban population growth rate (average annual %)[i]	1.4	0.9	0.8[b]
Fertility rate, total (live births per woman)[i]	2.8	2.6	2.5[b]
Life expectancy at birth (females/males, years)[i]	71.7 / 64.8	73.1 / 66.4	74.2 / 67.8[b]
Population age distribution (0-14 and 60+ years, %)	30.8 / 8.5	28.7 / 9.1	26.4 / 10.4[a]
International migrant stock (000/% of total pop.)[j]	33.7 / 6.8	39.7 / 7.7	46.8 / 8.6[b]
Refugees and others of concern to UNHCR (000)	...	~0.0[k]	~0.0[e]
Infant mortality rate (per 1 000 live births)[i]	24.2	22.2	17.4[b]
Health: Total expenditure (% of GDP)	6.8	5.8	5.7[d]
Health: Physicians (per 1 000 pop.)	0.8[l]	...	...
Education: Primary gross enrol. ratio (f/m per 100 pop.)	111.2 / 113.7	115.3 / 121.5	121.4 / 124.2[b]
Education: Secondary gross enrol. ratio (f/m per 100 pop.)	76.9 / 59.7	89.2 / 69.9	90.9 / 71.7[b]
Education: Tertiary gross enrol. ratio (f/m per 100 pop.)	16.1 / 9.4[m]	... / ...	... / ...
Intentional homicide rate (per 100 000 pop.)	3.1	9.5	10.7[b]
Seats held by women in national parliaments (%)	19.6	25.5	25.5

Environment and infrastructure indicators

	2005	2010	2017
Mobile-cellular subscriptions (per 100 inhabitants)	46.6	99.3	180.7[f,b]
Individuals using the Internet (per 100 inhabitants)	6.4	31.6	42.8[f,b]
Threatened species (number)	59[l]	65	83
Forested area (% of land area)[f]	98.5	98.4	98.3[d]
CO2 emission estimates (million tons/tons per capita)	1.6 / 3.2	2.4 / 4.6	2.0 / 3.7[d]
Energy production, primary (Petajoules)	32	43	44[d]
Energy supply per capita (Gigajoules)	53	77	62[d]
Tourist/visitor arrivals at national borders (000)	161	205	228[b]
Important sites for terrestrial biodiversity protected (%)	51.2	51.2	51.2
Pop. using improved drinking water (urban/rural, %)	97.9 / 79.2	98.0 / 85.8	98.1 / 88.4[b]
Pop. using improved sanitation facilities (urban/rural, %)	89.2 / 62.6	88.6 / 61.7	88.4 / 61.4[b]
Net Official Development Assist. received (% of GNI)	2.62	2.43	0.32[b]

a Projected estimate (medium fertility variant). b 2015. c Refers to the total population of the District of Paramaribo. d 2014. e 2016. f Estimate. g Index base: 2001=100. h Paramaribo i Data refers to a 5-year period preceding the reference year. j Refers to foreign citizens. k Data as at the end of December. l 2004. m 2002.

Swaziland

Region	Southern Africa	UN membership date	24 September 1968
Population (000, 2017)	1 367[a]	Surface area (km2)	17 363[b]
Pop. density (per km2, 2017)	79.5[a]	Sex ratio (m per 100 f, 2017)	93.9[a]
Capital city	Mbabane[c]	National currency	Lilangeni (SZL)
Capital city pop. (000)	66.0[d]	Exchange rate (per US$)	13.7[e]

Economic indicators

	2005	2010	2017
GDP: Gross domestic product (million current US$)	3 107	4 526	4 133[b]
GDP growth rate (annual %, const. 2005 prices)	5.2	1.8	1.7[b]
GDP per capita (current US$)	2 812.6	3 793.6	3 211.7[b]
Economy: Agriculture (% of GVA)[f]	8.0	7.5	6.6[b]
Economy: Industry (% of GVA)[f]	40.6	41.0	42.1[b]
Economy: Services and other activity (% of GVA)[f]	51.4	51.5	51.3[b]
Employment: Agriculture (% of employed)[g]	23.3	22.2	22.0
Employment: Industry (% of employed)[g]	17.5	17.9	17.0
Employment: Services (% of employed)[g]	59.2	59.9	61.0
Unemployment (% of labour force)[g]	25.5	27.8	25.1
Labour force participation (female/male pop. %)[g]	35.1 / 64.3	37.8 / 62.7	40.6 / 65.1
CPI: Consumer Price Index (2000=100)	140	127[h,i,j]	164[i,d]
Agricultural production index (2004-2006=100)	103	106	114[d]
Food production index (2004-2006=100)	103	107	115[d]
Index of industrial production (2005=100)	...	132	153[d]
International trade: Exports (million US$)	1 278	1 557	1 881[e]
International trade: Imports (million US$)	1 656	1 710	733[e]
International trade: Balance (million US$)	- 378	- 153	1 149[e]
Balance of payments, current account (million US$)	- 103	- 389	281[b]

Major trading partners

						2016
Export partners (% of exports)	South Africa	59.7	Nigeria	6.7	Mozambique	2.7
Import partners (% of imports)	South Africa	72.3	Nigeria	10.3	China	2.7

Social indicators

	2005	2010	2017
Population growth rate (average annual %)[k]	0.8	1.7	1.8[b]
Urban population (% of total population)	22.0	21.5	21.3[b]
Urban population growth rate (average annual %)[k]	0.2	1.0	1.3[b]
Fertility rate, total (live births per woman)[k]	4.0	3.8	3.3[b]
Life expectancy at birth (females/males, years)[k]	47.6 / 44.2	50.2 / 46.5	58.2 / 51.6[b]
Population age distribution (0-14 and 60+ years, %)	42.1 / 4.6	39.5 / 4.7	37.2 / 4.8[a]
International migrant stock (000/% of total pop.)[l]	27.1 / 2.5	30.5 / 2.6	31.6 / 2.5[b]
Refugees and others of concern to UNHCR (000)	1.0[m]	0.8[m]	1.1[e]
Infant mortality rate (per 1 000 live births)[k]	86.6	75.8	56.3[b]
Health: Total expenditure (% of GDP)	6.8	8.5	9.3[d]
Health: Physicians (per 1 000 pop.)	0.2[n]	0.1[o]	...
Education: Government expenditure (% of GDP)	6.5	6.1	7.0[d]
Education: Primary gross enrol. ratio (f/m per 100 pop.)	99.9 / 106.3	110.8 / 120.7	108.0 / 117.5[d]
Education: Secondary gross enrol. ratio (f/m per 100 pop.)	47.1 / 46.2	58.0 / 58.0	65.8 / 66.2[d]
Education: Tertiary gross enrol. ratio (f/m per 100 pop.)	4.9 / 4.6	4.4 / 4.5[p]	5.5 / 5.2[q]
Intentional homicide rate (per 100 000 pop.)	13.8	17.4	8.2[q]
Seats held by women in national parliaments (%)	10.8	13.6	6.2

Environment and infrastructure indicators

	2005	2010	2017
Mobile-cellular subscriptions (per 100 inhabitants)	18.1	60.8	73.2[g,b]
Individuals using the Internet (per 100 inhabitants)	3.7[g]	11.0	30.4[g,b]
Threatened species (number)	23[n]	29	34
Forested area (% of land area)[g]	31.5	32.7	33.8[d]
CO2 emission estimates (million tons/tons per capita)	1.0 / 0.9	1.0 / 0.9	1.2 / 1.0[d]
Energy production, primary (Petajoules)	36	33	39[d]
Energy supply per capita (Gigajoules)	36	37	40[d]
Tourist/visitor arrivals at national borders (000)	837	868	873[b]
Important sites for terrestrial biodiversity protected (%)	57.4	57.4	57.4
Pop. using improved drinking water (urban/rural, %)	90.8 / 52.7	92.8 / 64.2	93.6 / 68.9[b]
Pop. using improved sanitation facilities (urban/rural, %)	62.9 / 51.7	63.0 / 54.7	63.1 / 56.0[b]
Net Official Development Assist. received (% of GNI)	1.69	2.76	2.39[b]

a Projected estimate (medium fertility variant). **b** 2015. **c** Mbabane is the administrative capital and Lobamba is the legislative capital. **d** 2014. **e** 2016. **f** Data classified according to ISIC Rev. 4. **g** Estimate. **h** Break in the time series. **i** Index base: 2007=100. **j** Series linked to former series. **k** Data refers to a 5-year period preceding the reference year. **l** Including refugees. **m** Data as at the end of December. **n** 2004. **o** 2009. **p** 2006. **q** 2013.

Sweden

Region	Northern Europe	UN membership date	19 November 1946	
Population (000, 2017)	9 911[a]	Surface area (km2)	438 574[b]	
Pop. density (per km2, 2017)	24.2[a]	Sex ratio (m per 100 f, 2017)	100.2[a]	
Capital city	Stockholm	National currency	Swedish Krona (SEK)	
Capital city pop. (000)	1 485.7[c,b]	Exchange rate (per US$)	9.1[d]	

Economic indicators	2005	2010	2017
GDP: Gross domestic product (million current US$)	389 043	488 378	495 694[b]
GDP growth rate (annual %, const. 2005 prices)	2.8	6.0	4.1[b]
GDP per capita (current US$)	43 082.6	52 053.1	50 687.5[b]
Economy: Agriculture (% of GVA)[e]	1.1	1.6	1.3[b]
Economy: Industry (% of GVA)[e]	29.7	28.9	26.3[b]
Economy: Services and other activity (% of GVA)[e]	69.2	69.4	72.4[b]
Employment: Agriculture (% of employed)[f]	2.3	2.1	1.8
Employment: Industry (% of employed)[f]	22.0	19.9	18.2
Employment: Services (% of employed)[f]	75.6	78.0	79.9
Unemployment (% of labour force)	7.5	8.6	7.3[f]
Labour force participation (female/male pop. %)[f]	59.3 / 68.1	59.0 / 68.1	60.7 / 68.0
CPI: Consumer Price Index (2000=100)	108	116	120[g]
Agricultural production index (2004-2006=100)	100	94	100[g]
Food production index (2004-2006=100)	100	94	100[g]
Index of industrial production (2005=100)	100	93[h]	88[h,g]
International trade: Exports (million US$)	130 264	158 411	139 574[d]
International trade: Imports (million US$)	111 351	148 788	140 838[d]
International trade: Balance (million US$)	18 912	9 622	- 1 263[d]
Balance of payments, current account (million US$)	23 583	29 196	23 250[b]

Major trading partners						2016
Export partners (% of exports)	Germany	12.0	Norway	10.2	United States	7.4
Import partners (% of imports)	Germany	18.8	Netherlands	8.3	Norway	8.2

Social indicators	2005	2010	2017
Population growth rate (average annual %)[i]	0.4	0.8	0.8[b]
Urban population (% of total population)	84.3	85.1	85.8[b]
Urban population growth rate (average annual %)[i]	0.4	0.9	0.8[b]
Fertility rate, total (live births per woman)[i]	1.7	1.9	1.9[b]
Life expectancy at birth (females/males, years)[i]	82.3 / 77.9	83.1 / 79.0	83.7 / 80.0[b]
Population age distribution (0-14 and 60+ years, %)	17.4 / 23.5	16.5 / 24.9	17.5 / 25.5[a]
International migrant stock (000/% of total pop.)	1 125.8 / 12.5	1 384.9 / 14.8	1 639.8 / 16.8[b]
Refugees and others of concern to UNHCR (000)	96.4[j]	110.8[j]	348.5[d]
Infant mortality rate (per 1 000 live births)[i]	3.2	2.6	2.4[b]
Health: Total expenditure (% of GDP)[k]	9.1	9.5	11.9[l,g]
Health: Physicians (per 1 000 pop.)	...	3.9	4.1[m]
Education: Government expenditure (% of GDP)	6.6	6.6	7.7[g]
Education: Primary gross enrol. ratio (f/m per 100 pop.)	95.7 / 96.0	101.2 / 101.8	125.6 / 120.6[b]
Education: Secondary gross enrol. ratio (f/m per 100 pop.)	103.9 / 104.3	97.7 / 98.7	150.0 / 131.5[b]
Education: Tertiary gross enrol. ratio (f/m per 100 pop.)	100.0 / 64.8	90.8 / 59.3	75.7 / 49.6[b]
Intentional homicide rate (per 100 000 pop.)	0.9	1.0	1.2[b]
Seats held by women in national parliaments (%)	45.3	46.4	43.6

Environment and infrastructure indicators	2005	2010	2017
Mobile-cellular subscriptions (per 100 inhabitants)	100.8	117.2	130.4[b]
Individuals using the Internet (per 100 inhabitants)	84.8[n]	90.0[o]	90.6[n,b]
Research & Development expenditure (% of GDP)	3.4[l]	3.2[f]	3.2[p,g]
Threatened species (number)	36[q]	29	54
Forested area (% of land area)	68.8	68.4	68.9[f,g]
CO2 emission estimates (million tons/tons per capita)	51.6 / 5.7	52.0 / 5.5	43.4 / 4.5[g]
Energy production, primary (Petajoules)	1 430	1 364	1 428[g]
Energy supply per capita (Gigajoules)	237	225	206[g]
Tourist/visitor arrivals at national borders (000)	...	...	19 945[g]
Important sites for terrestrial biodiversity protected (%)	56.7	57.9	58.2
Pop. using improved drinking water (urban/rural, %)	100.0 / 100.0	100.0 / 100.0	100.0 / 100.0[b]
Pop. using improved sanitation facilities (urban/rural, %)	99.2 / 99.6	99.2 / 99.6	99.2 / 99.6[b]
Net Official Development Assist. disbursed (% of GNI)[r]	0.94	0.97	0.94[p,d]

a Projected estimate (medium fertility variant). **b** 2015. **c** Refers to "tätort" (according to the administrative divisions of 2005). **d** 2016. **e** Data classified according to ISIC Rev. 4. **f** Estimate. **g** 2014. **h** Excluding water and waste management. **i** Data refers to a 5-year period preceding the reference year. **j** Data as at the end of December. **k** Data is converted from SHA 2011. **l** Break in the time series. **m** 2013. **n** Population aged 16 to 74 years. **o** Population aged 16 to 75 years. **p** Provisional data. **q** 2004. **r** Development Assistance Committee member (OECD)

Switzerland

Region	Western Europe	UN membership date	10 September 2002
Population (000, 2017)	8 476 [a]	Surface area (km2)	41 291 [b]
Pop. density (per km2, 2017)	214.5 [a]	Sex ratio (m per 100 f, 2017)	98.2 [a]
Capital city	Bern	National currency	Swiss Franc (CHF)
Capital city pop. (000)	358.5 [b]	Exchange rate (per US$)	1.0 [c]

Economic indicators

	2005	2010	2017
GDP: Gross domestic product (million current US$)	407 543	581 209	670 790 [b]
GDP growth rate (annual %, const. 2005 prices)	3.0	3.0	0.8 [b]
GDP per capita (current US$)	55 009.4	74 223.4	80 831.1 [b]
Economy: Agriculture (% of GVA) [d]	0.9	0.7	0.7 [b]
Economy: Industry (% of GVA) [d]	26.8	26.3	25.5 [b]
Economy: Services and other activity (% of GVA) [d]	72.3	73.0	73.8 [b]
Employment: Agriculture (% of employed) [e]	3.7	3.5	3.5
Employment: Industry (% of employed) [e]	22.8	22.2	20.4
Employment: Services (% of employed) [e]	73.5	74.4	76.1
Unemployment (% of labour force)	4.4	4.5	4.6 [e]
Labour force participation (female/male pop. %) [e]	59.5 / 75.0	60.8 / 75.3	62.5 / 74.5
CPI: Consumer Price Index (2000=100)	104	109	108 [f]
Agricultural production index (2004-2006=100)	99	103	106 [f]
Food production index (2004-2006=100)	99	103	106 [f]
Index of industrial production (2005=100)	100	119 [g]	130 [g,f]
International trade: Exports (million US$)	130 930	195 609	304 691 [c]
International trade: Imports (million US$)	126 574	176 281	269 157 [c]
International trade: Balance (million US$)	4 356	19 329	35 534 [c]
Balance of payments, current account (million US$)	55 428	86 609	77 378 [b]

Major trading partners

						2016
Export partners (% of exports)	Germany	14.3	United States	12.1	United Kingdom	10.7
Import partners (% of imports)	Germany	19.3	United States	8.9	Italy	7.3

Social indicators

	2005	2010	2017
Population growth rate (average annual %) [h]	0.7	1.1	1.2 [b]
Urban population (% of total population)	73.5	73.7	73.9 [b]
Urban population growth rate (average annual %) [h]	0.7	1.2	1.1 [b]
Fertility rate, total (live births per woman) [h]	1.4	1.5	1.5 [b]
Life expectancy at birth (females/males, years) [h]	83.1 / 77.7	84.1 / 79.3	84.8 / 80.5 [b]
Population age distribution (0-14 and 60+ years, %)	16.3 / 21.3	15.1 / 22.8	14.9 / 24.1 [a]
International migrant stock (000/% of total pop.)	1 805.4 / 24.4	2 075.2 / 26.5	2 438.7 / 29.4 [b]
Refugees and others of concern to UNHCR (000)	63.4 [i]	61.9 [i]	110.1 [c]
Infant mortality rate (per 1 000 live births) [h]	4.6	4.2	3.9 [b]
Health: Total expenditure (% of GDP)	10.9	11.1	11.7 [f]
Health: Physicians (per 1 000 pop.)	...	3.8	4.1 [f]
Education: Government expenditure (% of GDP)	5.2	4.9	5.1 [f]
Education: Primary gross enrol. ratio (f/m per 100 pop.)	101.9 / 102.2	102.3 / 102.8	103.8 / 104.1 [b]
Education: Secondary gross enrol. ratio (f/m per 100 pop.)	92.2 / 98.0	94.4 / 97.3	99.4 / 103.0 [b]
Education: Tertiary gross enrol. ratio (f/m per 100 pop.)	42.4 / 49.0	52.5 / 53.1	58.5 / 56.9 [b]
Intentional homicide rate (per 100 000 pop.)	1.0	0.7	0.7 [b]
Seats held by women in national parliaments (%)	25.0	29.0	32.5

Environment and infrastructure indicators

	2005	2010	2017
Mobile-cellular subscriptions (per 100 inhabitants)	92.2	123.2	142.0 [e,b]
Individuals using the Internet (per 100 inhabitants) [j,k]	70.1	83.9	88.0 [b]
Research & Development expenditure (% of GDP)	2.7 [l]	2.7 [m]	3.0 [n]
Threatened species (number)	49 [l]	45	74
Forested area (% of land area)	30.8	31.3	31.6 [e,f]
CO2 emission estimates (million tons/tons per capita)	41.3 / 5.5	39.0 / 5.0	35.3 / 4.3 [f]
Energy production, primary (Petajoules) [o]	458	526	552 [f]
Energy supply per capita (Gigajoules) [o]	145	139	126 [f]
Tourist/visitor arrivals at national borders (000) [p]	7 229	8 628	9 305 [b]
Important sites for terrestrial biodiversity protected (%)	27.6	35.1	35.1
Pop. using improved drinking water (urban/rural, %)	100.0 / 100.0	100.0 / 100.0	100.0 / 100.0 [b]
Pop. using improved sanitation facilities (urban/rural, %)	99.9 / 99.9	99.9 / 99.8	99.9 / 99.8 [b]
Net Official Development Assist. disbursed (% of GNI) [q]	0.42	0.39	0.54 [r,c]

a Projected estimate (medium fertility variant). **b** 2015. **c** 2016. **d** Data classified according to ISIC Rev. 4. **e** Estimate. **f** 2014. **g** Excluding water and waste management. **h** Data refers to a 5-year period preceding the reference year. **i** Data as at the end of December. **j** Users in the last 6 months. **k** Population aged 14 years and over. **l** 2004. **m** 2008. **n** 2012. **o** Including Liechtenstein. **p** Including health establishments. **q** Development Assistance Committee member (OECD) **r** Provisional data.

Syrian Arab Republic

Region	Western Asia	UN membership date	24 October 1945	
Population (000, 2017)	18 270 [a]	Surface area (km2)	185 180 [b]	
Pop. density (per km2, 2017)	99.5 [a]	Sex ratio (m per 100 f, 2017)	102.1 [a]	
Capital city	Damascus	National currency	Syrian Pound (SYP)	
Capital city pop. (000)	2 565.7 [c,b]	Exchange rate (per US$)	514.8 [d,e]	

Economic indicators

	2005	2010	2017
GDP: Gross domestic product (million current US$)	28 397	60 465	28 393 [b]
GDP growth rate (annual %, const. 2005 prices)	6.2	3.4	- 5.3 [b]
GDP per capita (current US$)	1 566.1	2 918.1	1 534.5 [b]
Economy: Agriculture (% of GVA) [f]	20.3	19.7	20.7 [b]
Economy: Industry (% of GVA) [f]	31.2	30.7	30.0 [b]
Economy: Services and other activity (% of GVA) [f]	48.5	49.6	49.3 [b]
Employment: Agriculture (% of employed) [g]	21.6	14.3	18.5
Employment: Industry (% of employed) [g]	27.4	32.8	39.2
Employment: Services (% of employed) [g]	51.0	52.9	42.3
Unemployment (% of labour force)	9.2 [g]	8.4	13.8 [g]
Labour force participation (female/male pop. %) [g]	16.3 / 76.1	13.3 / 72.7	12.4 / 70.9
CPI: Consumer Price Index (2000=100)	122	173	473 [h]
Agricultural production index (2004-2006=100)	100	89	65 [i]
Food production index (2004-2006=100)	99	92	68 [i]
Index of industrial production (2005=100) [j]	100	98	...
International trade: Exports (million US$)	6 450	11 353	1 265 [e]
International trade: Imports (million US$)	7 898	17 562	2 383 [e]
International trade: Balance (million US$)	- 1 448	- 6 209	- 1 118 [e]
Balance of payments, current account (million US$)	295	- 367	...

Major trading partners

					2016
Export partners (% of exports)	Lebanon	15.9	Egypt	15.5	Jordan	11.4
Import partners (% of imports)	Turkey	28.3	China	20.1	Lebanon	5.3

Social indicators

	2005	2010	2017
Population growth rate (average annual %) [k]	2.2	2.8	- 2.3 [b]
Urban population (% of total population)	53.8	55.7	57.7 [b]
Urban population growth rate (average annual %) [k]	2.8	4.1	1.4 [b]
Fertility rate, total (live births per woman) [k]	3.8	3.4	3.1 [b]
Life expectancy at birth (females/males, years) [k]	75.9 / 71.4	77.3 / 72.0	76.3 / 64.4 [b]
Population age distribution (0-14 and 60+ years, %)	39.1 / 4.9	36.4 / 5.1	36.6 / 6.8 [a]
International migrant stock (000/% of total pop.) [l,m]	876.4 / 4.8	1 661.9 / 8.0	875.2 / 4.7 [b]
Refugees and others of concern to UNHCR (000)	328.0 [n]	1 308.1 [n]	6 768.5 [e]
Infant mortality rate (per 1 000 live births) [k]	17.7	15.0	17.9 [b]
Health: Total expenditure (% of GDP) [o]	4.1	3.3	3.3 [i]
Health: Physicians (per 1 000 pop.)	1.6	1.5	1.5 [i]
Education: Government expenditure (% of GDP)	5.4 [p]	5.1 [q]	...
Education: Primary gross enrol. ratio (f/m per 100 pop.)	119.5 / 123.0	120.0 / 124.4	78.7 / 81.4 [h]
Education: Secondary gross enrol. ratio (f/m per 100 pop.)	68.4 / 71.5	72.9 / 72.8	50.5 / 50.5 [h]
Education: Tertiary gross enrol. ratio (f/m per 100 pop.)	17.2 / 19.2	24.1 / 27.9	47.0 / 41.3 [b]
Intentional homicide rate (per 100 000 pop.)	2.4	2.2	...
Seats held by women in national parliaments (%)	12.0	12.4	13.2

Environment and infrastructure indicators

	2005	2010	2017
Mobile-cellular subscriptions (per 100 inhabitants)	16.2	54.3	62.4 [b]
Individuals using the Internet (per 100 inhabitants)	5.6 [g]	20.7	30.0 [g,b]
Threatened species (number)	29 [p]	78	132
Forested area (% of land area) [g]	2.5	2.7	2.7 [i]
CO2 emission estimates (million tons/tons per capita)	50.6 / 2.8	61.6 / 3.0	30.7 / 1.7 [i]
Energy production, primary (Petajoules)	1 171	1 165	237 [i]
Energy supply per capita (Gigajoules)	40	44	24 [i]
Tourist/visitor arrivals at national borders (000)	3 571	8 546 [r,s]	...
Important sites for terrestrial biodiversity protected (%)	1.1	1.1	1.1
Pop. using improved drinking water (urban/rural, %)	94.0 / 82.5	92.8 / 85.9	92.3 / 87.2 [b]
Pop. using improved sanitation facilities (urban/rural, %)	95.6 / 87.2	96.0 / 92.8	96.2 / 95.1 [b]
Net Official Development Assist. received (% of GNI)	0.25	...	...

a Projected estimate (medium fertility variant). **b** 2015. **c** Excluding refugees or internally displaced persons (if applicable). **d** UN operational exchange rate. **e** 2016. **f** Includes taxes less subsidies on production and imports. **g** Estimate. **h** 2013. **i** 2014. **j** Data classified according to ISIC Rev. 3. **k** Data refers to a 5-year period preceding the reference year. **l** Refers to foreign citizens. **m** Including refugees. **n** Data as at the end of December. **o** The exchange rate used for the Syrian Arab Republic is the rate for non-commercial transactions from the Central Bank of Syria. **p** 2004. **q** 2009. **r** Including nationals residing abroad. **s** Including Iraqi nationals.

Tajikistan

Region	Central Asia	UN membership date	02 March 1992
Population (000, 2017)	8 921 [a]	Surface area (km2)	142 600 [b]
Pop. density (per km2, 2017)	63.7 [a]	Sex ratio (m per 100 f, 2017)	100.9 [a]
Capital city	Dushanbe	National currency	Somoni (TJS)
Capital city pop. (000)	822.3 [b]	Exchange rate (per US$)	7.9 [c]

Economic indicators

	2005	2010	2017
GDP: Gross domestic product (million current US$)	2 312	5 642	7 853 [b]
GDP growth rate (annual %, const. 2005 prices)	6.7	6.5	4.2 [b]
GDP per capita (current US$)	339.8	744.2	925.9 [b]
Economy: Agriculture (% of GVA)	23.8	21.8	25.0 [b]
Economy: Industry (% of GVA)	30.7	27.9	28.0 [b]
Economy: Services and other activity (% of GVA)	45.6	50.3	47.1 [b]
Employment: Agriculture (% of employed) [d]	57.0	53.8	57.2
Employment: Industry (% of employed) [d]	16.3	15.3	13.4
Employment: Services (% of employed) [d]	26.7	31.0	29.4
Unemployment (% of labour force) [d]	11.7	11.6	10.8
Labour force participation (female/male pop. %) [d]	57.7 / 74.7	58.3 / 76.3	59.6 / 77.9
Agricultural production index (2004-2006=100)	99	123	155 [e]
Food production index (2004-2006=100)	99	137	172 [e]
Index of industrial production (2005=100) [f]	100	114	145 [e]
International trade: Exports (million US$)	905	1 195	899 [c]
International trade: Imports (million US$)	1 329	2 657	3 030 [c]
International trade: Balance (million US$)	- 424	- 1 462	- 2 132 [c]
Balance of payments, current account (million US$)	- 19	- 540 [g]	- 472 [b]

Major trading partners

						2016
Export partners (% of exports)	Kazakhstan	27.3	Turkey	20.3	Italy	10.0
Import partners (% of imports)	China	52.0	Russian Federation	20.1	Kazakhstan	11.3

Social indicators

	2005	2010	2017
Population growth rate (average annual %) [h]	2.0	2.2	2.2 [b]
Urban population (% of total population)	26.4	26.5	26.8 [b]
Urban population growth rate (average annual %) [h]	1.9	2.3	2.6 [b]
Fertility rate, total (live births per woman) [h]	3.6	3.5	3.5 [b]
Life expectancy at birth (females/males, years) [h]	69.6 / 63.6	71.9 / 66.0	73.5 / 67.7 [b]
Population age distribution (0-14 and 60+ years, %)	38.1 / 5.1	35.7 / 4.9	35.3 / 5.8 [a]
International migrant stock (000/% of total pop.)	280.4 / 4.1	278.2 / 3.7	275.1 / 3.2 [b]
Refugees and others of concern to UNHCR (000)	1.1 [i]	7.1 [i]	21.8 [c]
Infant mortality rate (per 1 000 live births) [h]	62.9	48.9	38.9 [b]
Health: Total expenditure (% of GDP)	5.9	6.0	6.9 [e]
Health: Physicians (per 1 000 pop.)	2.0	1.7	1.7 [a]
Education: Government expenditure (% of GDP)	3.5	4.0	5.2 [b]
Education: Primary gross enrol. ratio (f/m per 100 pop.)	97.2 / 100.6	98.5 / 101.5	101.2 / 99.8 [c]
Education: Secondary gross enrol. ratio (f/m per 100 pop.)	72.9 / 87.7	78.5 / 90.2	83.1 / 92.5 [i]
Education: Tertiary gross enrol. ratio (f/m per 100 pop.)	13.5 / 28.3	15.6 / 29.7	24.0 / 33.6 [c]
Intentional homicide rate (per 100 000 pop.)	...	2.0	1.4 [i]
Seats held by women in national parliaments (%)	12.7	17.5	19.0

Environment and infrastructure indicators

	2005	2010	2017
Mobile-cellular subscriptions (per 100 inhabitants)	3.9	77.9	98.6 [d,b]
Individuals using the Internet (per 100 inhabitants)	0.3	11.6 [d]	19.0 [d,b]
Research & Development expenditure (% of GDP)	0.1	0.1 [k,l]	0.1 [k,l,j]
Threatened species (number)	24 [m]	40	45
Forested area (% of land area)	2.9	2.9 [d]	3.0 [d,e]
CO2 emission estimates (million tons/tons per capita)	2.4 / 0.4	2.5 / 0.3	5.2 / 0.6 [e]
Energy production, primary (Petajoules)	66	65	76 [e]
Energy supply per capita (Gigajoules)	15	12	14 [e]
Tourist/visitor arrivals at national borders (000)	...	160	414 [b]
Important sites for terrestrial biodiversity protected (%)	20.5	20.5	21.0
Pop. using improved drinking water (urban/rural, %)	92.6 / 54.5	92.8 / 61.3	93.1 / 66.7 [b]
Pop. using improved sanitation facilities (urban/rural, %)	92.9 / 91.7	93.4 / 93.8	93.8 / 95.5 [b]
Net Official Development Assist. received (% of GNI)	11.30	7.79	4.55 [b]

a Projected estimate (medium fertility variant). b 2015. c 2016. d Estimate. e 2014. f Data classified according to ISIC Rev. 3. g Break in the time series. h Data refers to a 5-year period preceding the reference year. i Data as at the end of December. j 2013. k Excluding private non-profit. l Excluding business enterprise. m 2004.

Thailand

Region	South-eastern Asia	UN membership date	16 December 1946
Population (000, 2017)	69 038 [a]	Surface area (km2)	513 120 [b]
Pop. density (per km2, 2017)	135.1 [a]	Sex ratio (m per 100 f, 2017)	95.2 [a]
Capital city	Bangkok	National currency	Baht (THB)
Capital city pop. (000)	9 269.8 [b]	Exchange rate (per US$)	35.8 [c]

Economic indicators	2005	2010	2017
GDP: Gross domestic product (million current US$)	189 318	340 923	395 168 [b]
GDP growth rate (annual %, const. 2005 prices)	4.2	7.5	2.8 [b]
GDP per capita (current US$)	2 874.4	5 111.9	5 814.8 [b]
Economy: Agriculture (% of GVA) [d]	9.2	10.5	9.1 [b]
Economy: Industry (% of GVA) [d]	38.6	40.0	35.7 [b]
Economy: Services and other activity (% of GVA) [d]	52.2	49.4	55.1 [b]
Employment: Agriculture (% of employed) [e]	42.6	38.2	34.0
Employment: Industry (% of employed) [e]	20.2	20.7	22.7
Employment: Services (% of employed) [e]	37.2	41.0	43.3
Unemployment (% of labour force)	1.4	1.0	0.6 [e]
Labour force participation (female/male pop. %) [e]	66.0 / 81.4	64.4 / 81.0	62.7 / 79.8
CPI: Consumer Price Index (2000=100)	112	129	144 [f]
Agricultural production index (2004-2006=100)	98	113	129 [f]
Food production index (2004-2006=100)	98	115	126 [f]
International trade: Exports (million US$)	110 110	195 312	213 927 [c]
International trade: Imports (million US$)	118 164	182 393	195 666 [c]
International trade: Balance (million US$)	- 8 054	12 918	18 260 [c]
Balance of payments, current account (million US$)	- 7 642 [g]	11 486	32 149 [b]

Major trading partners						2016
Export partners (% of exports)	United States	11.2	China	11.1	Japan	9.4
Import partners (% of imports)	China	20.3	Japan	15.4	United States	6.9

Social indicators	2005	2010	2017
Population growth rate (average annual %) [h]	0.8	0.5	0.4 [b]
Urban population (% of total population)	37.5	44.1	50.4 [b]
Urban population growth rate (average annual %) [h]	4.6	3.5	3.0 [b]
Fertility rate, total (live births per woman) [h]	1.6	1.6	1.5 [b]
Life expectancy at birth (females/males, years) [h]	74.9 / 67.7	76.6 / 69.8	78.4 / 70.8 [b]
Population age distribution (0-14 and 60+ years, %)	21.3 / 11.1	19.2 / 12.9	17.3 / 16.9 [a]
International migrant stock (000/% of total pop.) [i]	2 163.4 / 3.3	3 224.1 / 4.8	3 913.3 / 5.8 [b]
Refugees and others of concern to UNHCR (000)	149.4 [j]	649.4 [j]	554.1 [c]
Infant mortality rate (per 1 000 live births) [h]	16.7	13.4	11.2 [b]
Health: Total expenditure (% of GDP) [k]	3.5	3.8	4.1 [f]
Health: Physicians (per 1 000 pop.)	0.3 [l]	0.4	...
Education: Government expenditure (% of GDP)	3.9	3.5	4.1 [m]
Education: Primary gross enrol. ratio (f/m per 100 pop.)	96.9 / 99.7	95.0 / 97.1	99.2 / 106.1 [b]
Education: Secondary gross enrol. ratio (f/m per 100 pop.)	73.6 / 69.6 [e]	86.1 / 81.2	125.3 / 132.6 [b]
Education: Tertiary gross enrol. ratio (f/m per 100 pop.)	47.2 / 41.4	56.3 / 44.1	57.3 / 40.5 [b]
Intentional homicide rate (per 100 000 pop.)	7.3	5.5	3.5 [b]
Seats held by women in national parliaments (%)	8.8	13.3	4.9

Environment and infrastructure indicators	2005	2010	2017
Mobile-cellular subscriptions (per 100 inhabitants)	46.5	108.0	125.8 [b]
Individuals using the Internet (per 100 inhabitants)	15.0	22.4	39.3 [n,b]
Research & Development expenditure (% of GDP)	0.2	0.2 [o]	0.5 [f]
Threatened species (number)	221 [l]	477	611
Forested area (% of land area) [e]	31.5	31.8	32.0 [f]
CO2 emission estimates (million tons/tons per capita)	247.5 / 3.7	281.9 / 4.2	316.2 / 4.7 [f]
Energy production, primary (Petajoules)	2 144	2 952	3 338 [f]
Energy supply per capita (Gigajoules)	61	74	83 [f]
Tourist/visitor arrivals at national borders (000)	11 567 [p]	15 936	29 923 [b]
Important sites for terrestrial biodiversity protected (%)	68.0	71.0	71.7
Pop. using improved drinking water (urban/rural, %)	97.0 / 92.6	97.4 / 95.6	97.6 / 98.0 [b]
Pop. using improved sanitation facilities (urban/rural, %)	89.6 / 95.3	89.9 / 96.1	89.9 / 96.1 [b]
Net Official Development Assist. disbursed (% of GNI)	...	~0.00	0.02 [b]
Net Official Development Assist. received (% of GNI)	- 0.09	- 0.01	0.02 [b]

a Projected estimate (medium fertility variant). b 2015. c 2016. d At producers' prices. e Estimate. f 2014. g Break in the time series. h Data refers to a 5-year period preceding the reference year. i Including refugees. j Data as at the end of December. k Data revision. l 2004. m 2013. n Population aged 6 years and over. o 2009. p Including nationals residing abroad.

The former Yugoslav Republic of Macedonia

Region	Southern Europe	UN membership date	08 April 1993
Population (000, 2017)	2 083 [a]	Surface area (km2)	25 713 [b]
Pop. density (per km2, 2017)	82.6 [a]	Sex ratio (m per 100 f, 2017)	100.0 [a]
Capital city	Skopje	National currency	Denar (MKD)
Capital city pop. (000)	502.7 [b]	Exchange rate (per US$)	58.3 [c]

Economic indicators

	2005	2010	2017
GDP: Gross domestic product (million current US$)	6 259	9 407	10 052 [b]
GDP growth rate (annual %, const. 2005 prices)	4.7	3.4	3.8 [b]
GDP per capita (current US$)	3 063.6	4 561.2	4 836.1 [b]
Economy: Agriculture (% of GVA) [d]	11.3	11.7	12.0 [b]
Economy: Industry (% of GVA) [d]	23.7	24.4	27.9 [b]
Economy: Services and other activity (% of GVA) [d]	64.9	63.9	65.1 [b]
Employment: Agriculture (% of employed) [e]	18.1	18.0	16.2
Employment: Industry (% of employed) [e]	29.4	29.4	29.2
Employment: Services (% of employed) [e]	52.4	52.7	54.5
Unemployment (% of labour force)	37.3	32.0	27.3 [e]
Labour force participation (female/male pop. %) [e]	42.6 / 64.6	43.1 / 69.3	43.9 / 67.8
CPI: Consumer Price Index (2000=100)	109 [f]	125 [g]	...
Agricultural production index (2004-2006=100)	99	115	111 [h]
Food production index (2004-2006=100)	99	115	112 [h]
Index of industrial production (2005=100)	100	100 [i]	113 [i,h]
International trade: Exports (million US$)	2 041	3 351	4 785 [c]
International trade: Imports (million US$)	3 228	5 474	6 757 [c]
International trade: Balance (million US$)	- 1 187	- 2 123	- 1 972 [c]
Balance of payments, current account (million US$)	- 159	- 198	- 204 [b]

Major trading partners

						2016
Export partners (% of exports)	Germany	47.0	Serbia	8.9	Bulgaria	5.2
Import partners (% of imports)	Germany	12.3	United Kingdom	10.8	Serbia	8.0

Social indicators

	2005	2010	2017
Population growth rate (average annual %) [j]	0.2	0.1	0.1 [b]
Urban population (% of total population)	57.5	57.0	57.1 [b]
Urban population growth rate (average annual %) [j]	−0.0	- 0.1	0.1 [b]
Fertility rate, total (live births per woman) [j]	1.6	1.5	1.5 [b]
Life expectancy at birth (females/males, years) [j]	76.4 / 71.3	76.3 / 72.1	77.2 / 73.2 [b]
Population age distribution (0-14 and 60+ years, %)	20.2 / 15.3	17.9 / 16.4	16.7 / 19.5 [a]
International migrant stock (000/% of total pop.)	127.7 / 6.2	129.7 / 6.3	130.7 / 6.3 [b]
Refugees and others of concern to UNHCR (000)	4.4 [k]	3.3 [k]	1.4 [c]
Infant mortality rate (per 1 000 live births) [j]	12.9	10.8	9.0 [b]
Health: Total expenditure (% of GDP)	8.0	6.8	6.5 [h]
Health: Physicians (per 1 000 pop.)	...	2.7	2.8 [l]
Education: Government expenditure (% of GDP)	3.3 [m]	...	...
Education: Primary gross enrol. ratio (f/m per 100 pop.)	93.3 / 95.2	84.9 / 86.3	92.8 / 93.6 [b]
Education: Secondary gross enrol. ratio (f/m per 100 pop.)	83.6 / 86.1	82.4 / 84.6	78.2 / 80.3 [b]
Education: Tertiary gross enrol. ratio (f/m per 100 pop.)	34.1 / 24.8	42.3 / 36.2	46.8 / 37.5 [b]
Intentional homicide rate (per 100 000 pop.)	2.2	2.1	1.6 [b]
Seats held by women in national parliaments (%)	19.2	32.5	31.7

Environment and infrastructure indicators

	2005	2010	2017
Mobile-cellular subscriptions (per 100 inhabitants)	54.1	102.4	105.4 [b]
Individuals using the Internet (per 100 inhabitants)	26.4 [e,n]	51.9 [o]	70.4 [n,b]
Research & Development expenditure (% of GDP)	0.2 [p]	0.2	0.4 [l]
Threatened species (number)	29 [p]	90	110
Forested area (% of land area) [e]	38.3	39.6	39.6 [h]
CO2 emission estimates (million tons/tons per capita)	11.3 / 5.5	8.6 / 4.2	7.5 / 3.6 [h]
Energy production, primary (Petajoules)	108	68	53 [h]
Energy supply per capita (Gigajoules)	80	59	53 [h]
Tourist/visitor arrivals at national borders (000)	197	262	486 [b]
Important sites for terrestrial biodiversity protected (%)	20.8	21.1	21.1
Pop. using improved drinking water (urban/rural, %)	99.8 / 98.6	99.8 / 98.8	99.8 / 98.9 [b]
Pop. using improved sanitation facilities (urban/rural, %)	93.8 / 84.7	96.5 / 83.4	97.2 / 82.6 [b]
Net Official Development Assist. received (% of GNI)	3.70	2.10	2.18 [b]

a Projected estimate (medium fertility variant). **b** 2015. **c** 2016. **d** Data classified according to ISIC Rev. 4. **e** Estimate. **f** Annual average is weighted mean of monthly data. **g** Series linked to former series. **h** 2014. **i** Excluding water and waste management. **j** Data refers to a 5-year period preceding the reference year. **k** Data as at the end of December. **l** 2013. **m** 2002. **n** Population aged 16 to 74 years. **o** Population aged 15 to 74 years. **p** 2004.

Timor-Leste

Region	South-eastern Asia	UN membership date	27 September 2002
Population (000, 2017)	1 296 [a]	Surface area (km2)	14 919 [b]
Pop. density (per km2, 2017)	87.2 [a]	Sex ratio (m per 100 f, 2017)	103.2 [a]
Capital city	Dili	National currency	US Dollar (USD)
Capital city pop. (000)	228.1 [c]		

Economic indicators	2005	2010	2017
GDP: Gross domestic product (million current US$)	1 850	4 274	2 873 [b]
GDP growth rate (annual %, const. 2005 prices)	52.7	- 1.3	4.3 [b]
GDP per capita (current US$)	1 869.5	4 042.7	2 425.4 [b]
Economy: Agriculture (% of GVA) [d]	7.3	4.5	5.2 [b]
Economy: Industry (% of GVA) [d]	76.8	82.3	79.9 [b]
Economy: Services and other activity (% of GVA) [d]	15.8	13.2	14.9 [b]
Employment: Agriculture (% of employed) [e]	55.4	50.7	50.8
Employment: Industry (% of employed) [e]	1.6	1.5	2.0
Employment: Services (% of employed) [e]	42.9	47.8	47.2
Unemployment (% of labour force)	7.3 [e]	3.1	4.3 [e]
Labour force participation (female/male pop. %) [e]	32.0 / 66.2	26.1 / 55.3	26.9 / 55.6
Agricultural production index (2004-2006=100)	98	121	111 [c]
Food production index (2004-2006=100)	97	126	117 [c]
International trade: Exports (million US$)	43	42	94 [f]
International trade: Imports (million US$)	102	246	647 [f]
International trade: Balance (million US$)	- 58	- 205	- 553 [f]
Balance of payments, current account (million US$)	...	1 671	238 [g,b]

Major trading partners						2016
Export partners (% of exports)	Thailand	40.2	United States	12.0	Singapore	10.6
Import partners (% of imports)	Indonesia	41.0	China	30.3	Singapore	7.7

Social indicators	2005	2010	2017
Population growth rate (average annual %) [h]	3.3	1.6	2.2 [b]
Urban population (% of total population)	26.3	29.5	32.8 [b]
Urban population growth rate (average annual %) [h]	4.7	3.9	3.8 [b]
Fertility rate, total (live births per woman) [h]	7.0	6.5	5.9 [b]
Life expectancy at birth (females/males, years) [h]	63.0 / 60.0	67.6 / 65.2	69.5 / 66.1 [b]
Population age distribution (0-14 and 60+ years, %)	49.2 / 4.3	45.6 / 5.1	43.6 / 5.4 [a]
International migrant stock (000/% of total pop.)	11.3 / 1.1	11.0 / 1.0	10.8 / 0.9 [b]
Refugees and others of concern to UNHCR (000)	~0.0 [i]	~0.0 [i]	~0.0 [f]
Infant mortality rate (per 1 000 live births) [h]	64.0	50.2	43.9 [b]
Health: Total expenditure (% of GDP) [j]	1.0	0.9	1.5 [c]
Health: Physicians (per 1 000 pop.)	0.1 [k]	0.1	0.1 [l]
Education: Government expenditure (% of GDP)		10.4	7.8 [c]
Education: Primary gross enrol. ratio (f/m per 100 pop.)	90.1 / 98.4	128.4 / 133.8	136.2 / 137.5 [b]
Education: Secondary gross enrol. ratio (f/m per 100 pop.)	52.8 / 54.3	67.7 / 67.2	79.6 / 74.1 [b]
Education: Tertiary gross enrol. ratio (f/m per 100 pop.)	9.5 / 8.3 [e,m]	15.2 / 21.1	... / ...
Intentional homicide rate (per 100 000 pop.)	4.6	3.7	...
Seats held by women in national parliaments (%)	25.3	29.2	38.5

Environment and infrastructure indicators	2005	2010	2017
Mobile-cellular subscriptions (per 100 inhabitants)	3.3	43.8	117.4 [b]
Individuals using the Internet (per 100 inhabitants)	0.1	0.2 [e]	13.4 [e,b]
Threatened species (number)	11 [k]	18	24
Forested area (% of land area) [e]	53.7	49.9	46.9 [c]
CO2 emission estimates (million tons/tons per capita)	0.2 / 0.2	0.2 / 0.2	0.5 / 0.4 [c]
Energy production, primary (Petajoules)	201	186	143 [c]
Energy supply per capita (Gigajoules) [e]	4	4	7 [c]
Tourist/visitor arrivals at national borders (000) [n]	...	40	62 [b]
Important sites for terrestrial biodiversity protected (%)	14.9	38.7	38.7
Pop. using improved drinking water (urban/rural, %)	79.9 / 54.2	90.8 / 58.7	95.2 / 60.5 [b]
Pop. using improved sanitation facilities (urban/rural, %)	59.5 / 30.1	66.3 / 27.7	69.0 / 26.8 [b]
Net Official Development Assist. received (% of GNI)	22.16	9.57	8.89 [b]

a Projected estimate (medium fertility variant). **b** 2015. **c** 2014. **d** Data classified according to ISIC Rev. 4. **e** Estimate. **f** 2016. **g** Break in the time series. **h** Data refers to a 5-year period preceding the reference year. **i** Data as at the end of December. **j** From this year oil GDP (includes the income from petroleum) is being used for denominators. Hence the changes in ratios since last year's reporting. The country became independent in 2002. Expenditure data have been allocated exceptionally to the previous calendar year (i.e. 2000 data covers the fiscal year 1999-2000). Drop in health expenditures from previous year is mainly due to revision of Out of pocket expenditure estimates. **k** 2004. **l** 2011. **m** 2002. **n** Arrivals by air at Dili Airport.

Togo

Region	Western Africa	UN membership date	20 September 1960
Population (000, 2017)	7 798 [a]	Surface area (km2)	56 785 [b]
Pop. density (per km2, 2017)	143.4 [a]	Sex ratio (m per 100 f, 2017)	99.4 [a]
Capital city	Lomé	National currency	CFA Franc (XOF)
Capital city pop. (000)	956.3 [b]	Exchange rate (per US$)	622.3 [c]

Economic indicators

	2005	2010	2017
GDP: Gross domestic product (million current US$)	2 110	3 173	4 086 [b]
GDP growth rate (annual %, const. 2005 prices)	1.2	4.0	5.5 [b]
GDP per capita (current US$)	378.3	496.4	559.4 [b]
Economy: Agriculture (% of GVA)	43.2	46.1	45.7 [b]
Economy: Industry (% of GVA)	18.9	18.2	19.7 [b]
Economy: Services and other activity (% of GVA)	37.5	35.7	34.6 [b]
Employment: Agriculture (% of employed) [d]	64.7	63.1	62.5
Employment: Industry (% of employed) [d]	8.2	8.6	8.7
Employment: Services (% of employed) [d]	27.1	28.2	28.7
Unemployment (% of labour force) [d]	7.0	6.9	6.8
Labour force participation (female/male pop. %) [d]	79.8 / 80.4	81.0 / 80.3	81.0 / 80.7
CPI: Consumer Price Index (2000=100) [e]	114	134 [f]	145 [g]
Agricultural production index (2004-2006=100)	97	124	140 [g]
Food production index (2004-2006=100)	100	130	143 [g]
Index of industrial production (2005=100)	100 [h]	124	156 [g]
International trade: Exports (million US$)	360	648	715 [c]
International trade: Imports (million US$)	593	1 205	1 716 [c]
International trade: Balance (million US$)	- 233	- 557	- 1 001 [c]
Balance of payments, current account (million US$)	- 204	- 200	- 461 [b]

Major trading partners

						2016
Export partners (% of exports)	Benin	17.6	Burkina Faso	16.0	India	7.7
Import partners (% of imports)	China	28.7	France	8.9	Netherlands	4.3

Social indicators

	2005	2010	2017
Population growth rate (average annual %) [i]	2.7	2.7	2.6 [b]
Urban population (% of total population)	35.2	37.5	40.0 [b]
Urban population growth rate (average annual %) [i]	3.9	3.9	3.8 [b]
Fertility rate, total (live births per woman) [i]	5.3	5.0	4.7 [b]
Life expectancy at birth (females/males, years) [i]	54.7 / 53.0	56.4 / 55.1	59.8 / 58.3 [b]
Population age distribution (0-14 and 60+ years, %)	42.6 / 4.5	42.5 / 4.4	41.6 / 4.6 [a]
International migrant stock (000/% of total pop.) [j,k]	203.4 / 3.6	255.3 / 4.0	276.8 / 3.8 [b]
Refugees and others of concern to UNHCR (000)	18.7 [l]	14.2 [l]	13.8 [c]
Infant mortality rate (per 1 000 live births) [i]	77.3	63.2	55.7 [b]
Health: Total expenditure (% of GDP)	5.2	5.4	5.2 [g]
Health: Physicians (per 1 000 pop.)	~0.0 [m]	0.1 [n]	...
Education: Government expenditure (% of GDP)	3.4	4.4	5.2 [b]
Education: Primary gross enrol. ratio (f/m per 100 pop.)	103.5 / 121.9	121.8 / 134.9	118.5 / 125.1 [b]
Education: Secondary gross enrol. ratio (f/m per 100 pop.)	31.2 / 58.9	30.5 / 57.6 [d,o]	... / ...
Education: Tertiary gross enrol. ratio (f/m per 100 pop.)	... / ...	... / ...	6.4 / 14.9 [b]
Intentional homicide rate (per 100 000 pop.)	10.9	9.8	9.1 [b]
Seats held by women in national parliaments (%)	6.2	11.1	17.6

Environment and infrastructure indicators

	2005	2010	2017
Mobile-cellular subscriptions (per 100 inhabitants)	7.8	41.3 [p]	65.0 [b]
Individuals using the Internet (per 100 inhabitants) [d]	1.8	3.0	7.1 [b]
Research & Development expenditure (% of GDP) [q]	...	0.3	0.3 [r,g]
Threatened species (number)	32 [m]	54	80
Forested area (% of land area) [d]	7.1	5.3	3.8 [g]
CO2 emission estimates (million tons/tons per capita)	1.3 / 0.3	2.6 / 0.4	2.6 / 0.4 [g]
Energy production, primary (Petajoules)	84	99	111 [g]
Energy supply per capita (Gigajoules)	18	20	20 [g]
Tourist/visitor arrivals at national borders (000)	81	202	273 [b]
Important sites for terrestrial biodiversity protected (%)	75.0	97.0	97.0
Pop. using improved drinking water (urban/rural, %)	86.6 / 40.5	89.0 / 42.3	91.4 / 44.2 [b]
Pop. using improved sanitation facilities (urban/rural, %)	24.1 / 4.5	24.4 / 3.7	24.7 / 2.9 [b]
Net Official Development Assist. received (% of GNI)	3.97	14.61	5.51 [b]

a Projected estimate (medium fertility variant). **b** 2015. **c** 2016. **d** Estimate. **e** Lomé **f** Series linked to former series. **g** 2014. **h** Country data supplemented with data from the Observatoire Economique et Statistique d'Afrique Subsaharienne (Afristat). **i** Data refers to a 5-year period preceding the reference year. **j** Refers to foreign citizens. **k** Including refugees. **l** Data as at the end of December. **m** 2004. **n** 2008. **o** 2007. **p** Includes active subscriptions using CDMA (Code Division Multiple Access) and GSM (Global System for Mobiles). **q** Excluding business enterprise. **r** Excluding private non-profit.

Tokelau

Region	Polynesia	Population (000, 2017)	1[a]	
Surface area (km2)	12[b]	Pop. density (per km2, 2017)	130.0[a]	
Sex ratio (m per 100 f, 2017)	100.0[c,d]	Capital city	Tokelau[e]	
National currency	New Zealand Dollar (NZD)	Exchange rate (per US$)	1.4[d]	

Economic indicators	2005	2010	2017
Agricultural production index (2004-2006=100)	100	107	112[f]
Food production index (2004-2006=100)	100	107	112[f]
International trade: Exports (million US$)	~0	~0	~0[d]
International trade: Imports (million US$)	1	1	1[d]
International trade: Balance (million US$)	- 1	- 1	- 1[d]

Major trading partners						2016
Export partners (% of exports)	Bangladesh	21.4	Myanmar	16.5	France	13.1
Import partners (% of imports)	United States	30.6	Samoa	21.0	Netherlands	14.8

Social indicators	2005	2010	2017
Population growth rate (average annual %)[g]	- 5.0	- 1.3	1.9[b]
Urban population (% of total population)	...	0.0	0.0[b]
Urban population growth rate (average annual %)[g]	0.0	0.0	0.0[b]
Fertility rate, total (live births per woman)	...	...	2.1[h]
Population age distribution (0-14 and 60+ years, %)	40.7 / 9.5[i]	36.6 / 11.3[i]	28.3 / 12.2[c,d]
International migrant stock (000/% of total pop.)	0.3 / 21.3	0.4 / 37.8	0.5 / 39.0[b]
Education: Primary gross enrol. ratio (f/m per 100 pop.)	132.6 / 101.8[k,l]	... / ...	114.3 / 121.0[k,d]
Education: Secondary gross enrol. ratio (f/m per 100 pop.)	75.8 / 83.3[k,l]	... / ...	120.7 / 129.1[k,d]

Environment and infrastructure indicators	2005	2010	2017
Mobile-cellular subscriptions (per 100 inhabitants)	0.0	...	...
Threatened species (number)	6[m]	41	49
Forested area (% of land area)[k]	0.0	0.0	0.0[f]
Important sites for terrestrial biodiversity protected (%)	0.0	0.0	0.0
Pop. using improved drinking water (urban/rural, %)	... / 96.2	... / 99.1	... / 100.0[b]
Pop. using improved sanitation facilities (urban/rural, %)	... / 71.4	... / 83.3	... / 90.5[b]

a Projected estimate (medium fertility variant). b 2015. c Break in the time series. d 2016. e The "capital" rotates yearly between the three atolls of Atafu, Fakaofo and Nukunomu, each with fewer than 500 inhabitants in 2011. f 2014. g Data refers to a 5-year period preceding the reference year. h 2012. i 2001. j 2006. k Estimate. l 2003. m 2004.

Tonga

Region	Polynesia	UN membership date	14 September 1999
Population (000, 2017)	108[a]	Surface area (km2)	747[b]
Pop. density (per km2, 2017)	150.0[a]	Sex ratio (m per 100 f, 2017)	100.7[a]
Capital city	Nuku'alofa	National currency	Pa'anga (TOP)
Capital city pop. (000)	25.0[c]	Exchange rate (per US$)	2.2[d]

Economic indicators

	2005	2010	2017
GDP: Gross domestic product (million current US$)	262	374	402[b]
GDP growth rate (annual %, const. 2005 prices)	1.6	3.6	3.8[b]
GDP per capita (current US$)	2 593.2	3 596.8	3 784.5[b]
Economy: Agriculture (% of GVA)	20.2	18.3	22.4[b]
Economy: Industry (% of GVA)	19.1	20.0	21.5[b]
Economy: Services and other activity (% of GVA)	60.6	61.7	56.1[b]
Employment: Agriculture (% of employed)[e]	32.0	33.2	33.3
Employment: Industry (% of employed)[e]	30.0	29.7	28.2
Employment: Services (% of employed)[e]	38.0	37.1	38.5
Unemployment (% of labour force)[e]	5.2	5.0	4.8
Labour force participation (female/male pop. %)[e]	53.1 / 75.0	53.1 / 75.2	52.9 / 73.9
CPI: Consumer Price Index (2000=100)[f]	160	210	233[c]
Agricultural production index (2004-2006=100)	98	135	134[c]
Food production index (2004-2006=100)	98	135	134[c]
International trade: Exports (million US$)	10	8	14[d]
International trade: Imports (million US$)	120	159	209[d]
International trade: Balance (million US$)	- 110	- 151	- 196[d]
Balance of payments, current account (million US$)	- 21	- 80	- 33[g]

Major trading partners

					2016
Export partners (% of exports)	New Zealand	23.2	China, Hong Kong SAR	17.7	Areas nes[h] 15.5
Import partners (% of imports)	New Zealand	28.6	Singapore	21.1	United States 10.9

Social indicators

	2005	2010	2017
Population growth rate (average annual %)[i]	0.6	0.6	0.4[b]
Urban population (% of total population)	23.2	23.4	23.7[b]
Urban population growth rate (average annual %)[i]	0.7	0.8	0.7[b]
Fertility rate, total (live births per woman)[i]	4.2	4.0	3.8[b]
Life expectancy at birth (females/males, years)[i]	73.5 / 68.8	74.7 / 69.0	75.6 / 69.6[b]
Population age distribution (0-14 and 60+ years, %)	38.2 / 8.3	37.4 / 8.0	35.8 / 8.5[a]
International migrant stock (000/% of total pop.)	4.3 / 4.3	5.0 / 4.8	5.7 / 5.4[b]
Refugees and others of concern to UNHCR (000)	...	~0.0[j]	...
Infant mortality rate (per 1 000 live births)[i]	23.5	22.0	20.6[b]
Health: Total expenditure (% of GDP)	6.5	4.6	5.2[c]
Health: Physicians (per 1 000 pop.)	0.3[k]	0.6	...
Education: Government expenditure (% of GDP)	3.9[l]	...	...
Education: Primary gross enrol. ratio (f/m per 100 pop.)	110.3 / 113.6	107.2 / 109.3	107.5 / 108.6[c]
Education: Secondary gross enrol. ratio (f/m per 100 pop.)	116.6 / 105.7[k]	107.7 / 100.9	94.2 / 86.4[c]
Education: Tertiary gross enrol. ratio (f/m per 100 pop.)	8.0 / 4.8[m]	... / ...	... / ...
Intentional homicide rate (per 100 000 pop.)	4.0	1.0	1.0[n]
Seats held by women in national parliaments (%)	0.0	3.1	3.8

Environment and infrastructure indicators

	2005	2010	2017
Mobile-cellular subscriptions (per 100 inhabitants)	29.6[e]	52.2[e]	65.6[o,b]
Individuals using the Internet (per 100 inhabitants)[e]	4.9	16.0	45.0[b]
Threatened species (number)	16[l]	58	79
Forested area (% of land area)	12.5[e]	12.5	12.5[e,c]
CO2 emission estimates (million tons/tons per capita)	0.1 / 1.1	0.1 / 1.1	0.1 / 1.1[c]
Energy production, primary (Petajoules)	0	0	0[c]
Energy supply per capita (Gigajoules)	16[e]	16	15[c]
Tourist/visitor arrivals at national borders (000)[p]	42	47	54[b]
Important sites for terrestrial biodiversity protected (%)	11.3	11.3	11.3
Pop. using improved drinking water (urban/rural, %)	97.6 / 99.0	98.8 / 99.3	99.7 / 99.6[b]
Pop. using improved sanitation facilities (urban/rural, %)	97.4 / 90.7	97.5 / 89.7	97.6 / 89.0[b]
Net Official Development Assist. received (% of GNI)	12.36	18.44	18.30[c]

a Projected estimate (medium fertility variant). b 2015. c 2014. d 2016. e Estimate. f Excluding "Rent". g 2013. h Areas not elsewhere specified. i Data refers to a 5-year period preceding the reference year. j Data as at the end of December. k 2002. l 2004. m 2003. n 2012. o Provisional data. p Arrivals by air.

Trinidad and Tobago

Region	Caribbean	UN membership date	18 September 1962
Population (000, 2017)	1 369 [a]	Surface area (km2)	5 127 [b]
Pop. density (per km2, 2017)	266.9 [a]	Sex ratio (m per 100 f, 2017)	97.1 [a]
Capital city	Port of Spain	National currency	TT Dollar (TTD) [c]
Capital city pop. (000)	34.4 [d]	Exchange rate (per US$)	6.8 [e]

Economic indicators	2005	2010	2017
GDP: Gross domestic product (million current US$)	15 982	22 158	25 927 [b]
GDP growth rate (annual %, const. 2005 prices)	6.2	0.2	0.2 [b]
GDP per capita (current US$)	12 323.2	16 684.0	19 062.9 [b]
Economy: Agriculture (% of GVA)	0.5	0.5	0.5 [b]
Economy: Industry (% of GVA)	56.7	51.3	42.5 [b]
Economy: Services and other activity (% of GVA)	42.8	48.2	57.0 [b]
Employment: Agriculture (% of employed) [f]	4.5	4.2	4.1
Employment: Industry (% of employed) [f]	32.8	33.7	31.6
Employment: Services (% of employed) [f]	62.7	62.2	64.3
Unemployment (% of labour force)	8.0	5.9	4.2 [f]
Labour force participation (female/male pop. %) [f]	53.5 / 76.2	52.5 / 75.4	52.4 / 73.2
CPI: Consumer Price Index (2000=100)	126	196	250 [d]
Agricultural production index (2004-2006=100)	99	96	95 [d]
Food production index (2004-2006=100)	99	96	95 [d]
Index of industrial production (2005=100) [g]	100	159	142 [d]
International trade: Exports (million US$)	9 611	10 982	4 576 [e]
International trade: Imports (million US$)	5 694	6 480	4 826 [e]
International trade: Balance (million US$)	3 918	4 502	- 249 [e]
Balance of payments, current account (million US$)	3 881	4 172	...

Major trading partners						2016
Export partners (% of exports)	United States	41.7	Argentina	6.8	Colombia	4.1
Import partners (% of imports)	United States	32.0	Gabon	12.5	China	7.1

Social indicators	2005	2010	2017
Population growth rate (average annual %) [h]	0.5	0.5	0.5 [b]
Urban population (% of total population)	9.9	9.1	8.4 [b]
Urban population growth rate (average annual %) [h]	- 1.2	- 1.2	- 1.2 [b]
Fertility rate, total (live births per woman) [h]	1.8	1.8	1.8 [b]
Life expectancy at birth (females/males, years) [h]	72.5 / 65.1	73.0 / 65.8	73.8 / 66.9 [b]
Population age distribution (0-14 and 60+ years, %)	21.8 / 10.8	20.7 / 12.4	20.7 / 15.0 [a]
International migrant stock (000/% of total pop.)	44.8 / 3.5	48.2 / 3.6	49.9 / 3.7 [b]
Refugees and others of concern to UNHCR (000)	...	0.1 [i]	0.2 [e]
Infant mortality rate (per 1 000 live births) [h]	28.9	26.6	24.8 [b]
Health: Total expenditure (% of GDP) [j]	5.3	5.3	5.9 [d]
Health: Physicians (per 1 000 pop.)	0.8 [k]	1.2 [l]	...
Education: Government expenditure (% of GDP)	3.1 [k]	...	...
Education: Primary gross enrol. ratio (f/m per 100 pop.)	97.8 / 100.7 [f]	104.3 / 108.0	... / ...
Education: Secondary gross enrol. ratio (f/m per 100 pop.)	88.5 / 82.6 [f,m]	... / ...	... / ...
Education: Tertiary gross enrol. ratio (f/m per 100 pop.)	13.4 / 10.6 [m]	... / ...	... / ...
Intentional homicide rate (per 100 000 pop.)	29.8	35.6	30.9 [b]
Seats held by women in national parliaments (%)	19.4	26.8	31.0

Environment and infrastructure indicators	2005	2010	2017
Mobile-cellular subscriptions (per 100 inhabitants)	71.2	142.6	157.7 [b]
Individuals using the Internet (per 100 inhabitants) [f]	29.0	48.5	69.2 [b]
Research & Development expenditure (% of GDP)	0.1	0.1	0.1 [d]
Threatened species (number)	33 [m]	48	69
Forested area (% of land area)	44.8	44.1	45.4 [f,d]
CO2 emission estimates (million tons/tons per capita)	38.2 / 29.0	47.9 / 36.1	46.3 / 34.2 [d]
Energy production, primary (Petajoules)	1 464	1 786	1 663 [d]
Energy supply per capita (Gigajoules)	516	636	607 [d]
Tourist/visitor arrivals at national borders (000) [n]	463	388	440 [b]
Important sites for terrestrial biodiversity protected (%)	40.7	40.7	40.7
Pop. using improved drinking water (urban/rural, %)	94.1 / 94.1	95.0 / 95.0	95.1 / 95.1 [b]
Pop. using improved sanitation facilities (urban/rural, %)	91.1 / 91.1	91.4 / 91.4	91.5 / 91.5 [b]
Net Official Development Assist. received (% of GNI)	- 0.01	0.02	...

a Projected estimate (medium fertility variant). b 2015. c Trinidad and Tobago Dollar. d 2014. e 2016. f Estimate. g Data classified according to ISIC Rev. 3. h Data refers to a 5-year period preceding the reference year. i Data as at the end of December. j Data revision. k 2003. l 2007. m 2004. n Arrivals by air.

Tunisia

Region	Northern Africa	UN membership date	12 November 1956
Population (000, 2017)	11 532[a]	Surface area (km2)	163 610[b]
Pop. density (per km2, 2017)	74.2[a]	Sex ratio (m per 100 f, 2017)	97.6[a]
Capital city	Tunis	National currency	Tunisian Dinar (TND)
Capital city pop. (000)	1 993.5[c,b]	Exchange rate (per US$)	2.3[d]

Economic indicators	2005	2010	2017
GDP: Gross domestic product (million current US$)	32 272	44 051	41 199[b]
GDP growth rate (annual %, const. 2005 prices)	4.0	3.0	0.8[b]
GDP per capita (current US$)	3 194.5	4 140.5	3 660.9[b]
Economy: Agriculture (% of GVA)[e]	10.0	8.1	10.3[b]
Economy: Industry (% of GVA)[e]	28.8	31.1	27.8[b]
Economy: Services and other activity (% of GVA)[e]	61.3	60.8	62.0[b]
Employment: Agriculture (% of employed)[f]	16.4	15.1	11.7
Employment: Industry (% of employed)[f]	28.6	29.4	29.4
Employment: Services (% of employed)[f]	55.1	55.6	58.9
Unemployment (% of labour force)	12.9	13.1	14.6[f]
Labour force participation (female/male pop. %)[f]	24.0 / 68.0	24.5 / 69.7	25.1 / 71.3
CPI: Consumer Price Index (2000=100)	114	139[g]	170[h]
Agricultural production index (2004-2006=100)	101	106	108[h]
Food production index (2004-2006=100)	101	106	108[h]
Index of industrial production (2005=100)	100	115	112[h]
International trade: Exports (million US$)	10 494	16 427	13 483[d]
International trade: Imports (million US$)	13 174	22 215	19 456[d]
International trade: Balance (million US$)	- 2 681	- 5 789	- 5 973[d]
Balance of payments, current account (million US$)	- 299	- 2 104	- 3 850[b]

Major trading partners						2016
Export partners (% of exports)	France	29.3	Italy	18.5	Germany	10.5
Import partners (% of imports)	France	17.8	Italy	14.9	China	8.4

Social indicators	2005	2010	2017
Population growth rate (average annual %)[i]	0.8	1.0	1.2[b]
Urban population (% of total population)	65.1	65.9	66.8[b]
Urban population growth rate (average annual %)[i]	1.5	1.4	1.4[b]
Fertility rate, total (live births per woman)[i]	2.0	2.0	2.3[b]
Life expectancy at birth (females/males, years)[i]	76.3 / 71.4	77.0 / 72.3	77.1 / 73.0[b]
Population age distribution (0-14 and 60+ years, %)	25.5 / 10.0	23.3 / 10.4	24.0 / 12.3[a]
International migrant stock (000/% of total pop.)[i]	35.0 / 0.3	43.2 / 0.4	56.7 / 0.5[b]
Refugees and others of concern to UNHCR (000)	0.1[k]	0.1[k]	0.7[d]
Infant mortality rate (per 1 000 live births)[i]	23.0	18.7	18.5[b]
Health: Total expenditure (% of GDP)[l]	5.6	6.5	7.0[h]
Health: Physicians (per 1 000 pop.)	0.9	1.2	1.6[h]
Education: Government expenditure (% of GDP)	6.5	6.3	6.3[m]
Education: Primary gross enrol. ratio (f/m per 100 pop.)	109.3 / 114.0	105.4 / 109.0	112.5 / 115.8[b]
Education: Secondary gross enrol. ratio (f/m per 100 pop.)	88.3 / 81.4	93.4 / 87.6	94.2 / 90.0[n]
Education: Tertiary gross enrol. ratio (f/m per 100 pop.)	35.1 / 28.6	42.6 / 27.8	43.3 / 26.2[b]
Intentional homicide rate (per 100 000 pop.)	2.6	2.7	3.0[m]
Seats held by women in national parliaments (%)	22.8	27.6	31.3

Environment and infrastructure indicators	2005	2010	2017
Mobile-cellular subscriptions (per 100 inhabitants)	56.5	104.5	129.9[b]
Individuals using the Internet (per 100 inhabitants)	9.7	36.8	48.5[f,b]
Research & Development expenditure (% of GDP)	0.7	0.7	0.6[h]
Threatened species (number)	36[o]	75	96
Forested area (% of land area)	5.9	6.4	6.6[f,h]
CO2 emission estimates (million tons/tons per capita)	22.7 / 2.3	27.7 / 2.6	28.8 / 2.6[h]
Energy production, primary (Petajoules)	274	341	274[h]
Energy supply per capita (Gigajoules)	35	40	39[h]
Tourist/visitor arrivals at national borders (000)	6 378[p]	7 828	5 359[b]
Important sites for terrestrial biodiversity protected (%)	17.3	27.2	40.8
Pop. using improved drinking water (urban/rural, %)	98.6 / 82.4	99.6 / 88.4	100.0 / 93.2[b]
Pop. using improved sanitation facilities (urban/rural, %)	96.2 / 66.0	96.9 / 73.7	97.4 / 79.8[b]
Net Official Development Assist. received (% of GNI)	1.20	1.31	1.14[b]

a Projected estimate (medium fertility variant). **b** 2015. **c** Refers to Grand Tunis. **d** 2016. **e** At factor cost. **f** Estimate. **g** Series linked to former series. **h** 2014. **i** Data refers to a 5-year period preceding the reference year. **j** Refers to foreign citizens. **k** Data as at the end of December. **l** Data revision. **m** 2012. **n** 2011. **o** 2004. **p** Excluding nationals residing abroad.

Turkey

Region	Western Asia	UN membership date	24 October 1945
Population (000, 2017)	80 745 [a]	Surface area (km2)	783 562 [b]
Pop. density (per km2, 2017)	104.9 [a]	Sex ratio (m per 100 f, 2017)	97.0 [a]
Capital city	Ankara	National currency	Turkish Lira (TRY)
Capital city pop. (000)	4 750.0 [c,b]	Exchange rate (per US$)	3.5 [d]

Economic indicators	2005	2010	2017
GDP: Gross domestic product (million current US$)	482 986	731 144	717 888 [b]
GDP growth rate (annual %, const. 2005 prices)	8.4	9.2	4.0 [b]
GDP per capita (current US$)	7 117.3	10 111.2	9 125.8 [b]
Economy: Agriculture (% of GVA) [e]	10.7	9.7	8.6 [b]
Economy: Industry (% of GVA) [e]	28.3	27.0	26.4 [b]
Economy: Services and other activity (% of GVA) [e]	61.0	63.4	65.0 [b]
Employment: Agriculture (% of employed) [f]	29.4	23.7	19.6
Employment: Industry (% of employed) [f]	24.8	26.1	27.5
Employment: Services (% of employed) [f]	45.8	50.2	52.9
Unemployment (% of labour force)	10.6	10.7	10.8 [f]
Labour force participation (female/male pop. %) [f]	23.4 / 70.3	27.6 / 70.7	30.4 / 71.4
CPI: Consumer Price Index (2000=100)	381 [g,h]	578	784 [i]
Agricultural production index (2004-2006=100)	101	110	120 [i]
Food production index (2004-2006=100)	101	111	122 [i]
Index of industrial production (2005=100)	100	116 [j]	140 [j,i]
International trade: Exports (million US$)	73 476	113 883	142 606 [d]
International trade: Imports (million US$)	116 774	185 544	198 602 [d]
International trade: Balance (million US$)	- 43 298	- 71 661	- 55 996 [d]
Balance of payments, current account (million US$)	- 20 980 [g]	- 44 616	- 32 278 [b]

Major trading partners						2016
Export partners (% of exports)	Germany	9.8	United Kingdom	8.2	Iraq	5.4
Import partners (% of imports)	China	12.8	Germany	10.8	Russian Federation	7.6

Social indicators	2005	2010	2017
Population growth rate (average annual %) [k]	1.4	1.3	1.6 [b]
Urban population (% of total population)	67.8	70.7	73.4 [b]
Urban population growth rate (average annual %) [k]	2.3	2.1	2.0 [b]
Fertility rate, total (live births per woman) [k]	2.4	2.2	2.1 [b]
Life expectancy at birth (females/males, years) [k]	74.9 / 68.0	76.9 / 69.9	78.1 / 71.5 [b]
Population age distribution (0-14 and 60+ years, %)	28.6 / 9.6	26.9 / 10.4	25.0 / 12.0 [a]
International migrant stock (000/% of total pop.) [l]	1 319.2 / 1.9	1 367.0 / 1.9	2 964.9 / 3.8 [b]
Refugees and others of concern to UNHCR (000)	8.7 [m]	17.8 [m]	3 006.3 [d]
Infant mortality rate (per 1 000 live births) [k]	24.7	16.4	12.6 [b]
Health: Total expenditure (% of GDP)	5.4	5.6	5.4 [i]
Health: Physicians (per 1 000 pop.)	1.5	1.7	1.7 [i]
Education: Government expenditure (% of GDP)	3.1 [n]	2.9 [o]	4.8 [p]
Education: Primary gross enrol. ratio (f/m per 100 pop.)	100.5 / 105.8	100.8 / 102.3	102.1 / 102.8 [b]
Education: Secondary gross enrol. ratio (f/m per 100 pop.)	75.6 / 91.0	80.5 / 87.8	101.1 / 103.8 [b]
Education: Tertiary gross enrol. ratio (f/m per 100 pop.)	27.6 / 37.8	50.2 / 61.7	88.3 / 101.0 [b]
Intentional homicide rate (per 100 000 pop.)	4.9	4.2	4.3 [q]
Seats held by women in national parliaments (%)	4.4	9.1	14.9

Environment and infrastructure indicators	2005	2010	2017
Mobile-cellular subscriptions (per 100 inhabitants)	64.4	85.6	96.0 [b]
Individuals using the Internet (per 100 inhabitants) [s]	15.5 [r]	39.8 [r]	53.7 [b]
Research & Development expenditure (% of GDP)	0.6	0.8	1.0 [i]
Threatened species (number)	92 [n]	150	388
Forested area (% of land area)	13.9	14.6	15.1 [f,i]
CO2 emission estimates (million tons/tons per capita)	237.4 / 3.5	298.0 / 4.1	346.0 / 4.5 [i]
Energy production, primary (Petajoules)	1 004	1 352	1 303 [i]
Energy supply per capita (Gigajoules)	52	61	65 [i]
Tourist/visitor arrivals at national borders (000) [t]	20 273	31 364	39 478 [b]
Important sites for terrestrial biodiversity protected (%)	2.1	2.2	2.3
Pop. using improved drinking water (urban/rural, %)	98.3 / 90.3	99.7 / 95.9	100.0 / 100.0 [b]
Pop. using improved sanitation facilities (urban/rural, %)	97.3 / 76.5	97.8 / 81.0	98.3 / 85.5 [b]
Net Official Development Assist. disbursed (% of GNI)	0.17	0.13	0.79 [u,d]
Net Official Development Assist. received (% of GNI)	0.08	0.14	0.30 [b]

a Projected estimate (medium fertility variant). b 2015. c Refers to Altindag, Cankaya, Etimesgut, Golbasi, Kecioren, Mamak, Sincan and Yenimahalle. d 2016. e Data classified according to ISIC Rev. 4. f Estimate. g Break in the time series. h Series linked to former series. i 2014. j Excluding water and waste management. k Data refers to a 5-year period preceding the reference year. l Including refugees. m Data as at the end of December. n 2004. o 2006. p 2013. q 2012. r Users in the last 12 months. s Population aged 16 to 74 years. t Turkish citizens resident abroad are included. u Provisional data.

Turkmenistan

Region	Central Asia		UN membership date	02 March 1992	
Population (000, 2017)	5 758 [a]		Surface area (km2)	488 100 [b]	
Pop. density (per km2, 2017)	12.3 [a]		Sex ratio (m per 100 f, 2017)	97.0 [a]	
Capital city	Ashgabat		National currency	Turkmen. Manat (TMT) [c]	
Capital city pop. (000)	746.0 [b]		Exchange rate (per US$)	3.5 [d,e]	

Economic indicators	2005	2010	2017
GDP: Gross domestic product (million current US$)	14 182	22 583	37 597 [b]
GDP growth rate (annual %, const. 2005 prices)	13.0	9.2	6.5 [b]
GDP per capita (current US$)	2 987.0	4 479.0	6 996.7 [b]
Economy: Agriculture (% of GVA)	18.8	14.5	13.4 [b]
Economy: Industry (% of GVA)	37.6	48.4	51.0 [b]
Economy: Services and other activity (% of GVA)	43.6	37.0	35.6 [b]
Employment: Agriculture (% of employed) [f]	22.2	19.4	17.9
Employment: Industry (% of employed) [f]	35.7	41.0	37.4
Employment: Services (% of employed) [f]	42.1	39.6	44.7
Unemployment (% of labour force) [f]	9.2	9.2	8.6
Labour force participation (female/male pop. %) [f]	47.0 / 74.8	46.4 / 75.7	47.3 / 77.7
Agricultural production index (2004-2006=100)	104	98	103 [g]
Food production index (2004-2006=100)	102	102	109 [g]
International trade: Exports (million US$)	3 009	3 335	3 741 [e]
International trade: Imports (million US$)	2 217	2 400	2 616 [e]
International trade: Balance (million US$)	792	935	1 125 [e]

Major trading partners					2016
Export partners (% of exports)	China	70.9	Turkey	5.4	Italy	5.4
Import partners (% of imports)	Turkey	24.9	Russian Federation	11.4	Japan	7.9

Social indicators	2005	2010	2017
Population growth rate (average annual %) [h]	1.0	1.4	1.8 [b]
Urban population (% of total population)	47.0	48.4	50.0 [b]
Urban population growth rate (average annual %) [h]	1.6	1.8	1.9 [b]
Fertility rate, total (live births per woman) [h]	2.8	2.6	3.0 [b]
Life expectancy at birth (females/males, years) [h]	68.2 / 60.3	69.6 / 62.2	70.8 / 63.9 [b]
Population age distribution (0-14 and 60+ years, %)	32.6 / 6.1	29.5 / 6.1	30.9 / 7.3 [a]
International migrant stock (000/% of total pop.)	213.1 / 4.5	198.0 / 3.9	196.4 / 3.7 [b]
Refugees and others of concern to UNHCR (000)	12.0 [i]	20.1 [i]	7.2 [e]
Infant mortality rate (per 1 000 live births) [h]	62.1	54.2	46.9 [b]
Health: Total expenditure (% of GDP) [j]	3.5	2.0	2.1 [g]
Health: Physicians (per 1 000 pop.)	4.4 [k]	2.3	2.3 [g]
Education: Government expenditure (% of GDP)	...	...	3.1 [l]
Education: Primary gross enrol. ratio (f/m per 100 pop.)	... / ...	... / ...	88.6 / 90.1 [g]
Education: Secondary gross enrol. ratio (f/m per 100 pop.)	... / ...	... / ...	83.7 / 86.9 [g]
Education: Tertiary gross enrol. ratio (f/m per 100 pop.)	... / ...	... / ...	6.2 / 9.7 [g]
Intentional homicide rate (per 100 000 pop.)	4.9	4.5	4.2 [b]
Seats held by women in national parliaments (%)	26.0 [m]	16.8	25.8

Environment and infrastructure indicators	2005	2010	2017
Mobile-cellular subscriptions (per 100 inhabitants)	2.2 [f]	63.4	145.9 [f,b]
Individuals using the Internet (per 100 inhabitants) [f]	1.0	3.0	15.0 [b]
Threatened species (number)	40 [n]	45	54
Forested area (% of land area) [f]	8.8	8.8	8.8 [g]
CO2 emission estimates (million tons/tons per capita)	48.3 / 10.2	57.3 / 11.4	68.4 / 12.9 [g]
Energy production, primary (Petajoules)	2 584	1 982	3 270 [g]
Energy supply per capita (Gigajoules)	170	189	212 [g]
Tourist/visitor arrivals at national borders (000)	12	...	...
Important sites for terrestrial biodiversity protected (%)	14.4	14.6	14.6
Pop. using improved drinking water (urban/rural, %)	89.1 / 34.6	... / ...	... / ...
Pop. using improved sanitation facilities (urban/rural, %)	77.0 / 49.9	... / ...	... / ...
Net Official Development Assist. received (% of GNI)	0.39	0.21	0.07 [b]

a Projected estimate (medium fertility variant). **b** 2015. **c** Turkmenistan New Manat. **d** UN operational exchange rate. **e** 2016. **f** Estimate. **g** 2014. **h** Data refers to a 5-year period preceding the reference year. **i** Data as at the end of December. **j** Estimates should be viewed with caution as these are derived from scarce data. **k** 2002. **l** 2012. **m** 2000. **n** 2004.

Turks and Caicos Islands

Region	Caribbean	Population (000, 2017)	35[a]	
Surface area (km2)	948[b,c]	Pop. density (per km2, 2017)	37.3[a]	
Sex ratio (m per 100 f, 2017)	104.1[d,e]	Capital city	Cockburn Town	
National currency	US Dollar (USD)	Capital city pop. (000)	0.1[f]	

Economic indicators	2005	2010	2017
GDP: Gross domestic product (million current US$)	579	687	863[c]
GDP growth rate (annual %, const. 2005 prices)	14.4	1.0	4.1[c]
GDP per capita (current US$)	21 877.0	22 159.4	25 121.8[c]
Economy: Agriculture (% of GVA)	1.2	0.6	0.6[c]
Economy: Industry (% of GVA)	19.7	12.4	10.4[c]
Economy: Services and other activity (% of GVA)	79.1	86.9	89.0[c]
Employment: Agriculture (% of employed)[g]	1.4	1.2[h,i]	...
Employment: Industry (% of employed)[g]	16.8	23.1[h,i]	...
Employment: Services (% of employed)[g]	70.9	74.0[h,i]	...
Unemployment (% of labour force)	8.0	8.3[h,i]	...
International trade: Exports (million US$)	15	16	4[j]
International trade: Imports (million US$)	304	302	389[j]
International trade: Balance (million US$)	- 289	- 286	- 385[j]

Major trading partners						2016
Export partners (% of exports)	Bahamas	30.7	United States	29.6	Zimbabwe	22.4
Import partners (% of imports)	United States	89.3	Japan	2.0	United Kingdom	1.1

Social indicators	2005	2010	2017
Population growth rate (average annual %)[k]	6.7	3.2	2.0[c]
Urban population (% of total population)	87.7	90.2	92.2[c]
Urban population growth rate (average annual %)[k]	7.5	3.7	2.5[c]
Life expectancy at birth (females/males, years)	77.3 / 75.1[l]	... / ...	77.8 / 75.8[m]
Population age distribution (0-14 and 60+ years, %)	28.6 / 5.2[f]	... / ...	19.2 / 7.6[e,d]
International migrant stock (000/% of total pop.)	9.9 / 37.6	10.9 / 35.1	11.7 / 34.0[c]
Refugees and others of concern to UNHCR (000)	...	...	~0.0[j]
Education: Government expenditure (% of GDP)	...	...	3.3[c]
Intentional homicide rate (per 100 000 pop.)	...	6.6[n]	...

Environment and infrastructure indicators	2005	2010	2017
Threatened species (number)	20[o]	34	60
Forested area (% of land area)[p]	36.2	36.2	36.2[q]
CO2 emission estimates (million tons/tons per capita)	0.1 / 4.0	0.2 / 6.1	0.2 / 6.1[q]
Energy production, primary (Petajoules)	0	0	0[q]
Energy supply per capita (Gigajoules)[p]	57	86	86[q]
Tourist/visitor arrivals at national borders (000)	176	281	386[c]
Important sites for terrestrial biodiversity protected (%)	28.0	28.0	28.0
Pop. using improved drinking water (urban/rural, %)	87.0 / 87.0	... / ...	... / ...
Pop. using improved sanitation facilities (urban/rural, %)	81.4 / 81.4	... / ...	... / ...

a Projected estimate (medium fertility variant). **b** Including low water level for all islands (area to shoreline). **c** 2015. **d** Estimates should be viewed with caution as these are derived from scarce data. **e** De jure population. **f** 2001. **g** Data classified according to ISIC Rev. 3. **h** Break in the time series. **i** 2008. **j** 2016. **k** Data refers to a 5-year period preceding the reference year. **l** 2002. **m** 2012. **n** 2009. **o** 2004. **p** Estimate. **q** 2014.

Tuvalu

Region	Polynesia	UN membership date	05 September 2000
Population (000, 2017)	11 [a]	Surface area (km2)	26 [b]
Pop. density (per km2, 2017)	373.1 [a]	Sex ratio (m per 100 f, 2017)	102.0 [c]
Capital city	Funafuti	National currency	Australian Dollar (AUD)
Capital city pop. (000)	5.8 [d]	Exchange rate (per US$)	1.4 [c]

Economic indicators	2005	2010	2017
GDP: Gross domestic product (million current US$)	22	32	33 [b]
GDP growth rate (annual %, const. 2005 prices)	- 3.9	- 2.7	3.5 [b]
GDP per capita (current US$)	2 258.8	3 238.5	3 362.4 [b]
Economy: Agriculture (% of GVA)	21.6	27.6	26.0 [b]
Economy: Industry (% of GVA)	8.5	5.7	7.6 [b]
Economy: Services and other activity (% of GVA)	69.9	66.7	66.4 [b]
Unemployment (% of labour force)	6.5	...	...
Labour force participation (female/male pop. %)	47.9 / 69.6	... / ...	... / ...
CPI: Consumer Price Index (2000=100)	117 [e]	...	...
Agricultural production index (2004-2006=100)	100	105	110 [d]
Food production index (2004-2006=100)	100	105	110 [d]
International trade: Exports (million US$)	~0	~0	~0 [c]
International trade: Imports (million US$)	13	12	12 [c]
International trade: Balance (million US$)	- 13	- 12	- 12 [c]
Balance of payments, current account (million US$)	- 4	- 14	7 [f]

Major trading partners						2016
Export partners (% of exports)	Thailand	86.2	Japan	5.5	China, Hong Kong SAR	1.8
Import partners (% of imports)	Singapore	30.1	Japan	26.7	Fiji	16.6

Social indicators	2005	2010	2017
Population growth rate (average annual %) [g]	1.2	1.0	0.9 [b]
Urban population (% of total population)	49.7	54.8	59.7 [b]
Urban population growth rate (average annual %) [g]	2.1	2.2	1.9 [b]
Fertility rate, total (live births per woman)	3.7 [h]	...	3.6 [i,j]
Life expectancy at birth (females/males, years)	... / ...	71.9 / 67.4	... / ...
Population age distribution (0-14 and 60+ years, %)	36.2 / 8.6 [h]	... / ...	31.1 / 9.9 [c]
International migrant stock (000/% of total pop.) [k]	0.2 / 1.9	0.2 / 1.6	0.1 / 1.4 [b]
Infant mortality rate (per 1 000 live births)	...	10.3	...
Health: Total expenditure (% of GDP)	18.4	16.8	16.5 [d]
Health: Physicians (per 1 000 pop.)	1.0 [l]	1.2 [m]	...
Education: Primary gross enrol. ratio (f/m per 100 pop.) [n]	97.6 / 101.4	97.6 / 102.4 [o]	104.3 / 103.0 [b]
Education: Secondary gross enrol. ratio (f/m per 100 pop.)	74.1 / 67.4 [n,p]	... / ...	97.5 / 76.0 [n,b]
Intentional homicide rate (per 100 000 pop.)	...	10.2	20.3 [i]
Seats held by women in national parliaments (%)	0.0	0.0	6.7

Environment and infrastructure indicators	2005	2010	2017
Mobile-cellular subscriptions (per 100 inhabitants)	13.4	16.3	40.3 [n,b]
Individuals using the Internet (per 100 inhabitants)	5.2 [q]	25.0 [n]	42.7 [n,b]
Threatened species (number)	8 [r]	85	96
Forested area (% of land area) [n]	33.3	33.3	33.3 [d]
CO2 emission estimates (million tons/tons per capita)	~0.0 / ...	~0.0 / ...	~0.0 / ... [d]
Energy supply per capita (Gigajoules)	13 [n]	13	13 [n,d]
Tourist/visitor arrivals at national borders (000)	1	2	2 [b]
Pop. using improved drinking water (urban/rural, %)	96.9 / 95.3	98.3 / 97.0	98.3 / 97.0 [b]
Pop. using improved sanitation facilities (urban/rural, %)	84.0 / 78.3	86.3 / 80.2	86.3 / 80.2 [b,f]
Net Official Development Assist. received (% of GNI)	24.65	27.46	63.52 [d]

a Projected estimate (medium fertility variant). b 2015. c 2016. d 2014. e Funafuti f 2013. g Data refers to a 5-year period preceding the reference year. h 2002. i Break in the time series. j 2012. k Refers to foreign citizens. l 2003. m 2009. n Estimate. o 2006. p 2001. q 2000. r 2004.

Uganda

Region	Eastern Africa	
Population (000, 2017)	42 863[a]	
Pop. density (per km2, 2017)	214.5[a]	
Capital city	Kampala	
Capital city pop. (000)	1 935.7[b]	

UN membership date	25 October 1962
Surface area (km2)	241 550[b]
Sex ratio (m per 100 f, 2017)	99.0[a]
National currency	Uganda Shilling (UGX)
Exchange rate (per US$)	3 610.5[c]

Economic indicators

	2005	2010	2017
GDP: Gross domestic product (million current US$)	11 154	19 803	25 282[b]
GDP growth rate (annual %, const. 2005 prices)	10.0	8.2	5.4[b]
GDP per capita (current US$)	397.8	597.4	647.7[b]
Economy: Agriculture (% of GVA)[d]	28.6	26.1	25.6[b]
Economy: Industry (% of GVA)[d]	22.2	20.4	21.5[b]
Economy: Services and other activity (% of GVA)[d]	49.1	53.5	52.9[b]
Employment: Agriculture (% of employed)[e]	73.7	73.7	72.0
Employment: Industry (% of employed)[e]	5.6	6.9	7.4
Employment: Services (% of employed)[e]	20.7	19.4	20.5
Unemployment (% of labour force)	1.9	3.1[e]	2.4[e]
Labour force participation (female/male pop. %)[e]	77.1 / 79.7	80.6 / 85.4	82.3 / 87.7
CPI: Consumer Price Index (2000=100)	124	186	277[f]
Agricultural production index (2004-2006=100)	100	102	93[f]
Food production index (2004-2006=100)	100	101	90[f]
International trade: Exports (million US$)	813	1 619	2 755[c]
International trade: Imports (million US$)	2 054	4 664	3 750[c]
International trade: Balance (million US$)	- 1 241	- 3 046	- 996[c]
Balance of payments, current account (million US$)	- 13	- 1 659	- 2 353[b]

Major trading partners

						2016
Export partners (% of exports)	Kenya	18.8	South Sudan	11.7	Rwanda	10.5
Import partners (% of imports)	India	20.9	China	15.8	Kenya	10.0

Social indicators

	2005	2010	2017
Population growth rate (average annual %)[g]	3.4	3.4	3.4[b]
Urban population (% of total population)	13.0	14.5	16.1[b]
Urban population growth rate (average annual %)[g]	4.9	5.5	5.4[b]
Fertility rate, total (live births per woman)[g]	6.7	6.4	5.9[b]
Life expectancy at birth (females/males, years)[g]	52.1 / 47.8	56.7 / 53.6	60.7 / 56.5[b]
Population age distribution (0-14 and 60+ years, %)	49.8 / 3.6	49.3 / 3.4	47.7 / 3.3[a]
International migrant stock (000/% of total pop.)[h]	653.0 / 2.3	529.2 / 1.6	749.5 / 1.9[b]
Refugees and others of concern to UNHCR (000)	260.7[i]	594.4[i]	727.1[c]
Infant mortality rate (per 1 000 live births)[g]	79.4	68.2	60.2[b]
Health: Total expenditure (% of GDP)[j]	9.4	11.0	7.2[f]
Health: Physicians (per 1 000 pop.)	0.1	...	...
Education: Government expenditure (% of GDP)	5.0[k]	2.4	2.2[f]
Education: Primary gross enrol. ratio (f/m per 100 pop.)	122.2 / 123.2	121.2 / 119.3	110.9 / 108.9[i]
Education: Secondary gross enrol. ratio (f/m per 100 pop.)	17.3 / 21.5[k]	22.1 / 26.9[m]	22.1 / 24.3[b]
Education: Tertiary gross enrol. ratio (f/m per 100 pop.)	2.8 / 4.4[k]	3.5 / 4.5	4.2 / 5.4[f]
Intentional homicide rate (per 100 000 pop.)	8.9	9.5	11.8[f]
Seats held by women in national parliaments (%)	23.9	31.5	34.3

Environment and infrastructure indicators

	2005	2010	2017
Mobile-cellular subscriptions (per 100 inhabitants)	4.6	37.7[i]	50.4[i,b]
Individuals using the Internet (per 100 inhabitants)	1.7	12.5	19.2[e,b]
Research & Development expenditure (% of GDP)	0.2	0.5	...
Threatened species (number)	134[k]	166	196
Forested area (% of land area)	17.2	13.7	11.0[e,f]
CO2 emission estimates (million tons/tons per capita)	2.2 / 0.1	3.9 / 0.1	5.2 / 0.1[f]
Energy production, primary (Petajoules)	350	379	409[f]
Energy supply per capita (Gigajoules)	13	13	12[f]
Tourist/visitor arrivals at national borders (000)	468	946	1 303[b]
Important sites for terrestrial biodiversity protected (%)	62.4	73.6	73.6
Pop. using improved drinking water (urban/rural, %)	89.0 / 60.8	92.6 / 69.1	95.5 / 75.8[b]
Pop. using improved sanitation facilities (urban/rural, %)	28.4 / 15.1	28.5 / 16.3	28.5 / 17.3[b]
Net Official Development Assist. received (% of GNI)	13.66	8.52	6.35[b]

a Projected estimate (medium fertility variant). b 2015. c 2016. d Data classified according to ISIC Rev. 4. e Estimate. f 2014. g Data refers to a 5-year period preceding the reference year. h Including refugees. i Data as at the end of December. j Unlike other countries, in Uganda fiscal year 2010/2011 corresponds to calendar year 2010. k 2004. l 2013. m 2007.

Ukraine

Region	Eastern Europe	UN membership date	24 October 1945
Population (000, 2017)	44 223[a,b]	Surface area (km2)	603 500[c]
Pop. density (per km2, 2017)	76.3[a,b]	Sex ratio (m per 100 f, 2017)	86.0[a,b]
Capital city	Kyiv	National currency	Hryvnia (UAH)
Capital city pop. (000)	2 941.9[c]	Exchange rate (per US$)	27.2[d]

Economic indicators	2005	2010	2017
GDP: Gross domestic product (million current US$)	89 239	141 209	90 615[e,c]
GDP growth rate (annual %, const. 2005 prices)	3.1	4.1	- 9.9[e,c]
GDP per capita (current US$)	1 907.0	3 093.5	2 021.6[e,c]
Economy: Agriculture (% of GVA)[f]	10.0	8.4	14.0[e,c]
Economy: Industry (% of GVA)[f]	34.1	29.0	26.3[e,c]
Economy: Services and other activity (% of GVA)[f]	55.8	62.7	59.7[e,c]
Employment: Agriculture (% of employed)[g]	27.9	20.3	15.7
Employment: Industry (% of employed)[g]	22.7	25.7	24.6
Employment: Services (% of employed)[g]	49.4	54.0	59.7
Unemployment (% of labour force)	7.2	8.1	8.8[g]
Labour force participation (female/male pop. %)[g]	52.2 / 65.6	52.4 / 65.9	52.3 / 67.5
CPI: Consumer Price Index (2000=100)	147	287[h]	311[i]
Agricultural production index (2004-2006=100)	100	106	137[i]
Food production index (2004-2006=100)	100	106	137[i]
Index of industrial production (2005=100)[k]	100	94	99[l]
International trade: Exports (million US$)	34 228	51 430	36 369[d]
International trade: Imports (million US$)	36 122	60 737	39 184[d]
International trade: Balance (million US$)	- 1 894	- 9 307	- 2 815[d]
Balance of payments, current account (million US$)	2 534[m]	- 3 016	- 189[c]

Major trading partners						2016
Export partners (% of exports)	Russian Federation	12.7	Turkey	7.3	China	6.3
Import partners (% of imports)	Russian Federation	20.0	Germany	10.6	China	10.1

Social indicators	2005	2010	2017
Population growth rate (average annual %)[a,n]	- 0.8	- 0.5	- 0.5[c]
Urban population (% of total population)	67.8	68.7	69.7[c]
Urban population growth rate (average annual %)[n]	- 0.6	- 0.2	- 0.3[c]
Fertility rate, total (live births per woman)[a,n]	1.1	1.4	1.5[c]
Life expectancy at birth (females/males, years)[a,n]	73.4 / 61.8	73.8 / 62.2	76.0 / 66.1[c]
Population age distribution (0-14 and 60+ years, %)[a]	14.6 / 20.4	14.1 / 21.0	15.5 / 23.2[b]
International migrant stock (000/% of total pop.)	5 050.3 / 10.8	4 818.8 / 10.6	4 834.9 / 10.8[c]
Refugees and others of concern to UNHCR (000)	76.9[o]	46.4[o]	1 644.8[d]
Infant mortality rate (per 1 000 live births)[a,n]	14.8	12.6	8.8[c]
Health: Total expenditure (% of GDP)	6.4	7.8	7.1[e,j]
Health: Physicians (per 1 000 pop.)	...	3.5	3.0[i]
Education: Government expenditure (% of GDP)	6.1	7.3[p]	5.9[i]
Education: Primary gross enrol. ratio (f/m per 100 pop.)	105.7 / 106.1	103.1 / 102.4	105.1 / 102.8[i]
Education: Secondary gross enrol. ratio (f/m per 100 pop.)	93.2 / 100.6[q]	93.9 / 96.2[q]	98.2 / 100.2[i]
Education: Tertiary gross enrol. ratio (f/m per 100 pop.)	78.8 / 63.8	91.5 / 72.8	88.4 / 76.5[i]
Intentional homicide rate (per 100 000 pop.)	6.5	4.4	...
Seats held by women in national parliaments (%)	5.3	8.0	12.3

Environment and infrastructure indicators	2005	2010	2017
Mobile-cellular subscriptions (per 100 inhabitants)	63.7	117.1	144.0[c]
Individuals using the Internet (per 100 inhabitants)	3.7[g,q,r]	23.3	49.3[g,c]
Research & Development expenditure (% of GDP)	1.2	0.8	0.7[s,j]
Threatened species (number)	55[t]	61	102
Forested area (% of land area)	16.5	16.5	16.6[g,j]
CO2 emission estimates (million tons/tons per capita)	333.9 / 7.1	304.6 / 6.7	227.3 / 5.1[i]
Energy production, primary (Petajoules)	3 328	3 238	3 203[i]
Energy supply per capita (Gigajoules)	125	120	98[i]
Tourist/visitor arrivals at national borders (000)	17 631	21 203	12 428[c]
Important sites for terrestrial biodiversity protected (%)	23.3	23.3	23.3
Pop. using improved drinking water (urban/rural, %)	98.4 / 94.6	97.0 / 96.2	95.5 / 97.8[c]
Pop. using improved sanitation facilities (urban/rural, %)	97.2 / 90.7	97.3 / 91.8	97.4 / 92.6[c]
Net Official Development Assist. received (% of GNI)	0.48	0.49	1.63[c]

a Including Crimea. **b** Projected estimate (medium fertility variant). **c** 2015. **d** 2016. **e** Excludes the temporarily occupied territory of the Autonomous Republic of Crimea and Sevastopol. **f** Data classified according to ISIC Rev. 4. **g** Estimate. **h** Series linked to former series. **i** 2013. **j** 2014. **k** Data classified according to ISIC Rev. 3. **l** 2012. **m** Break in the time series. **n** Data refers to a 5-year period preceding the reference year. **o** Data as at the end of December. **p** 2009. **q** Users in the last month. **r** Population aged 15 to 59 years. **s** Excluding data from some regions, provinces or states. **t** 2004.

United Arab Emirates

Region	Western Asia	UN membership date	09 December 1971
Population (000, 2017)	9 400[a]	Surface area (km2)	83 600[b]
Pop. density (per km2, 2017)	112.4[a]	Sex ratio (m per 100 f, 2017)	262.4[a]
Capital city	Abu Dhabi	National currency	UAE Dirham (AED)[c]
Capital city pop. (000)	1 144.9[b]	Exchange rate (per US$)	3.7[d]

Economic indicators

	2005	2010	2017
GDP: Gross domestic product (million current US$)	180 617	286 185	370 296[b]
GDP growth rate (annual %, const. 2005 prices)	4.9	1.6	3.8[b]
GDP per capita (current US$)	40 298.6	34 358.3	40 438.8[b]
Economy: Agriculture (% of GVA)[e]	1.4	0.8	0.7[b]
Economy: Industry (% of GVA)[e]	53.8	52.4	44.9[b]
Economy: Services and other activity (% of GVA)[e]	44.8	46.8	54.4[b]
Employment: Agriculture (% of employed)[f]	4.9	3.8	3.5
Employment: Industry (% of employed)[f]	40.1	23.1	21.1
Employment: Services (% of employed)[f]	54.9	73.1	75.4
Unemployment (% of labour force)	3.1	4.2[f]	3.7[f]
Labour force participation (female/male pop. %)[f]	37.1 / 91.2	42.4 / 91.3	41.7 / 90.8
Agricultural production index (2004-2006=100)	105	112	70[g]
Food production index (2004-2006=100)	105	112	70[g]
International trade: Exports (million US$)	115 453	198 362	195 613[d]
International trade: Imports (million US$)	80 814	187 001	201 908[d]
International trade: Balance (million US$)	34 639	11 361	- 6 296[d]

Major trading partners

						2016
Export partners (% of exports)	Areas nes[h]	53.3	Asia nes[i]	14.0	Iran (Islamic Rep.)	3.2
Import partners (% of imports)	Areas nes[h]	35.8	China	8.0	United States	6.7

Social indicators

	2005	2010	2017
Population growth rate (average annual %)[j]	7.5	11.8	2.0[b]
Urban population (% of total population)	82.3	84.1	85.5[b]
Urban population growth rate (average annual %)[j]	6.8	14.6	2.9[b]
Fertility rate, total (live births per woman)[j]	2.4	2.0	1.8[b]
Life expectancy at birth (females/males, years)[j]	76.3 / 74.1	77.3 / 75.2	78.2 / 76.0[b]
Population age distribution (0-14 and 60+ years, %)	18.4 / 1.7	13.4 / 1.5	13.9 / 2.4[a]
International migrant stock (000/% of total pop.)[k,l]	3 281.0 / 73.2	7 316.6 / 87.8	8 095.1 / 88.4[b]
Refugees and others of concern to UNHCR (000)	0.2[m]	0.6[m]	1.3[d]
Infant mortality rate (per 1 000 live births)[j]	9.2	6.9	6.2[b]
Health: Total expenditure (% of GDP)	2.3	3.9	3.6[g]
Health: Physicians (per 1 000 pop.)	1.6	1.5	1.6[g]
Education: Primary gross enrol. ratio (f/m per 100 pop.)	105.2 / 105.8	101.5 / 98.1	116.0 / 116.7[b]
Intentional homicide rate (per 100 000 pop.)	...	0.8	0.7[b]
Seats held by women in national parliaments (%)	0.0	22.5	20.0

Environment and infrastructure indicators

	2005	2010	2017
Mobile-cellular subscriptions (per 100 inhabitants)	109.3	129.4	187.4[b]
Individuals using the Internet (per 100 inhabitants)	40.0[f]	68.0	91.2[f,b]
Research & Development expenditure (% of GDP)	...	...	0.7[g]
Threatened species (number)	23[n]	48	56
Forested area (% of land area)[f]	3.7	3.8	3.8[g]
CO2 emission estimates (million tons/tons per capita)	116.1 / 28.5	160.8 / 19.3	211.4 / 23.2[g]
Energy production, primary (Petajoules)	7 293	7 541	8 642[g]
Energy supply per capita (Gigajoules)	453	311	366[g]
Tourist/visitor arrivals at national borders (000)	7 126[o]	...	...
Important sites for terrestrial biodiversity protected (%)	0.0	14.8	29.9
Pop. using improved drinking water (urban/rural, %)	99.6 / 100.0	99.6 / 100.0	99.6 / 100.0[b]
Pop. using improved sanitation facilities (urban/rural, %)	98.0 / 95.2	98.0 / 95.2	98.0 / 95.2[b]
Net Official Development Assist. disbursed (% of GNI)	...	0.14	1.12[p,d]

a Projected estimate (medium fertility variant). **b** 2015. **c** United Arab Emirates Dirham. **d** 2016. **e** At producers' prices. **f** Estimate. **g** 2014. **h** Areas not elsewhere specified. **i** Asia not elsewhere specified. **j** Data refers to a 5-year period preceding the reference year. **k** Refers to foreign citizens. **l** Including refugees. **m** Data as at the end of December. **n** 2004. **o** Arrivals in hotels only. Including domestic tourism and nationals of the country residing abroad. **p** Provisional data.

United Kingdom

Region	Northern Europe	UN membership date	24 October 1945
Population (000, 2017)	66 182 [a]	Surface area (km2)	242 495 [b]
Pop. density (per km2, 2017)	273.6 [a]	Sex ratio (m per 100 f, 2017)	97.4 [a]
Capital city	London	National currency	Pound Sterling (GBP)
Capital city pop. (000)	10 313.3 [b]	Exchange rate (per US$)	0.8 [c]

Economic indicators	2005	2010	2017
GDP: Gross domestic product (million current US$)	2 508 111	2 429 680	2 858 003 [b]
GDP growth rate (annual %, const. 2005 prices)	3.0	1.9	2.2 [b]
GDP per capita (current US$)	41 656.0	38 740.6	44 162.4 [b]
Economy: Agriculture (% of GVA) [d]	0.6	0.7	0.7 [b]
Economy: Industry (% of GVA) [d]	22.0	20.1	19.4 [b]
Economy: Services and other activity (% of GVA) [d]	77.3	79.2	79.9 [b]
Employment: Agriculture (% of employed) [e]	1.4	1.2	1.2
Employment: Industry (% of employed) [e]	22.2	19.3	18.4
Employment: Services (% of employed) [e]	76.4	79.5	80.4
Unemployment (% of labour force)	4.8	7.8	5.0 [e]
Labour force participation (female/male pop. %) [e]	54.9 / 69.3	55.8 / 68.7	57.0 / 68.6
CPI: Consumer Price Index (2000=100)	113	131	150 [f]
Agricultural production index (2004-2006=100)	100	102	108 [f]
Food production index (2004-2006=100)	100	102	108 [f]
Index of industrial production (2005=100)	100	92	90 [f]
International trade: Exports (million US$)	392 744	422 014	415 856 [c]
International trade: Imports (million US$)	528 461	627 618	635 570 [c]
International trade: Balance (million US$)	- 135 717	- 205 603	- 219 713 [c]
Balance of payments, current account (million US$)	- 30 220	- 66 842	- 122 571 [b]

Major trading partners						2016
Export partners (% of exports)	United States	15.0	Germany	10.6	France	6.4
Import partners (% of imports)	Germany	14.0	United States	9.7	China	9.3

Social indicators	2005	2010	2017
Population growth rate (average annual %) [g]	0.4	1.0	0.6 [b]
Urban population (% of total population)	79.9	81.3	82.6 [b]
Urban population growth rate (average annual %) [g]	0.8	0.9	0.9 [b]
Fertility rate, total (live births per woman) [g]	1.7	1.9	1.9 [b]
Life expectancy at birth (females/males, years) [g]	80.6 / 76.1	81.8 / 77.5	82.8 / 79.0 [b]
Population age distribution (0-14 and 60+ years, %)	18.0 / 21.2	17.5 / 22.7	17.7 / 23.9 [a]
International migrant stock (000/% of total pop.)	5 926.2 / 9.8	7 604.6 / 12.1	8 543.1 / 13.2 [b]
Refugees and others of concern to UNHCR (000)	316.6 [h]	253.3 [h]	151.7 [c]
Infant mortality rate (per 1 000 live births) [g]	5.3	4.8	4.1 [b]
Health: Total expenditure (% of GDP)	8.2	9.5	9.1 [f]
Health: Physicians (per 1 000 pop.)	...	2.7	2.8 [b]
Education: Government expenditure (% of GDP)	5.0	5.8	5.7 [b]
Education: Primary gross enrol. ratio (f/m per 100 pop.)	106.2 / 106.3	105.6 / 106.1	108.1 / 108.4 [f]
Education: Secondary gross enrol. ratio (f/m per 100 pop.)	107.0 / 103.9	101.7 / 102.1	130.4 / 125.3 [f]
Education: Tertiary gross enrol. ratio (f/m per 100 pop.)	68.9 / 49.5	68.1 / 50.4	64.1 / 49.0 [f]
Intentional homicide rate (per 100 000 pop.)	1.5	1.2	0.9 [f]
Seats held by women in national parliaments (%)	18.1	19.5	30.0

Environment and infrastructure indicators	2005	2010	2017
Mobile-cellular subscriptions (per 100 inhabitants)	108.6	123.6	125.8 [b]
Individuals using the Internet (per 100 inhabitants) [i]	70.0	85.0	92.0 [b]
Research & Development expenditure (% of GDP)	1.6	1.7 [e]	1.7 [e,f]
Threatened species (number)	55 [j]	73	102
Forested area (% of land area)	12.5	12.6	12.9 [e,f]
CO2 emission estimates (million tons/tons per capita)	542.6 / 9.0	493.2 / 7.8	419.8 / 6.5 [f]
Energy production, primary (Petajoules) [k]	8 483	6 217	4 482 [f]
Energy supply per capita (Gigajoules) [k]	153	135	116 [f]
Tourist/visitor arrivals at national borders (000)	28 039	28 295	34 436 [b]
Important sites for terrestrial biodiversity protected (%)	77.6	80.0	80.2
Pop. using improved drinking water (urban/rural, %)	100.0 / 100.0	100.0 / 100.0	100.0 / 100.0 [b]
Pop. using improved sanitation facilities (urban/rural, %)	99.1 / 99.6	99.1 / 99.6	99.1 / 99.6 [b]
Net Official Development Assist. disbursed (% of GNI) [l]	0.47	0.57	0.70 [m,c]

a Projected estimate (medium fertility variant). **b** 2015. **c** 2016. **d** Data classified according to ISIC Rev. 4. **e** Estimate. **f** 2014. **g** Data refers to a 5-year period preceding the reference year. **h** Data as at the end of December. **i** Population aged 16 to 74 years. **j** 2004. **k** Shipments of coal and oil to Jersey, Guernsey and the Isle of Man from the United Kingdom are not classed as exports. Supplies of coal and oil to these islands are, therefore, included as part of UK supply. Exports of natural gas to the Isle of Man included with the exports to Ireland. **l** Development Assistance Committee member (OECD). **m** Provisional data.

United Republic of Tanzania

Region	Eastern Africa	UN membership date	14 December 1961
Population (000, 2017)	57 310 [a,b]	Surface area (km2)	947 303 [c]
Pop. density (per km2, 2017)	64.7 [a,b]	Sex ratio (m per 100 f, 2017)	97.8 [a,b]
Capital city	Dodoma	National currency	Tanzanian Shilling (TZS)
Capital city pop. (000)	227.8 [d]	Exchange rate (per US$)	2 172.6 [e]

Economic indicators

	2005	2010	2017
GDP: Gross domestic product (million current US$) [f]	18 072	31 105	45 628 [c]
GDP growth rate (annual %, const. 2005 prices) [f]	7.4	6.4	7.0 [c]
GDP per capita (current US$) [f]	475.7	700.9	877.3 [c]
Economy: Agriculture (% of GVA) [f,g]	30.1	31.7	31.1 [c]
Economy: Industry (% of GVA) [f,g]	20.8	21.5	26.1 [c]
Economy: Services and other activity (% of GVA) [f,g]	49.1	46.8	42.9 [c]
Employment: Agriculture (% of employed) [h]	75.5	72.2	66.9
Employment: Industry (% of employed) [h]	4.2	5.5	6.4
Employment: Services (% of employed) [h]	20.3	22.3	26.7
Unemployment (% of labour force) [h]	3.1	2.9	2.7
Labour force participation (female/male pop. %) [h]	88.7 / 90.6	83.6 / 86.0	73.9 / 83.2
CPI: Consumer Price Index (2000=100) [i]	128	192 [j]	287 [d]
Agricultural production index (2004-2006=100)	98	128	176 [d]
Food production index (2004-2006=100)	97	130	180 [d]
International trade: Exports (million US$)	1 672	4 051	4 742 [e]
International trade: Imports (million US$)	3 247	8 013	7 876 [e]
International trade: Balance (million US$)	- 1 575	- 3 962	- 3 134 [e]
Balance of payments, current account (million US$)	- 1 570	- 2 211 [k]	- 3 312 [c]

Major trading partners

						2016
Export partners (% of exports)	Switzerland	16.2	India	14.8	South Africa	13.3
Import partners (% of imports)	China	20.8	India	18.1	United Arab Emirates	7.5

Social indicators

	2005	2010	2017
Population growth rate (average annual %) [b,l]	2.8	3.1	3.1 [c]
Urban population (% of total population) [b]	24.8	28.1	31.6 [c]
Urban population growth rate (average annual %) [b,l]	4.8	5.4	5.4 [c]
Fertility rate, total (live births per woman) [b,l]	5.7	5.6	5.2 [c]
Life expectancy at birth (females/males, years) [b,l]	55.4 / 52.0	60.1 / 57.5	64.8 / 60.8 [c]
Population age distribution (0-14 and 60+ years, %) [b]	45.3 / 4.6	45.3 / 4.7	44.9 / 4.7 [a]
International migrant stock (000/% of total pop.) [m]	770.8 / 2.0	308.6 / 0.7	261.2 / 0.5 [c]
Refugees and others of concern to UNHCR (000)	630.6 [n]	273.8 [n]	402.1 [e]
Infant mortality rate (per 1 000 live births) [b,l]	67.1	52.4	44.0 [c]
Health: Total expenditure (% of GDP)	4.7	5.3	5.6 [d]
Health: Physicians (per 1 000 pop.)	~0.0 [o]	~0.0 [p]	~0.0 [q]
Education: Government expenditure (% of GDP)	4.6	4.6	3.5 [d]
Education: Primary gross enrol. ratio (f/m per 100 pop.)	101.0 / 106.2	99.3 / 98.6	82.9 / 80.5 [c]
Education: Secondary gross enrol. ratio (f/m per 100 pop.)	... / ...	27.5 / 34.8	30.8 / 33.7 [r]
Education: Tertiary gross enrol. ratio (f/m per 100 pop.)	0.9 / 2.0 [h]	1.9 / 2.4	2.5 / 4.9 [r]
Intentional homicide rate (per 100 000 pop.)	...	8.5	7.0 [c]
Seats held by women in national parliaments (%)	21.4	30.7	36.4

Environment and infrastructure indicators

	2005	2010	2017
Mobile-cellular subscriptions (per 100 inhabitants)	7.6	46.7	75.9 [c]
Individuals using the Internet (per 100 inhabitants) [h]	1.1	2.9	5.4 [c]
Research & Development expenditure (% of GDP) [t]	...	0.4 [s]	0.5 [r]
Threatened species (number)	416 [u]	691	1 082
Forested area (% of land area)	56.4	54.1 [h]	52.4 [h,d]
CO2 emission estimates (million tons/tons per capita)	5.5 / 0.1	7.1 / 0.1	11.6 / 0.2 [d]
Energy production, primary (Petajoules)	665	789	935 [d]
Energy supply per capita (Gigajoules)	19	19	20 [d]
Tourist/visitor arrivals at national borders (000)	590	754	1 104 [c]
Important sites for terrestrial biodiversity protected (%)	50.9	53.6	53.6
Pop. using improved drinking water (urban/rural, %)	83.0 / 45.4	80.1 / 45.5	77.2 / 45.5 [c]
Pop. using improved sanitation facilities (urban/rural, %)	21.3 / 7.6	26.3 / 7.9	31.3 / 8.3 [c]
Net Official Development Assist. received (% of GNI)	9.00	9.53	5.85 [c]

a Projected estimate (medium fertility variant). b Including Zanzibar. c 2015. d 2014. e 2016. f Tanzania mainland only. g Data classified according to ISIC Rev. 4. h Estimate. i Excluding Zanzibar. j Series linked to former series. k Break in the time series. l Data refers to a 5-year period preceding the reference year. m Including refugees. n Data as at the end of December. o 2002. p 2006. q 2012. r 2013. s Partial data. t Excluding business enterprise. u 2004.

United States of America

Region	Northern America	UN membership date	24 October 1945
Population (000, 2017)	324 460[a]	Surface area (km2)	9 833 517[b]
Pop. density (per km2, 2017)	35.5[a]	Sex ratio (m per 100 f, 2017)	98.0[a]
Capital city	Washington, D.C.	National currency	US Dollar (USD)
Capital city pop. (000)	4 955.1[b]		

Economic indicators	2005	2010	2017
GDP: Gross domestic product (million current US$)	13 093 726	14 964 372	18 036 648[b]
GDP growth rate (annual %, const. 2005 prices)	3.3	2.5	2.6[b]
GDP per capita (current US$)	44 214.7	48 291.5	56 053.8[b]
Economy: Agriculture (% of GVA)[c,d]	1.0	1.1	1.0[b]
Economy: Industry (% of GVA)[c,d]	21.5	20.2	19.7[b]
Economy: Services and other activity (% of GVA)[c,d]	77.5	78.8	79.3[b]
Employment: Agriculture (% of employed)[e]	1.6	1.6	1.5
Employment: Industry (% of employed)[e]	20.2	17.8	17.2
Employment: Services (% of employed)[e]	78.2	80.6	81.3
Unemployment (% of labour force)	5.1	9.6	4.9[e]
Labour force participation (female/male pop. %)[e]	58.3 / 72.2	57.6 / 70.0	55.7 / 68.1
CPI: Consumer Price Index (2000=100)[f]	113	127	139[g]
Agricultural production index (2004-2006=100)	100	106	119[g]
Food production index (2004-2006=100)	100	107	113[g]
Index of industrial production (2005=100)	100	96[h]	108[h,g]
International trade: Exports (million US$)[i]	904 339	1 278 099	1 453 167[j]
International trade: Imports (million US$)[i]	1 732 321	1 968 260	2 249 661[j]
International trade: Balance (million US$)[i]	- 827 981	- 690 161	- 796 494[j]
Balance of payments, current account (million US$)	- 745 445	- 441 963	- 462 961[b]

Major trading partners						2016
Export partners (% of exports)	Canada	18.3	Mexico	15.9	China	8.0
Import partners (% of imports)	China	21.4	Mexico	13.2	Canada	12.6

Social indicators	2005	2010	2017
Population growth rate (average annual %)[k]	0.9	0.9	0.7[b]
Urban population (% of total population)	79.9	80.8	81.6[b]
Urban population growth rate (average annual %)[k]	1.2	1.1	1.0[b]
Fertility rate, total (live births per woman)[k]	2.0	2.0	1.9[b]
Life expectancy at birth (females/males, years)[k]	79.7 / 74.5	80.6 / 75.6	81.2 / 76.5[b]
Population age distribution (0-14 and 60+ years, %)	20.9 / 16.7	20.2 / 18.4	18.9 / 21.5[a]
International migrant stock (000/% of total pop.)	39 258.3 / 13.3	44 183.6 / 14.3	46 627.1 / 14.5[b]
Refugees and others of concern to UNHCR (000)	549.2[l]	270.9[l]	616.5[j]
Infant mortality rate (per 1 000 live births)[k]	7.0	6.8	6.0[b]
Health: Total expenditure (% of GDP)	15.2	17.0	17.1[g]
Health: Physicians (per 1 000 pop.)	2.7[m]	2.4	2.6[n]
Education: Government expenditure (% of GDP)	5.1	5.4	5.4[g]
Education: Primary gross enrol. ratio (f/m per 100 pop.)	100.3 / 101.1	100.2 / 101.0	100.0 / 100.3[b]
Education: Secondary gross enrol. ratio (f/m per 100 pop.)	97.1 / 94.4	95.2 / 93.5	98.5 / 96.7[g]
Education: Tertiary gross enrol. ratio (f/m per 100 pop.)	96.8 / 68.2	110.7 / 78.6	99.6 / 72.8[b]
Intentional homicide rate (per 100 000 pop.)	5.6	4.8	4.9[b]
Seats held by women in national parliaments (%)	14.9	16.8	19.1

Environment and infrastructure indicators	2005	2010	2017
Mobile-cellular subscriptions (per 100 inhabitants)	68.3	91.3	117.6[b]
Individuals using the Internet (per 100 inhabitants)	68.0[e]	71.7[o]	74.6[o,b]
Research & Development expenditure (% of GDP)[p]	2.5	2.7	2.7[e,n]
Threatened species (number)	1 143[m]	1 152	1 513
Forested area (% of land area)	33.3	33.7	33.9[e,g]
CO2 emission estimates (million tons/tons per capita)[q]	5 789.7 / 19.3	5 395.5 / 17.2	5 254.3 / 16.2[g]
Energy production, primary (Petajoules)[r]	68 344	71 997	83 887[g]
Energy supply per capita (Gigajoules)[r]	326	297	289[g]
Tourist/visitor arrivals at national borders (000)	49 206	60 010	77 510[b]
Important sites for terrestrial biodiversity protected (%)	26.7	30.1	31.2
Pop. using improved drinking water (urban/rural, %)	99.5 / 96.7	99.4 / 97.6	99.4 / 98.2[b]
Pop. using improved sanitation facilities (urban/rural, %)	99.9 / 99.6	100.0 / 99.9	100.0 / 100.0[b]
Net Official Development Assist. disbursed (% of GNI)[s]	0.0	0.20	0.18[t,j]

a Projected estimate (medium fertility variant). b 2015. c Data classified according to ISIC Rev. 4. d Includes taxes less subsidies on production and imports. e Estimate. f All urban consumers. g 2014. h Excluding water and waste management. i Including the trade with the U.S. Virgin Islands and Puerto Rico but excluding with Guam and American Samoa. Including non-monetary gold imports and exports. j 2016. k Data refers to a 5-year period preceding the reference year. l Data as at the end of December. m 2004. n 2013. o Population aged 3 years and over. p Excluding most or all capital expenditures. q Including overseas territories. r Oil and coal trade statistics include overseas territories. s Development Assistance Committee member (OECD) t Provisional data.

United States Virgin Islands

Region	Caribbean	Population (000, 2017)	105[a]	
Surface area (km2)	347[b]	Pop. density (per km2, 2017)	299.7[a]	
Sex ratio (m per 100 f, 2017)	91.1[a]	Capital city	Charlotte Amalie	
National currency	US Dollar (USD)	Capital city pop. (000)	51.6[c]	

Economic indicators	2005	2010	2017
Employment: Agriculture (% of employed)[d]	10.1	9.7	10.9
Employment: Industry (% of employed)[d]	23.9	23.9	24.0
Employment: Services (% of employed)[d]	66.1	66.4	65.2
Unemployment (% of labour force)[d]	9.3	9.0	9.0
Labour force participation (female/male pop. %)[d]	54.9 / 76.1	55.2 / 73.9	52.5 / 70.7
Agricultural production index (2004-2006=100)	99	108	109[c]
Food production index (2004-2006=100)	99	108	109[c]

Social indicators	2005	2010	2017
Population growth rate (average annual %)[e]	- 0.2	- 0.3	- 0.2[b]
Urban population (% of total population)	93.7	94.6	95.3[b]
Urban population growth rate (average annual %)[e]	0.1	- 0.1	0.3[b]
Fertility rate, total (live births per woman)[e]	2.1	2.4	2.3[b]
Life expectancy at birth (females/males, years)[e]	79.5 / 74.9	80.3 / 75.5	81.5 / 76.7[b]
Population age distribution (0-14 and 60+ years, %)	22.4 / 16.6	20.8 / 20.4	20.1 / 25.3[a]
International migrant stock (000/% of total pop.)	56.6 / 52.6	56.7 / 53.3	56.7 / 53.4[b]
Infant mortality rate (per 1 000 live births)[e]	11.6	10.7	9.3[b]
Intentional homicide rate (per 100 000 pop.)	32.5	52.6	...

Environment and infrastructure indicators	2005	2010	2017
Mobile-cellular subscriptions (per 100 inhabitants)	74.5[d]	...	...
Individuals using the Internet (per 100 inhabitants)[d]	27.3	31.2	54.8[b]
Threatened species (number)	31[f]	33	58
Forested area (% of land area)	53.5	51.9	50.6[d,c]
Tourist/visitor arrivals at national borders (000)	594	572	637[b]
Important sites for terrestrial biodiversity protected (%)	32.8	32.8	39.4
Pop. using improved drinking water (urban/rural, %)	100.0 / 100.0	100.0 / 100.0	100.0 / 100.0[b]
Pop. using improved sanitation facilities (urban/rural, %)	96.4 / 96.4	96.4 / 96.4	96.4 / 96.4[b]

a Projected estimate (medium fertility variant). b 2015. c 2014. d Estimate. e Data refers to a 5-year period preceding the reference year. f 2004.

Uruguay

Region	South America	UN membership date	18 December 1945
Population (000, 2017)	3 457[a]	Surface area (km2)	173 626[b]
Pop. density (per km2, 2017)	19.8[a]	Sex ratio (m per 100 f, 2017)	93.5[a]
Capital city	Montevideo	National currency	Peso Uruguayo (UYU)
Capital city pop. (000)	1 706.8[b]	Exchange rate (per US$)	29.3[c]

Economic indicators	2005	2010	2017
GDP: Gross domestic product (million current US$)	17 363	40 287	53 442[b]
GDP growth rate (annual %, const. 2005 prices)	7.5	7.8	1.0[b]
GDP per capita (current US$)	5 221.0	11 939.0	15 573.8[b]
Economy: Agriculture (% of GVA)	9.8	8.0	6.8[b]
Economy: Industry (% of GVA)	26.6	27.3	28.0[b]
Economy: Services and other activity (% of GVA)	63.6	64.7	65.2[b]
Employment: Agriculture (% of employed)[d]	11.1	11.6	8.7
Employment: Industry (% of employed)[d]	23.1	21.4	20.5
Employment: Services (% of employed)[d]	65.8	67.0	70.8
Unemployment (% of labour force)	12.2	6.8	8.8[d]
Labour force participation (female/male pop. %)[d]	52.7 / 74.1	55.1 / 76.7	55.6 / 76.3
CPI: Consumer Price Index (2000=100)[e]	162	230	320[f]
Agricultural production index (2004-2006=100)	101	119	129[f]
Food production index (2004-2006=100)	101	120	130[f]
International trade: Exports (million US$)	3 422	6 724	6 964[c]
International trade: Imports (million US$)	3 879	8 622	8 137[c]
International trade: Balance (million US$)	- 457	- 1 898	- 1 173[c]
Balance of payments, current account (million US$)	24	- 756	- 1 141[b]

Major trading partners					2016
Export partners (% of exports)	China	17.8	Brazil	17.5	Free zones 9.6
Import partners (% of imports)	China	18.8	Brazil	18.0	Argentina 13.3

Social indicators	2005	2010	2017
Population growth rate (average annual %)[g]	~0.0	0.3	0.3[b]
Urban population (% of total population)	93.3	94.4	95.3[b]
Urban population growth rate (average annual %)[g]	0.3	0.5	0.5[b]
Fertility rate, total (live births per woman)[g]	2.2	2.1	2.0[b]
Life expectancy at birth (females/males, years)[g]	78.9 / 71.6	79.7 / 72.5	80.4 / 73.2[b]
Population age distribution (0-14 and 60+ years, %)	23.8 / 17.9	22.5 / 18.4	21.1 / 19.5[a]
International migrant stock (000/% of total pop.)	82.3 / 2.5	76.3 / 2.3	71.8 / 2.1[b]
Refugees and others of concern to UNHCR (000)	0.1[h]	0.2[h]	0.5[c]
Infant mortality rate (per 1 000 live births)[g]	14.4	13.4	12.7[b]
Health: Total expenditure (% of GDP)[i]	11.1	8.6	8.6[f]
Health: Physicians (per 1 000 pop.)	3.7[i]	3.9[k]	
Education: Government expenditure (% of GDP)	2.7	2.9[l]	4.4[m]
Education: Primary gross enrol. ratio (f/m per 100 pop.)	112.4 / 115.3	110.2 / 113.9	107.3 / 109.8[f]
Education: Secondary gross enrol. ratio (f/m per 100 pop.)	108.5 / 94.2	96.2 / 84.6	100.0 / 90.3[f]
Education: Tertiary gross enrol. ratio (f/m per 100 pop.)	57.9 / 33.2	80.3 / 46.5	... / ...
Intentional homicide rate (per 100 000 pop.)	5.6	6.1	8.4[b]
Seats held by women in national parliaments (%)	12.1	14.1	20.2

Environment and infrastructure indicators	2005	2010	2017
Mobile-cellular subscriptions (per 100 inhabitants)	34.7	131.6[n]	160.2[n,b]
Individuals using the Internet (per 100 inhabitants)	20.1	46.4[o]	64.6[o,b]
Research & Development expenditure (% of GDP)	0.2[j]	0.3	0.3[f]
Threatened species (number)	50[p]	80	106
Forested area (% of land area)	8.7	9.9	10.4[d,f]
CO2 emission estimates (million tons/tons per capita)	5.8 / 1.7	6.4 / 1.9	6.7 / 2.0[f]
Energy production, primary (Petajoules)	45	89	113[f]
Energy supply per capita (Gigajoules)	38	51	58[f]
Tourist/visitor arrivals at national borders (000)	1 808	2 353	2 773[b]
Important sites for terrestrial biodiversity protected (%)	10.4	20.7	20.8
Pop. using improved drinking water (urban/rural, %)	99.0 / 82.6	99.6 / 88.3	100.0 / 93.9[b]
Pop. using improved sanitation facilities (urban/rural, %)	95.0 / 87.1	95.8 / 89.8	96.6 / 92.6[b]
Net Official Development Assist. received (% of GNI)	0.10	0.12	0.04[b]

a Projected estimate (medium fertility variant). b 2015. c 2016. d Estimate. e Montevideo f 2014. g Data refers to a 5-year period preceding the reference year. h Data as at the end of December. i Data revision. j 2002. k 2008. l 2006. m 2011. n Includes data-only subscriptions. o Population aged 6 years and over. p 2004.

Uzbekistan

Region	Central Asia	UN membership date	02 March 1992
Population (000, 2017)	31 911 [a]	Surface area (km2)	448 969 [b]
Pop. density (per km2, 2017)	75.0 [a]	Sex ratio (m per 100 f, 2017)	99.4 [a]
Capital city	Tashkent	National currency	Uzbekistan Sum (UZS)
Capital city pop. (000)	2 251.2 [b]	Exchange rate (per US$)	3 218.0 [c,d]

Economic indicators

	2005	2010	2017
GDP: Gross domestic product (million current US$)	14 396	39 526	69 004 [b]
GDP growth rate (annual %, const. 2005 prices)	7.0	8.5	6.8 [b]
GDP per capita (current US$)	555.4	1 424.9	2 308.3 [b]
Economy: Agriculture (% of GVA)	29.5	19.8	19.2 [b]
Economy: Industry (% of GVA)	29.1	33.4	32.9 [b]
Economy: Services and other activity (% of GVA)	41.4	46.8	47.9 [b]
Employment: Agriculture (% of employed) [e]	39.3	32.6	29.0
Employment: Industry (% of employed) [e]	20.9	23.0	23.9
Employment: Services (% of employed) [e]	39.7	44.4	47.1
Unemployment (% of labour force) [e]	9.3	9.3	8.9
Labour force participation (female/male pop. %) [e]	47.2 / 72.1	47.6 / 74.4	48.5 / 76.6
Agricultural production index (2004-2006=100)	100	127	158 [f]
Food production index (2004-2006=100)	99	135	174 [f]
Index of industrial production (2005=100) [g]	100	165	175 [h]
International trade: Exports (million US$)	4 458	11 587	27 947 [d]
International trade: Imports (million US$)	3 657	8 381	25 652 [d]
International trade: Balance (million US$)	801	3 206	2 295 [d]

Major trading partners

						2016
Export partners (% of exports)	Switzerland	38.1	China	21.4	Russian Federation	10.1
Import partners (% of imports)	China	21.0	Russian Federation	20.3	Republic of Korea	9.6

Social indicators

	2005	2010	2017
Population growth rate (average annual %) [i]	1.3	1.5	1.6 [b]
Urban population (% of total population)	36.7	36.2	36.4 [b]
Urban population growth rate (average annual %) [i]	0.5	1.0	1.4 [b]
Fertility rate, total (live births per woman) [i]	2.5	2.5	2.4 [b]
Life expectancy at birth (females/males, years) [i]	71.0 / 64.5	72.2 / 66.1	73.5 / 68.1 [b]
Population age distribution (0-14 and 60+ years, %)	32.6 / 6.6	29.1 / 6.2	28.0 / 7.6 [a]
International migrant stock (000/% of total pop.)	1 329.3 / 5.1	1 220.1 / 4.4	1 170.9 / 3.9 [b]
Refugees and others of concern to UNHCR (000)	44.5 [j]	0.3 [j]	86.7 [d]
Infant mortality rate (per 1 000 live births) [i]	49.5	40.7	31.3 [b]
Health: Total expenditure (% of GDP)	5.1	5.3	5.8 [f]
Health: Physicians (per 1 000 pop.)	...	2.6	2.5 [f]
Education: Primary gross enrol. ratio (f/m per 100 pop.)	102.6 / 102.7	95.8 / 97.7	103.2 / 105.6 [d]
Education: Secondary gross enrol. ratio (f/m per 100 pop.)	88.3 / 91.2	94.8 / 95.0	95.1 / 96.8 [d]
Education: Tertiary gross enrol. ratio (f/m per 100 pop.)	8.2 / 12.0	7.6 / 11.2	7.1 / 11.0 [d]
Intentional homicide rate (per 100 000 pop.)	3.6	3.2	3.0 [b]
Seats held by women in national parliaments (%)	17.5	22.0	16.0

Environment and infrastructure indicators

	2005	2010	2017
Mobile-cellular subscriptions (per 100 inhabitants)	2.8	75.4 [e]	73.3 [b]
Individuals using the Internet (per 100 inhabitants)	3.3	15.9 [e]	42.8 [e,b]
Research & Development expenditure (% of GDP)	...	...	0.2 [f]
Threatened species (number)	31 [k]	50	59
Forested area (% of land area)	7.7	7.7 [e]	7.6 [e,f]
CO2 emission estimates (million tons/tons per capita)	117.2 / 4.5	104.2 / 3.7	105.2 / 3.6 [f]
Energy production, primary (Petajoules)	2 446	2 309	2 339 [f]
Energy supply per capita (Gigajoules)	79	65	62 [f]
Tourist/visitor arrivals at national borders (000)	242	975	1 969 [l]
Important sites for terrestrial biodiversity protected (%)	11.9	16.1	16.1
Pop. using improved drinking water (urban/rural, %)	98.1 / 81.8	98.5 / 80.9	98.5 / 80.9 [b,m]
Pop. using improved sanitation facilities (urban/rural, %)	99.2 / 96.2	100.0 / 100.0	100.0 / 100.0 [b]
Net Official Development Assist. received (% of GNI)	1.18	0.58	0.66 [b]

a Projected estimate (medium fertility variant). b 2015. c UN operational exchange rate. d 2016. e Estimate. f 2014.
g Data classified according to ISIC Rev. 3. h 2011. i Data refers to a 5-year period preceding the reference year. j
Data as at the end of December. k 2004. l 2013. m 2012.

Vanuatu

Region	Melanesia	UN membership date	15 September 1981	
Population (000, 2017)	276[a]	Surface area (km2)	12 189[b]	
Pop. density (per km2, 2017)	22.7[a]	Sex ratio (m per 100 f, 2017)	102.4[a]	
Capital city	Port Vila	National currency	Vatu (VUV)	
Capital city pop. (000)	52.5[c]	Exchange rate (per US$)	112.3[d]	

Economic indicators	2005	2010	2017
GDP: Gross domestic product (million current US$)	395	701	737[b]
GDP growth rate (annual %, const. 2005 prices)	5.3	1.6	- 1.0[b]
GDP per capita (current US$)	1 886.4	2 965.8	2 783.0[b]
Economy: Agriculture (% of GVA)[e]	24.1	21.9	26.7[b]
Economy: Industry (% of GVA)[e]	8.5	13.0	8.4[b]
Economy: Services and other activity (% of GVA)[e]	67.4	65.0	64.9[b]
Employment: Agriculture (% of employed)[f]	63.3	60.9	61.4
Employment: Industry (% of employed)[f]	6.2	7.3	6.8
Employment: Services (% of employed)[f]	30.5	31.8	31.8
Unemployment (% of labour force)[f]	5.6	5.4	5.3
Labour force participation (female/male pop. %)[f]	65.3 / 81.7	61.5 / 80.7	61.7 / 80.5
CPI: Consumer Price Index (2000=100)	112	133	139[c]
Agricultural production index (2004-2006=100)	100	128	123[c]
Food production index (2004-2006=100)	100	128	122[c]
International trade: Exports (million US$)	38	46	50[d]
International trade: Imports (million US$)	149	276	416[d]
International trade: Balance (million US$)	- 111	- 230	- 366[d]
Balance of payments, current account (million US$)	- 53	- 42[g]	- 82[b]

Major trading partners						2016
Export partners (% of exports)	Mauritania	37.9	Japan	25.1	Republic of Korea	5.7
Import partners (% of imports)	China	18.4	Australia	16.8	Japan	9.9

Social indicators	2005	2010	2017
Population growth rate (average annual %)[h]	2.5	2.4	2.3[b]
Urban population (% of total population)	23.1	24.6	26.1[b]
Urban population growth rate (average annual %)[h]	3.7	3.7	3.4[b]
Fertility rate, total (live births per woman)[h]	4.1	3.6	3.4[b]
Life expectancy at birth (females/males, years)[h]	70.3 / 66.7	72.1 / 68.2	73.6 / 69.4[b]
Population age distribution (0-14 and 60+ years, %)	39.7 / 5.2	38.2 / 5.7	35.9 / 6.7[a]
International migrant stock (000/% of total pop.)	2.8 / 1.3	3.0 / 1.3	3.2 / 1.2[b]
Refugees and others of concern to UNHCR (000)	...	~0.0[i]	~0.0[b]
Infant mortality rate (per 1 000 live births)[h]	34.6	28.6	24.3[b]
Health: Total expenditure (% of GDP)	3.9	4.7	5.0[c]
Health: Physicians (per 1 000 pop.)	0.1[j]	0.1[k]	0.2[l]
Education: Government expenditure (% of GDP)	8.4[m]	5.0[n]	5.5[b]
Education: Primary gross enrol. ratio (f/m per 100 pop.)	116.1 / 119.2	121.9 / 123.0	118.7 / 120.6[b]
Education: Secondary gross enrol. ratio (f/m per 100 pop.)	39.5 / 45.8[j]	59.5 / 59.6	56.4 / 53.4[b]
Education: Tertiary gross enrol. ratio (f/m per 100 pop.)	3.5 / 5.9[f,j]	... / ...	... / ...
Intentional homicide rate (per 100 000 pop.)	2.5	2.3	2.1[b]
Seats held by women in national parliaments (%)	3.8	3.8	0.0

Environment and infrastructure indicators	2005	2010	2017
Mobile-cellular subscriptions (per 100 inhabitants)	6.1	71.9	66.2[b]
Individuals using the Internet (per 100 inhabitants)	5.1	8.0	22.4[f,b]
Threatened species (number)	29[j]	121	137
Forested area (% of land area)[f]	36.1	36.1	36.1[c]
CO2 emission estimates (million tons/tons per capita)	0.1 / 0.3	0.1 / 0.5	0.2 / 0.6[c]
Energy production, primary (Petajoules)	1	1	1[c]
Energy supply per capita (Gigajoules)	8	11	12[c]
Tourist/visitor arrivals at national borders (000)	62	97	90[b]
Important sites for terrestrial biodiversity protected (%)	6.4	6.4	6.4
Pop. using improved drinking water (urban/rural, %)	96.8 / 77.8	97.8 / 85.4	98.9 / 92.9[b]
Pop. using improved sanitation facilities (urban/rural, %)	59.3 / 46.0	64.1 / 53.8	65.1 / 55.4[b]
Net Official Development Assist. received (% of GNI)	10.81	15.96	12.32[c]

a Projected estimate (medium fertility variant). b 2015. c 2014. d 2016. e Data classified according to ISIC Rev. 4. f Estimate. g Break in the time series. h Data refers to a 5-year period preceding the reference year. i Data as at the end of December. j 2004. k 2008. l 2012. m 2003. n 2009.

Venezuela (Bolivarian Republic of)

Region	South America	UN membership date	15 November 1945
Population (000, 2017)	31 977[a]	Surface area (km2)	912 050[b]
Pop. density (per km2, 2017)	36.3[a]	Sex ratio (m per 100 f, 2017)	99.0[a]
Capital city	Caracas	National currency	Bolívar (VEF)
Capital city pop. (000)	2 916.2[c,b]	Exchange rate (per US$)	10.0[d]

Economic indicators

	2005	2010	2017
GDP: Gross domestic product (million current US$)	145 514	393 806	344 331[b]
GDP growth rate (annual %, const. 2005 prices)	10.3	- 1.5	- 6.2[b]
GDP per capita (current US$)	5 435.9	13 581.5	11 068.9[b]
Economy: Agriculture (% of GVA)	4.0	5.7	5.3[b]
Economy: Industry (% of GVA)	56.9	51.0	44.7[b]
Economy: Services and other activity (% of GVA)	39.2	43.4	50.0[b]
Employment: Agriculture (% of employed)[e]	10.6	10.3	11.9
Employment: Industry (% of employed)[e]	26.9	25.8	26.8
Employment: Services (% of employed)[e]	62.5	63.9	61.3
Unemployment (% of labour force)	11.4	8.5	6.6[e]
Labour force participation (female/male pop. %)[e]	51.7 / 81.5	50.6 / 79.3	51.5 / 78.3
CPI: Consumer Price Index (2000=100)	255[f,g]	156[h,i]	544[h,j]
Agricultural production index (2004-2006=100)	101	109	118[j]
Food production index (2004-2006=100)	101	109	119[j]
International trade: Exports (million US$)	55 413	66 963	19 731[d]
International trade: Imports (million US$)	21 848	32 343	16 324[d]
International trade: Balance (million US$)	33 565	34 620	3 407[d]
Balance of payments, current account (million US$)	25 447[i]	5 585	- 20 360[b]

Major trading partners

						2016
Export partners (% of exports)	United States	38.3	China	18.4	India	17.0
Import partners (% of imports)	United States	33.8	China	16.3	Brazil	8.2

Social indicators

	2005	2010	2017
Population growth rate (average annual %)[k]	1.8	1.6	1.4[b]
Urban population (% of total population)	88.6	88.8	89.0[b]
Urban population growth rate (average annual %)[k]	1.9	1.7	1.5[b]
Fertility rate, total (live births per woman)[k]	2.7	2.5	2.4[b]
Life expectancy at birth (females/males, years)[k]	77.2 / 68.8	77.7 / 69.4	78.2 / 69.9[b]
Population age distribution (0-14 and 60+ years, %)	31.7 / 7.4	29.8 / 8.3	27.6 / 9.9[a]
International migrant stock (000/% of total pop.)	1 070.6 / 4.0	1 331.5 / 4.6	1 404.4 / 4.5[b]
Refugees and others of concern to UNHCR (000)	206.3[l]	217.4[l]	174.2[d]
Infant mortality rate (per 1 000 live births)[k]	18.1	15.9	13.8[b]
Health: Total expenditure (% of GDP)	4.7	5.0	5.3[j]
Health: Physicians (per 1 000 pop.)	1.9[m]	...	...
Education: Government expenditure (% of GDP)	...	6.9[n]	...
Education: Primary gross enrol. ratio (f/m per 100 pop.)	101.8 / 103.8	100.1 / 103.1	98.6 / 101.3[b]
Education: Secondary gross enrol. ratio (f/m per 100 pop.)	77.5 / 68.6	84.7 / 77.3	93.0 / 86.5[b]
Education: Tertiary gross enrol. ratio (f/m per 100 pop.)	41.2 / 38.4[e,o]	97.7 / 57.8[e,p]	... / ...
Intentional homicide rate (per 100 000 pop.)	37.2	45.1	57.2[b]
Seats held by women in national parliaments (%)	9.7	17.5	22.2

Environment and infrastructure indicators

	2005	2010	2017
Mobile-cellular subscriptions (per 100 inhabitants)	46.8	96.0	93.0[q,b]
Individuals using the Internet (per 100 inhabitants)	12.6	37.4[e]	61.9[e,b]
Threatened species (number)	219[r]	270	328
Forested area (% of land area)[e]	54.1	53.9	53.1[j]
CO2 emission estimates (million tons/tons per capita)	165.1 / 6.2	189.1 / 6.5	185.2 / 6.1[j]
Energy production, primary (Petajoules)	8 283	8 139	7 460[j]
Energy supply per capita (Gigajoules)	103	111	90[j]
Tourist/visitor arrivals at national borders (000)	706	526	789[b]
Important sites for terrestrial biodiversity protected (%)	67.0	67.0	67.0
Pop. using improved drinking water (urban/rural, %)	94.2 / 74.6	94.7 / 76.6	95.0 / 77.9[b]
Pop. using improved sanitation facilities (urban/rural, %)	94.5 / 61.3	96.4 / 66.7	97.5 / 69.9[b]
Net Official Development Assist. received (% of GNI)	0.03	0.01	0.01[s]

a Projected estimate (medium fertility variant). **b** 2015. **c** Refers to multiple municipalities and parishes (see source). **d** 2016. **e** Estimate. **f** Caracas **g** Metropolitan areas. **h** Index base: 2008=100. **i** Break in the time series. **j** 2014. **k** Data refers to a 5-year period preceding the reference year. **l** Data as at the end of December. **m** 2001. **n** 2009. **o** 2003. **p** 2008. **q** Provisional data. **r** 2004. **s** 2013.

Viet Nam

Region	South-eastern Asia	UN membership date	20 September 1977
Population (000, 2017)	95 541 [a]	Surface area (km2)	330 967 [b]
Pop. density (per km2, 2017)	308.1 [a]	Sex ratio (m per 100 f, 2017)	98.0 [a]
Capital city	Hanoi	National currency	Dong (VND)
Capital city pop. (000)	3 629.5 [c,b]	Exchange rate (per US$)	22 159.0 [d]

Economic indicators	2005	2010	2017
GDP: Gross domestic product (million current US$)	57 633	115 932	193 241 [b]
GDP growth rate (annual %, const. 2005 prices)	7.5	6.4	6.7 [b]
GDP per capita (current US$)	684.4	1 312.1	2 067.9 [b]
Economy: Agriculture (% of GVA) [e]	21.3	21.0	18.9 [b]
Economy: Industry (% of GVA) [e]	36.1	36.7	37.0 [b]
Economy: Services and other activity (% of GVA) [e]	42.6	42.2	44.2 [b]
Employment: Agriculture (% of employed) [f]	55.5	49.9	41.8
Employment: Industry (% of employed) [f]	18.8	21.3	22.9
Employment: Services (% of employed) [f]	25.7	28.9	35.2
Unemployment (% of labour force)	2.3 [f]	2.6	2.2 [f]
Labour force participation (female/male pop. %) [f]	72.5 / 81.8	72.5 / 81.6	73.9 / 83.3
CPI: Consumer Price Index (2000=100)	126 [g]	208 [g]	299 [h]
Agricultural production index (2004-2006=100)	100	120	136 [h]
Food production index (2004-2006=100)	100	118	134 [h]
Index of industrial production (2005=100)	100	156	199 [h]
International trade: Exports (million US$)	32 447	72 237	176 632 [d]
International trade: Imports (million US$)	36 761	84 839	174 111 [d]
International trade: Balance (million US$)	- 4 314	- 12 602	2 520 [d]
Balance of payments, current account (million US$)	- 560	- 4 276	906 [b]

Major trading partners					2016
Export partners (% of exports)	United States	20.7	China	10.6	Japan 8.7
Import partners (% of imports)	China	30.0	Republic of Korea	16.6	Japan 8.6

Social indicators	2005	2010	2017
Population growth rate (average annual %) [i]	1.0	1.0	1.1 [b]
Urban population (% of total population)	27.3	30.4	33.6 [b]
Urban population growth rate (average annual %) [i]	3.2	3.1	3.0 [b]
Fertility rate, total (live births per woman) [i]	1.9	1.9	2.0 [b]
Life expectancy at birth (females/males, years) [i]	78.7 / 68.9	79.6 / 69.7	80.3 / 70.7 [b]
Population age distribution (0-14 and 60+ years, %)	27.2 / 8.6	23.7 / 8.9	23.1 / 11.1 [a]
International migrant stock (000/% of total pop.) [j,k]	51.8 / 0.1	61.8 / 0.1	72.8 / 0.1 [b]
Refugees and others of concern to UNHCR (000)	17.4 [l]	12.1 [l]	11.0 [d]
Infant mortality rate (per 1 000 live births) [i]	25.3	22.2	19.3 [b]
Health: Total expenditure (% of GDP) [m]	5.4	6.4	7.1 [h]
Health: Physicians (per 1 000 pop.)	1.2	1.1	1.2 [n]
Education: Government expenditure (% of GDP)	...	5.1	5.7 [n]
Education: Primary gross enrol. ratio (f/m per 100 pop.)	94.6 / 99.6	102.3 / 107.7	108.4 / 109.3 [b]
Education: Tertiary gross enrol. ratio (f/m per 100 pop.)	13.3 / 18.7	22.7 / 22.7	28.9 / 28.8 [b]
Intentional homicide rate (per 100 000 pop.)	1.2	1.5	1.5 [o]
Seats held by women in national parliaments (%)	27.3	25.8	26.7

Environment and infrastructure indicators	2005	2010	2017
Mobile-cellular subscriptions (per 100 inhabitants)	11.3	125.3	130.6 [f,b]
Individuals using the Internet (per 100 inhabitants)	12.7	30.6	52.7 [f,b]
Research & Development expenditure (% of GDP)	0.2 [p]	...	0.2 [o]
Threatened species (number)	289 [q]	424	616
Forested area (% of land area) [f]	42.2	45.6	47.2 [h]
CO2 emission estimates (million tons/tons per capita)	98.1 / 1.2	142.7 / 1.6	166.9 / 1.8 [h]
Energy production, primary (Petajoules)	2 612	2 747	2 977 [h]
Energy supply per capita (Gigajoules)	21	26	30 [h]
Tourist/visitor arrivals at national borders (000)	3 477	5 050	7 944 [b]
Important sites for terrestrial biodiversity protected (%)	27.2	30.0	40.9
Pop. using improved drinking water (urban/rural, %)	95.5 / 80.4	97.3 / 88.6	99.1 / 96.9 [b]
Pop. using improved sanitation facilities (urban/rural, %)	82.6 / 53.4	88.5 / 61.6	94.4 / 69.7 [b]
Net Official Development Assist. received (% of GNI)	3.38	2.64	1.73 [b]

a Projected estimate (medium fertility variant). b 2015. c Refers to urban population in the city districts. d 2016. e Data classified according to ISIC Rev. 4. f Estimate. g Series linked to former series. h 2014. i Data refers to a 5-year period preceding the reference year. j Refers to foreign citizens. k Including refugees. l Data as at the end of December. m Data revision. n 2013. o 2011. p 2002. q 2004.

Wallis and Futuna Islands

Region	Polynesia	Population (000, 2017)	12 [a]
Surface area (km2)	142 [b]	Pop. density (per km2, 2017)	84.1 [a]
Sex ratio (m per 100 f, 2017)	93.4 [c,d]	Capital city	Matu-Utu
National currency	CFP Franc (XPF)	Capital city pop. (000)	1.1 [e]
Exchange rate (per US$)	113.2 [d]		

Economic indicators	2005	2010	2017
Agricultural production index (2004-2006=100)	102	104	115 [e]
Food production index (2004-2006=100)	102	104	115 [e]
International trade: Exports (million US$)	1	1	1 [d]
International trade: Imports (million US$)	51	35	53 [d]
International trade: Balance (million US$)	- 50	- 34	- 51 [d]

Major trading partners						2016
Export partners (% of exports)	United States	53.8	Cambodia	12.1	France	7.6
Import partners (% of imports)	France	26.2	Fiji	20.5	New Caledonia	20.4

Social indicators	2005	2010	2017
Population growth rate (average annual %) [f]	0.1	- 1.6	- 2.1 [b]
Urban population (% of total population)	...	0.0	0.0 [b]
Urban population growth rate (average annual %) [f]	0.0	0.0	0.0 [b]
Fertility rate, total (live births per woman)	...	...	2.1 [g]
Life expectancy at birth (females/males, years)	75.5 / 73.1 [h]	... / ...	78.7 / 72.8 [c,g]
Population age distribution (0-14 and 60+ years, %)	... / ...	... / ...	25.5 / 15.4 [d]
International migrant stock (000/% of total pop.)	2.4 / 16.6	2.8 / 20.5	2.8 / 21.7 [b]
Infant mortality rate (per 1 000 live births)	...	5.2 [i,j]	...

Environment and infrastructure indicators	2005	2010	2017
Individuals using the Internet (per 100 inhabitants)	6.7	8.2	9.0 [k,l]
Threatened species (number)	13 [m]	74	89
Forested area (% of land area)	41.5	41.6	41.6 [k,e]
CO2 emission estimates (million tons/tons per capita)	~0.0 / 1.9	~0.0 / 2.1	~0.0 / 1.6 [e]
Energy supply per capita (Gigajoules)	26	27	26 [e]
Important sites for terrestrial biodiversity protected (%)	0.0	0.0	0.0

a Projected estimate (medium fertility variant). b 2015. c Break in the time series. d 2016. e 2014. f Data refers to a 5-year period preceding the reference year. g 2013. h 2003. i Data refers to a 4-year period up to and including the reference year. j 2008. k Estimate. l 2012. m 2004.

Western Sahara

Region	Northern Africa	Population (000, 2017)	553 [a]
Surface area (km2)	266 000 [b,c]	Pop. density (per km2, 2017)	2.1 [a]
Sex ratio (m per 100 f, 2017)	110.1 [a]	Capital city	El Aaiún
National currency	Moroccan Dirham (MAD)	Capital city pop. (000)	262.4 [d]
Exchange rate (per US$)	10.1 [e]		

Economic indicators	2005	2010	2017
Employment: Agriculture (% of employed) [f]	38.6	38.0	37.4
Employment: Industry (% of employed) [f]	26.6	27.5	27.9
Employment: Services (% of employed) [f]	34.8	34.5	34.7
Unemployment (% of labour force) [f]	7.2	7.0	6.8
Labour force participation (female/male pop. %) [f]	24.1 / 83.1	27.7 / 83.5	28.6 / 83.3
Agricultural production index (2004-2006=100)	100	101	100 [d]
Food production index (2004-2006=100)	100	101	100 [d]

Social indicators	2005	2010	2017
Population growth rate (average annual %) [g]	6.6	1.9	1.8 [c]
Urban population (% of total population)	80.6	80.7	80.9 [c]
Urban population growth rate (average annual %) [g]	5.9	3.7	3.3 [c]
Fertility rate, total (live births per woman) [g]	2.8	2.6	2.6 [c]
Life expectancy at birth (females/males, years) [g]	65.8 / 62.3	68.1 / 64.7	70.3 / 66.9 [c]
Population age distribution (0-14 and 60+ years, %)	31.5 / 3.6	29.4 / 3.8	28.1 / 5.4 [a]
International migrant stock (000/% of total pop.) [f]	3.9 / 0.9	4.5 / 0.9	5.2 / 0.9 [c]
Infant mortality rate (per 1 000 live births) [g]	52.9	43.1	34.1 [c]

Environment and infrastructure indicators	2005	2010	2017
Threatened species (number) [f]	19 [h]	39	49
Forested area (% of land area) [f]	2.7	2.7	2.7 [d]

a Projected estimate (medium fertility variant). **b** Comprising the Northern Region (former Saguia el Hamra) and Southern Region (former Rio de Oro). **c** 2015. **d** 2014. **e** 2016. **f** Estimate. **g** Data refers to a 5-year period preceding the reference year. **h** 2004.

Yemen

Region	Western Asia	UN membership date	30 September 1947
Population (000, 2017)	28 250[a]	Surface area (km2)	527 968[b]
Pop. density (per km2, 2017)	53.5[a]	Sex ratio (m per 100 f, 2017)	102.1[a]
Capital city	Sana'a	National currency	Yemeni Rial (YER)
Capital city pop. (000)	2 961.9[b]	Exchange rate (per US$)	214.9[c]

Economic indicators	2005	2010	2017
GDP: Gross domestic product (million current US$)	19 041	30 907	29 688[b]
GDP growth rate (annual %, const. 2005 prices)	5.1	5.7	- 28.1[b]
GDP per capita (current US$)	928.6	1 310.1	1 106.4[b]
Economy: Agriculture (% of GVA)	9.6	12.0	14.7[b]
Economy: Industry (% of GVA)	43.8	38.3	36.9[b]
Economy: Services and other activity (% of GVA)	46.5	49.5	48.4[b]
Employment: Agriculture (% of employed)[d]	33.1	24.1	32.9
Employment: Industry (% of employed)[d]	15.9	19.0	17.9
Employment: Services (% of employed)[d]	51.0	56.9	49.2
Unemployment (% of labour force)	16.1	17.8	16.1[d]
Labour force participation (female/male pop. %)[d]	23.6 / 71.3	24.8 / 71.4	26.2 / 73.7
CPI: Consumer Price Index (2000=100)	174	292[e]	426[f]
Agricultural production index (2004-2006=100)	98	136	136[g]
Food production index (2004-2006=100)	98	137	137[g]
International trade: Exports (million US$)	5 608	6 437	570[c]
International trade: Imports (million US$)	5 400	9 255	6 861[c]
International trade: Balance (million US$)	208	- 2 818	- 6 291[c]
Balance of payments, current account (million US$)	624	- 1 398	- 3 026[b]

Major trading partners						2016
Export partners (% of exports)	Saudi Arabia	32.2	Oman	17.0	Areas nes[h]	10.5
Import partners (% of imports)	United Arab Emirates	11.5	China	10.8	Saudi Arabia	8.6

Social indicators	2005	2010	2017
Population growth rate (average annual %)[i]	2.8	2.7	2.6[b]
Urban population (% of total population)	28.9	31.7	34.6[b]
Urban population growth rate (average annual %)[i]	4.7	4.3	4.0[b]
Fertility rate, total (live births per woman)[i]	5.9	5.0	4.4[b]
Life expectancy at birth (females/males, years)[i]	62.4 / 59.7	64.1 / 61.4	65.6 / 62.8[b]
Population age distribution (0-14 and 60+ years, %)	45.7 / 4.2	42.5 / 4.4	39.9 / 4.6[a]
International migrant stock (000/% of total pop.)[j,k]	171.1 / 0.8	285.8 / 1.2	344.1 / 1.3[b]
Refugees and others of concern to UNHCR (000)	82.8[l]	508.6[l]	3 371.4[c]
Infant mortality rate (per 1 000 live births)	67.9	53.0	47.2[b]
Health: Total expenditure (% of GDP)[m]	4.6	5.2	5.6[g]
Health: Physicians (per 1 000 pop.)	0.3[n]	0.3[o]	0.3[g]
Education: Government expenditure (% of GDP)	9.3[d,p]	5.1[q]	...
Education: Primary gross enrol. ratio (f/m per 100 pop.)	74.5 / 100.7	81.5 / 99.8	88.9 / 105.7[f]
Education: Secondary gross enrol. ratio (f/m per 100 pop.)	29.8 / 61.0	33.1 / 53.3	39.5 / 57.4[f]
Education: Tertiary gross enrol. ratio (f/m per 100 pop.)	5.1 / 14.0	6.4 / 14.6	6.1 / 13.7[r]
Intentional homicide rate (per 100 000 pop.)	4.6	4.7	6.7[f]
Seats held by women in national parliaments (%)	0.3	0.3	0.0

Environment and infrastructure indicators	2005	2010	2017
Mobile-cellular subscriptions (per 100 inhabitants)	11.3	48.7	68.0[d,b]
Individuals using the Internet (per 100 inhabitants)	1.0[d]	12.4	25.1[d,b]
Threatened species (number)	195[n]	269	298
Forested area (% of land area)[d]	1.0	1.0	1.0[g]
CO2 emission estimates (million tons/tons per capita)	20.0 / 1.0	23.4 / 1.0	22.7 / 0.9[g]
Energy production, primary (Petajoules)	844	804	668[g]
Energy supply per capita (Gigajoules)	13	14	12[g]
Tourist/visitor arrivals at national borders (000)	336	1 025[s]	367[s,b]
Important sites for terrestrial biodiversity protected (%)	20.0	31.1	31.1
Pop. using improved drinking water (urban/rural, %)	75.9 / 48.5	72.0 / 46.5	72.0 / 46.5[t]
Pop. using improved sanitation facilities (urban/rural, %)	88.7 / 30.4	92.5 / 34.1	92.5 / 34.1[t]
Net Official Development Assist. received (% of GNI)	1.96	2.28	2.99[f]

a Projected estimate (medium fertility variant). **b** 2015. **c** 2016. **d** Estimate. **e** Series linked to former series. **f** 2013. **g** 2014. **h** Areas not elsewhere specified. **i** Data refers to a 5-year period preceding the reference year. **j** Refers to foreign citizens. **k** Including refugees. **l** Data as at the end of December. **m** Data revision. **n** 2004. **o** 2009. **p** 2001. **q** 2008. **r** 2011. **s** Including nationals residing abroad. **t** 2012.

Zambia

Region	Eastern Africa	UN membership date	01 December 1964
Population (000, 2017)	17 094 [a]	Surface area (km2)	752 612 [b]
Pop. density (per km2, 2017)	23.0 [a]	Sex ratio (m per 100 f, 2017)	98.5 [a]
Capital city	Lusaka	National currency	Zambian Kwacha (ZMW)
Capital city pop. (000)	2 179.5 [b]	Exchange rate (per US$)	9.9 [c]

Economic indicators	2005	2010	2017
GDP: Gross domestic product (million current US$)	8 332	20 265	21 255 [b]
GDP growth rate (annual %, const. 2005 prices)	7.2	10.3	2.9 [b]
GDP per capita (current US$)	691.8	1 456.1	1 311.1 [b]
Economy: Agriculture (% of GVA)	15.5	10.0 [d]	8.2 [d,b]
Economy: Industry (% of GVA)	28.6	34.1 [d]	32.3 [d,b]
Economy: Services and other activity (% of GVA)	55.9	55.9 [d]	59.5 [d,b]
Employment: Agriculture (% of employed) [e]	72.1	65.0	54.8
Employment: Industry (% of employed) [e]	7.1	8.7	9.9
Employment: Services (% of employed) [e]	20.8	26.3	35.3
Unemployment (% of labour force)	15.9	10.8 [e]	7.4 [e]
Labour force participation (female/male pop. %) [e]	73.5 / 85.6	70.4 / 79.8	69.9 / 80.9
CPI: Consumer Price Index (2000=100)	251	420	547 [f]
Agricultural production index (2004-2006=100)	101	169	179 [f]
Food production index (2004-2006=100)	98	172	180 [f]
Index of industrial production (2005=100) [g]	100	141	157 [h]
International trade: Exports (million US$)	1 810	7 200	6 505 [c]
International trade: Imports (million US$)	2 558	5 321	7 442 [c]
International trade: Balance (million US$)	- 748	1 879	- 937 [c]
Balance of payments, current account (million US$)	- 363 [i]	1 377	- 768 [b]

Major trading partners					2016
Export partners (% of exports)	Switzerland	44.3	China	14.5	Singapore 7.8
Import partners (% of imports)	South Africa	30.9	Dem. Rep. of Congo	11.2	China 8.2

Social indicators	2005	2010	2017
Population growth rate (average annual %) [j]	2.7	2.8	3.0 [b]
Urban population (% of total population)	36.6	38.7	40.9 [b]
Urban population growth rate (average annual %) [j]	3.6	4.0	4.3 [b]
Fertility rate, total (live births per woman) [j]	6.0	5.6	5.2 [b]
Life expectancy at birth (females/males, years) [j]	48.4 / 45.3	54.7 / 51.2	61.9 / 57.5 [b]
Population age distribution (0-14 and 60+ years, %)	47.0 / 3.9	46.8 / 3.8	44.8 / 3.7 [a]
International migrant stock (000/% of total pop.) [k]	252.7 / 2.1	149.6 / 1.1	127.9 / 0.8 [b]
Refugees and others of concern to UNHCR (000)	185.7 [l]	57.9 [l]	55.3 [c]
Infant mortality rate (per 1 000 live births) [j]	82.2	65.2	53.8 [b]
Health: Total expenditure (% of GDP)	7.6	4.4	5.0 [f]
Health: Physicians (per 1 000 pop.)	0.1	0.1	0.2 [m]
Education: Government expenditure (% of GDP)	1.7	1.1 [n]	...
Education: Primary gross enrol. ratio (f/m per 100 pop.)	108.0 / 113.1	108.3 / 106.9	104.0 / 103.3 [h]
Education: Tertiary gross enrol. ratio (f/m per 100 pop.)	... / ...	... / ...	3.4 / 4.5 [m]
Intentional homicide rate (per 100 000 pop.)	...	5.8	...
Seats held by women in national parliaments (%)	12.0	14.0	18.0

Environment and infrastructure indicators	2005	2010	2017
Mobile-cellular subscriptions (per 100 inhabitants)	8.3	41.2	74.5 [b]
Individuals using the Internet (per 100 inhabitants)	2.9 [e]	10.0	21.0 [e,b]
Research & Development expenditure (% of GDP)	-0.0 [o]	0.3 [i,n]	...
Threatened species (number)	39 [p]	67	88
Forested area (% of land area) [e]	67.7	66.5	65.6 [f]
CO2 emission estimates (million tons/tons per capita)	2.3 / 0.2	2.7 / 0.2	4.5 / 0.3 [f]
Energy production, primary (Petajoules)	280	319	374 [f]
Energy supply per capita (Gigajoules)	27	25	26 [f]
Tourist/visitor arrivals at national borders (000)	669	815	932 [b]
Important sites for terrestrial biodiversity protected (%)	46.3	48.3	48.3
Pop. using improved drinking water (urban/rural, %)	86.7 / 40.3	86.2 / 45.8	85.6 / 51.3 [b]
Pop. using improved sanitation facilities (urban/rural, %)	56.9 / 32.9	56.3 / 34.3	55.6 / 35.7 [b]
Net Official Development Assist. received (% of GNI)	15.18	4.86	3.96 [b]

a Projected estimate (medium fertility variant). **b** 2015. **c** 2016. **d** Data classified according to ISIC Rev. 4. **e** Estimate. **f** 2014. **g** Data classified according to ISIC Rev. 3. **h** 2013. **i** Break in the time series. **j** Data refers to a 5-year period preceding the reference year. **k** Including refugees. **l** Data as at the end of December. **m** 2012. **n** 2008. **o** Partial data. **p** 2004.

Zimbabwe

Region	Eastern Africa	UN membership date	25 August 1980
Population (000, 2017)	16 530[a]	Surface area (km2)	390 757[b]
Pop. density (per km2, 2017)	42.7[a]	Sex ratio (m per 100 f, 2017)	95.0[a]
Capital city	Harare	National currency	Zimbabwe Dollar (ZWL)
Capital city pop. (000)	1 501.4[b]		

Economic indicators

	2005	2010	2017
GDP: Gross domestic product (million current US$)	6 223	9 422	13 893[b]
GDP growth rate (annual %, const. 2005 prices)	- 4.1	11.4	1.1[b]
GDP per capita (current US$)	479.3	674.3	890.4[b]
Economy: Agriculture (% of GVA)	12.3	14.4	13.0[b]
Economy: Industry (% of GVA)	41.9	30.7	30.5[b]
Economy: Services and other activity (% of GVA)	45.9	54.9	56.5[b]
Employment: Agriculture (% of employed)[c]	70.1	68.4	67.5
Employment: Industry (% of employed)[c]	10.6	9.4	7.3
Employment: Services (% of employed)[c]	19.4	22.2	25.2
Unemployment (% of labour force)[c]	4.8	6.3	5.0
Labour force participation (female/male pop. %)[c]	82.5 / 90.2	78.0 / 88.7	78.0 / 87.5
CPI: Consumer Price Index (2000=100)	~0[d,e]	103[d,f]	112[f,g]
Agricultural production index (2004-2006=100)	93	102	99[g]
Food production index (2004-2006=100)	91	97	98[g]
International trade: Exports (million US$)	1 394	3 199	2 832[h]
International trade: Imports (million US$)	2 072	5 852	5 212[h]
International trade: Balance (million US$)	- 679	- 2 653	- 2 379[h]
Balance of payments, current account (million US$)	...	- 1 444	- 1 521[b]

Major trading partners

							2016
Export partners (% of exports)	South Africa	79.4	Mozambique	9.5	United Arab Emirates	4.1	
Import partners (% of imports)	South Africa	41.3	Singapore	21.5	China	7.0	

Social indicators

	2005	2010	2017
Population growth rate (average annual %)[i]	1.1	1.7	2.3[b]
Urban population (% of total population)	34.1	33.2	32.4[b]
Urban population growth rate (average annual %)[i]	0.5	-0.0	2.3[b]
Fertility rate, total (live births per woman)[i]	4.0	4.0	4.0[b]
Life expectancy at birth (females/males, years)[i]	45.5 / 42.7	49.4 / 47.2	59.0 / 56.1[b]
Population age distribution (0-14 and 60+ years, %)	41.8 / 4.5	41.5 / 4.3	41.2 / 4.2[a]
International migrant stock (000/% of total pop.)[j]	392.7 / 3.0	397.9 / 2.8	398.9 / 2.6[b]
Refugees and others of concern to UNHCR (000)	14.0[k]	4.9[k]	308.6[h]
Infant mortality rate (per 1 000 live births)[i]	67.2	58.3	46.5[b]
Health: Total expenditure (% of GDP)[l]	5.8	5.3	6.0[g]
Health: Physicians (per 1 000 pop.)	0.2[m]	0.1	0.1[n]
Education: Government expenditure (% of GDP)	...	2.0	8.4[g]
Education: Primary gross enrol. ratio (f/m per 100 pop.)	95.4 / 96.8[o]	... / ...	99.1 / 100.8[p]
Education: Secondary gross enrol. ratio (f/m per 100 pop.)	35.6 / 39.6[o]	... / ...	47.1 / 48.1[p]
Education: Tertiary gross enrol. ratio (f/m per 100 pop.)	... / ...	5.2 / 6.6	8.0 / 8.9[b]
Intentional homicide rate (per 100 000 pop.)	10.4	5.1	6.7[q]
Seats held by women in national parliaments (%)	10.0	15.0	32.6

Environment and infrastructure indicators

	2005	2010	2017
Mobile-cellular subscriptions (per 100 inhabitants)	5.1	58.9	84.8[b]
Individuals using the Internet (per 100 inhabitants)[c]	2.4	6.4	16.4[b]
Threatened species (number)	43[m]	55	89
Forested area (% of land area)[c]	44.6	40.4	37.2[g]
CO2 emission estimates (million tons/tons per capita)	10.8 / 0.8	7.8 / 0.6	12.0 / 0.8[g]
Energy production, primary (Petajoules)	379	368	482[g]
Energy supply per capita (Gigajoules)	33	28	30[g]
Tourist/visitor arrivals at national borders (000)	1 559	2 239	2 057[b]
Important sites for terrestrial biodiversity protected (%)	80.7	80.7	85.9
Pop. using improved drinking water (urban/rural, %)	98.0 / 68.9	97.5 / 68.1	97.0 / 67.3[b]
Pop. using improved sanitation facilities (urban/rural, %)	50.3 / 32.5	49.8 / 31.7	49.3 / 30.8[b]
Net Official Development Assist. received (% of GNI)	6.80	8.03	6.00[b]

a Projected estimate (medium fertility variant). b 2015. c Estimate. d Break in the time series. e Due to lack of space, multiply each figure by 1,000. Annual average is calculated as geometric mean of monthly indices. Index base: 2005=100. f Index base: 2009=100. g 2014. h 2016. i Data refers to a 5-year period preceding the reference year. j Including refugees. k Data as at the end of December. l Estimates should be viewed with caution as these are derived from scarce data. m 2004. n 2011. o 2003. p 2013. q 2012.

Below are brief descriptions of the indicators presented in the world, regional and country profiles. The terms are arranged in alphabetical order.

Agricultural production indices are calculated by the Laspeyres formula based on the sum of price-weighted quantities of different agricultural commodities produced. The commodities covered in the computation of indices of agricultural production are all crops and livestock products originating in each country. Practically all products are covered, with the main exception of fodder crops. Production quantities of each commodity are weighted by the average international commodity prices in the base period and summed for each year. To obtain the index, the aggregate for a given year is divided by the average aggregate for the base period 2004-2006. Indices are calculated without any deductions for feed and seed and are referred to as "gross" by the Food and Agriculture Organization of the United Nations (FAO).
Source of the data: Food and Agriculture Organization of the United Nations (FAO), Rome, FAOSTAT database, last accessed February 2017.

Balance of payments is a statement summarizing the economic transactions between the residents of a country and non-residents during a specific period, usually a year. It includes transactions in goods, services, income, transfers and financial assets and liabilities. Generally, the balance of payments is divided into two major components: the current account and the capital and financial account. The data on balance of payments correspond to the current account category. The current account is a record of all transactions in the balance of payments covering the exports and imports of goods and services, payments of income, and current transfers between residents of a country and non-residents.
Source of the data: International Monetary Fund (IMF), Washington, D.C., the database on International Financial Statistics, last accessed February 2017.

Capital city and capital city population is the designation of any specific city as a capital city as reported by the country or area. The city can be the seat of the government as determined by the country. Some countries designate more than one city to be a capital city with a specific title function (e.g., administrative and/or legislative capital). The data refer to the year 2015, unless otherwise stated in a footnote.
Source of the data: United Nations Population Division, New York, "World Urbanization Prospects: The 2014 Revision".

CO_2 emission estimates represent the volume of carbon dioxide (CO_2) produced during the combustion of solid, liquid, and gaseous fuels, from gas flaring and the manufacture of cement. Original data were converted to CO_2 emissions by using the conversion formula: 1 gram Carbon = 3.667 grams CO_2.

Technical notes (*continued*)

Source of the data: Carbon Dioxide Information Analysis Center (CDIAC) of the Oak Ridge National Laboratory, Oak Ridge, Tennessee, U.S.A., database on national CO2 emission estimates, last accessed March 2017.

Consumer price index (CPI) measures the period-to-period proportional change in the prices of a fixed set of consumer goods and services of constant quantity and characteristics, acquired, used or paid for by the reference population. The index is constructed as a weighted average of a large number of elementary aggregate indices. Each of the elementary aggregate indices is estimated using a sample of prices for a defined set of goods and services obtained in, or by residents of, a specific region from a given set of outlets or other sources of consumption. The indices here generally refer to "all items" and to the country as a whole, unless otherwise stated in a footnote.
Source of the data: International Labour Office (ILO), Geneva, the LABORSTA database, last accessed April 2016.

Economy: Agriculture, industry and services and other activity presents the shares of the components of Gross Value Added (GVA) at current prices by kind of economic activity; agriculture (agriculture, hunting, forestry and fishing), industry (mining and quarrying, manufacturing, electricity, gas and water supply; and construction) and in services and other sectors based on the sections of the International Standard Industrial Classification of All Economic Activities (ISIC), Revision 3, unless a different revision is stated in a footnote.
Source of the data: United Nations Statistics Division, New York, national accounts analysis of main aggregates (AMA) database, last accessed February 2017.

Education: Government expenditure shows the trends in general government expenditures for educational affairs and services at pre-primary, primary, secondary and tertiary levels and subsidiary services to education, expressed as a percentage of the gross domestic product.
Source of the data: United Nations Educational, Scientific and Cultural Organization (UNESCO) Institute for Statistics, Montreal, the UNESCO Institute for Statistics (UIS) statistics database, last accessed June 2017.

Education: Primary, secondary and tertiary gross enrolment ratio is the total enrolment in the primary, secondary and tertiary levels of education, regardless of age, expressed as a percentage of the <u>eligible</u> official school-age population corresponding to the same level of education in a given school year. Education at the primary level provides the basic elements of education (e.g. at elementary school or primary school). Education at the secondary level is provided at middle school, secondary school, high school, teacher-training school at this level and schools of a vocational or technical nature. Education at the tertiary level is that which is provided at university, teachers' college, higher professional school, and which requires, as a minimum condition of admission, the successful completion of education at the second level, or evidence of the attainment of an equivalent level of knowledge. Enrolment is measured at the beginning of the school or academic year. The gross enrolment ratio at each level will include all pupils whatever their ages, whereas the population is limited to the range of official school ages. Therefore, for countries with almost universal education among the school-age population, the gross enrolment ratio can exceed 100 if the actual age distribution of pupils extends beyond the official school ages. **Source of the data:** United Nations Educational, Scientific and Cultural Organization (UNESCO) Institute for Statistics, Montreal, the UNESCO Institute for Statistics (UIS) statistics database, last accessed June 2017.

Employment in agricultural, industrial and services and other sectors: The "employed" comprise all persons above a specified age who, during a specified brief period, either one week or one day, were in "paid employment" or in "self-employment", see ILO's Current International Recommendations on Labour Statistics. The data refer to those 15 years and over, unless otherwise stated in a footnote, who perform any work at all in the reference period, for pay or profit in agriculture (agriculture, forestry and fishing), industry (mining and quarrying; manufacturing; electricity, gas, steam and air conditioning supply; water supply, sewerage, waste management and remediation activities; and construction) and in services and other sectors based on the sections of the International Standard Industrial Classification of All Economic Activities (ISIC), Revision 4, unless an earlier revision is stated in a footnote.
Source of the data: International Labour Organization (ILO), Geneva, Key Indicators of the Labour Market (KILM 9th edition) and the ILOSTAT database, last accessed March 2017.

Energy production, primary, is the capture or extraction of fuels or energy from natural energy flows, the biosphere and natural reserves of fossil fuels within the national territory in a form suitable for use. Inert matter removed from the extracted fuels and quantities reinjected, flared or vented are not included. The resulting products are referred to as "primary" products. It excludes secondary production, that is, the manufacture of energy products through the process of transforming primary and/or other secondary fuels or energy. Data are provided in a common energy unit (Petajoule) and refer to the following primary energy sources: hard coal, brown coal, peat, oil shale, conventional crude oil, natural gas liquids (NGL), other hydrocarbons, additives and oxygenates, natural gas, fuelwood, wood residues and by-products, bagasse, animal waste, black liquor, other vegetal material and residues, biogasoline, biodiesels, bio jet kerosene, other liquid biofuels, biogases, industrial waste, municipal waste, nuclear, solar photovoltaic, solar thermal, hydro, wind, geothermal, and tide, wave and other marine sources. Peat, biomass and wastes are included only when the production is for energy purposes. See International Recommendations for Energy Statistics (2011) and 2012 Energy Balances for a complete description of the methodology.

Technical notes (*continued*)

Source of the data: United Nations Statistics Division, New York, Energy Statistics Yearbook 2014, last accessed January 2017.

Energy supply per capita is defined as primary energy production plus imports minus exports minus international marine bunkers minus international aviation bunkers minus stock changes. For imports, exports, international bunkers and stock changes, it includes secondary energy products, in addition to primary products.
Source of the data: United Nations Statistics Division, New York, Energy Statistics Yearbook 2014, last accessed January 2017.

Exchange rates are shown in units of national currency per US dollar and refer to end-of-period quotations. The exchange rates are classified into broad categories, reflecting both the role of the authorities in the determination of the exchange and/or the multiplicity of exchange rates in a country. The market rate is used to describe exchange rates determined largely by market forces; the official rate is an exchange rate determined by the authorities, sometimes in a flexible manner. For countries maintaining multiple exchange arrangements, the rates are labelled principal rate, secondary rate, and tertiary rate.
Source of the data: International Monetary Fund (IMF), Washington, D.C., the database on International Financial Statistics supplemented by operational rates of exchange for United Nations programmes, last accessed June 2017.

Fertility rate is the total fertility rate, a widely used summary indicator of fertility. It refers to the number of children that would be born per woman, assuming no female mortality at child bearing ages and the age-specific fertility rates of a specified country and reference period. The data are an average over five-year ranges; 2000-2005 labelled "2005", 2005-2010 labelled "2010" and 2010-2015 labelled "2017", unless otherwise stated in a footnote.
Source of the data: United Nations Population Division, New York, World Population Prospects: The 2017 Revision; supplemented by data from the United Nations Statistics Division, New York, Demographic Yearbook 2015 and Secretariat for the Pacific Community (SPC) for small countries or areas, last accessed June 2017.

Food production index covers commodities that are considered edible and contain nutrients. Accordingly, coffee and tea are excluded because they have practically no nutritive value. The index numbers shown may differ from those produced by countries themselves because of differences in concepts of production, coverage, weights, time reference of data, and methods of evaluation. The data include estimates made by FAO in cases where no official or semi-official figures are available from the countries.
Source of the data: Food and Agriculture Organization of the United Nations (FAO), Rome, FAOSTAT database, last accessed February 2017.

Forested area refers to the percentage of land area occupied by forest. Forest is defined in the Food and Agriculture Organization's Global Forest Resources Assessment as land spanning more than 0.5 hectares with trees higher than 5 metres and a canopy cover of more than 10 percent, or trees able to reach these thresholds in situ. It does not include land that is predominantly under agricultural or urban land use. Data are calculated from the forest estimates divided by the land area.
Source of the data: Food and Agriculture Organization of the United Nations (FAO), Rome, FAOSTAT database, last accessed December 2016.

Gross domestic product (GDP) is an aggregate measure of production equal to the sum of gross value added of all resident producer units plus that part (possibly the total) of taxes on products, less subsidies on products, that is not included in the valuation of output. It is also equal to the sum of the final uses of goods and services (all uses except intermediate consumption) measured at purchasers' prices, less the value of imports of goods and services, and equal to the sum of primary incomes distributed by resident producer units (see System of National Accounts 2008). The data are in current United States (US) dollars and are estimates of the total production of goods and services of the countries represented in economic terms, not as a measure of the standard of living of their inhabitants. In order to have comparable coverage for as many countries as possible, these US dollar estimates are based on official GDP data in national currency, supplemented by national currency estimates prepared by the Statistics Division using additional data from national and international sources. The estimates given here are in most cases those accepted by the United Nations General Assembly's Committee on Contributions for determining United Nations members' contributions to the United Nations regular budget. The exchange rates for the conversion of GDP national currency data into US dollars are the average market rates published by the International Monetary Fund, in International Financial Statistics. Official exchange rates are used only when free market rates are not available. For non-members of the Fund, the conversion rates used are the average of United Nations operational rates of exchange. It should be noted that the conversion from local currency into US dollars introduces deficiencies in comparability over time and among countries which should be considered when using the data. For example, comparability over time is distorted when exchange rate fluctuations differ substantially from domestic inflation rates.
Source of the data: United Nations Statistics Division, New York, national accounts analysis of main aggregates (AMA) database, last accessed February 2017.

GDP growth rate is derived on the basis of constant 2005 price series in national currency. The figures are computed as the geometric mean of annual rates of growth expressed in percentages.
Source of the data: United Nations Statistics Division, New York, national accounts analysis of main aggregates (AMA) database, last accessed February 2017.

Technical notes (*continued*)

GDP per capita estimates are the value of all goods and services produced in the economy divided by the population.
Source of the data: United Nations Statistics Division, New York, national accounts analysis of main aggregates (AMA) database, last accessed February 2017.

Health: Physicians (per 1 000 population) includes generalist medical practitioners and specialist medical practitioners. The classification of health workers used is based on criteria for vocational education and training, regulation of health professions, and activities and tasks of jobs, i.e. a framework for categorizing key workforce variables according to shared characteristics.
Source of the data: World Health Organisation (WHO), Geneva, WHO Global Health Workforce statistics database, last accessed June 2017.

Health: Total expenditure is the sum of all outlays for health maintenance, restoration or enhancement paid for in cash or supplied in kind expressed as a percentage of Gross Domestic Product. It is the sum of General Government Expenditure on Health and Private Expenditure on Health. General government expenditure on health is the sum of health outlays paid for in cash or supplied in kind by government entities, such as the Ministry of Health, other ministries, parastatal organizations or social security agencies (without double counting government transfers to social security and extra budgetary funds). It includes all expenditure made by these entities, regardless of the source, so includes any donor funding passing through them. It includes transfer payments to households to offset medical care costs and extra budgetary funds to finance health services and goods. It includes current and capital expenditure.
Source of the data: World Health Organization (WHO), Geneva, WHO Global Health Expenditure database, last accessed June 2017.

Important sites for terrestrial biodiversity protected (%) shows land which contributes significantly to the global persistence of biodiversity measured as a proportion of which is wholly covered by a designated protected area. Data are based on spatial overlap between polygons for Key Biodiversity Areas from the World Database of key Biodiversity Areas and polygons for protected areas from the World Database on Protected Areas. Figures for each region are calculated as the proportion of each Key Biodiversity Area covered by protected areas, averaged (i.e. calculated as the mean) across all Key Biodiversity Areas within the region.
Source of the data: United Nations Environment Programme (UNEP) World Conservation Monitoring Centre (WCWC), Cambridge, Sustainable Development Goals database, last accessed June 2017.

Index of Industrial production generally cover industry (mining and quarrying; manufacturing; electricity, gas, steam and air conditioning supply; water supply, sewerage, waste management and remediation activities; and construction) based on the sections (i.e. B, C, D and E) of the International Standard Industrial

Classification of All Economic Activities (ISIC), Revision 4, unless a different revision/set of sections is stated in a footnote.

Source of the data: United Nations Statistics Division, New York, Environment and energy statistics branch, Industrial and Energy Statistics Section, last accessed November 2015.

Individuals using the Internet refer to the percentage of people who used the Internet from any location and for any purpose, irrespective of the device and network used. It can be via a computer (i.e. desktop or laptop computer, tablet or similar handheld computer), mobile phone, games machine, digital TV, etc. Access can be via a fixed or mobile network. There are certain data limits to this indicator, insofar as estimates have to be calculated for many developing countries which do not yet collect information and communications technology household statistics.

Source of the data: International Telecommunication Union (ITU), Geneva, the ITU database, last accessed July 2016.

Infant mortality rate (per 1 000 live births) is the ratio of infant deaths (the deaths of children under one year of age) in a given year to the total number of live births in the same year. The data are an average over five-year ranges; 2000-2005 labelled "2005", 2005-2010 labelled "2010" and 2010-2015 labelled "2017", unless otherwise stated in a footnote.

Source of the data: United Nations Population Division, New York, World Population Prospects: The 2017 Revision; supplemented by data from the United Nations Statistics Division, New York, Demographic Yearbook 2015 and Secretariat for the Pacific Community (SPC) for small countries or areas, last accessed June 2017.

Intentional homicide rate: The rates are the annual number of unlawful deaths purposefully inflicted on a person by another person, reported for the year per 100 000. For most countries, country information on causes of death is not available for most causes. Estimates are therefore based on cause of death modelling and death registration data from other countries in the region. Further country-level information and data on specific causes was also used.

Source of the data: United Nations Office on Drugs and Crime, Vienna, UNODC Statistics database, last accessed June 2017.

International migrant stock generally represents the number of persons born in a country other than that in which they live. When information on country of birth was not recorded, data on the number of persons having foreign citizenship was used instead. In the absence of any empirical data, estimates were imputed. Data refer to mid-year. Figures for international migrant stock as a percentage of the population are the outcome of dividing the estimated international migrant stock by the estimated total population and multiplying the result by 100.

Technical notes (*continued*)

Source of the data: United Nations Population Division, New York, International migrant stock: The 2015 Revision, last accessed June 2016.

International trade: Exports, Imports and Balance show the movement of goods out of and into a country. Goods simply being transported through a country (goods in transit) or temporarily admitted (except for goods for inward processing) do not add to the stock of material resources of a country and are not included in the international merchandise trade statistics. In the "general trade system", the definition of the statistical territory of a country coincides with its economic territory. In the "special trade system", the definition of the statistical territory comprises only a particular part of the economic territory, mainly that part which coincides with the free circulation area for goods. "The free circulation area" is a part of the economic territory of a country within which goods "may be disposed of without Customs restrictions". In the case of exports, the transaction value is the value at which the goods were sold by the exporter, including the cost of transportation and insurance, to bring the goods onto the transporting vehicle at the frontier of the exporting country (an FOB-type valuation). In the case of imports, the transaction value is the value at which the goods were purchased by the importer plus the cost of transportation and insurance to the frontier of the importing country (a CIF-type valuation). Both imports and exports are shown in United States dollars. Conversion from national currencies is made by means of currency conversion factors based on official exchange rates (par values or weighted averages). All regional aggregations are calculated as the sum of their components.
Source of the data: United Nations Statistics Division, New York, UN Comtrade database, last accessed June 2017.

Labour force participation rate is calculated by expressing the number of persons in the labour force as a percentage of the working-age population. The labour force is the sum of the number of persons employed and the number of unemployed (see ILO's current International Recommendations on Labour Statistics). The working-age population is the population above a certain age, prescribed for the measurement of economic characteristics. The data refer to the age group of 15 years and over and are based on ILO's modelled estimates, unless otherwise stated in a footnote.
Source of the data: International Labour Organization (ILO), Geneva, Key Indicators of the Labour Market (KILM 9th edition) and the ILOSTAT database, last accessed March 2017.

Life expectancy at birth is the average number of years of life at birth (age 0) for males and females according to the expected mortality rates by age estimated for the reference year and population. The data are an average over five-year ranges; 2000-2005 labelled "2005", 2005-2010 labelled "2010" and 2010-2015 labelled "2017", unless otherwise stated in a footnote.

Technical notes (*continued*)

Source of the data: United Nations Population Division, New York, World Population Prospects: The 2017 Revision; supplemented by data from the United Nations Statistics Division, New York, Demographic Yearbook 2015 and Secretariat for the Pacific Community (SPC) for small countries or areas, last accessed June 2017.

Major trading partners show the three largest trade partners (countries of last known destination and origin or consignment) in international merchandise trade transactions. In some cases a special partner is shown (i.e. Areas nes, bunkers, etc.) instead of a country and refers to one of the following special categories. Areas not elsewhere specified (i.e. Areas nes) is used (a) for low value trade, (b) if the partner designation was unknown to the country or if an error was made in the partner assignment and (c) for reasons of confidentiality. If a specific geographical location can be identified within Areas nes, then they are recorded accordingly (i.e. Asia nes). Bunkers are ship stores and aircraft supplies, which consists mostly of fuels and food. Free zones belong to the geographical and economic territory of a country but not to its customs territory. For the purpose of trade statistics the transactions between the customs territory and the free zones are recorded, if the reporting country uses the Special Trade System. Free zones can be commercial free zones (duty free shops) or industrial free zones. Data are expressed as percentages of total exports and of total imports of the country, area or special partner.
Source of the data: United Nations Statistics Division, New York, UN Comtrade database, last accessed June 2017.

Mobile-cellular telephone subscriptions, per 100 inhabitants refer to the number of mobile cellular telephone subscriptions in a country for each 100 inhabitants. It is calculated by dividing the number of mobile cellular telephone subscriptions by the total population and multiplied by 100.
Source of the data: International Telecommunication Union (ITU), Geneva, the ITU database, last accessed July 2016.

National currency refers to those notes and coins in circulation that are commonly used to make payments. The official currency names and the ISO currency codes are those officially in use, and may be subject to change.
Source of the data: International Standards Organisation, Geneva, Currency Code Services – ISO 4217 Maintenance Agency, last accessed June 2017.

Net Official Development Assistance received or disbursed is defined as those flows to developing countries and multilateral institutions provided by official agencies, including state and local governments, or by their executive agencies, each transaction of which meets the following tests: i) it is administered with the promotion of the economic development and welfare of developing countries as its main objective; and ii) it is concessional in character and conveys a grant element of at least 25 per cent. It is expressed as a percentage of Gross National Income of

Technical notes (*continued*)

either the donor or recipient. The multilateral institutions include the World Bank Group, regional banks, financial institutions of the European Union and a number of United Nations institutions, programmes and trust funds.

Source of the data: Organisation for Economic Co-operation and Development (OECD), Paris, the OECD Development Assistance Committee database, last accessed April 2017.

Population refers to the medium fertility projected de facto population as of 1 July 2017, unless otherwise stated in a footnote. The total population of a country may comprise either all usual residents of the country (de jure population) or all persons present in the country (de facto population) at the time of the census; for purposes of international comparisons, the de facto definition is used, unless otherwise stated in a footnote.

Source of the data: United Nations Population Division, New York, "World Population Prospects: The 2017 Revision", last accessed June 2017.

Population aged 0-14 years / 60 years and over refers to the percentage of the medium fertility projected population aged 0-14 years and aged 60 years and older, respectively as of 1 July 2017, unless otherwise stated in a footnote.

Source of the data: United Nations Population Division, New York, World Population Prospects: The 2017 Revision; supplemented by data from the United Nations Statistics Division, New York, Demographic Yearbook 2015 and Secretariat for the Pacific Community (SPC) for small countries or areas, last accessed June 2017.

Population density refers to the medium fertility projected population as of 1 July 2017 per square kilometre of surface area, unless otherwise stated in a footnote.

Source of the data: United Nations Population Division, New York, "World Population Prospects: The 2017 Revision", last accessed June 2017.

Population growth rate is the average annual percentage change in total population size. The data are an average over five-year ranges; 2000-2005 labelled "2005", 2005-2010 labelled "2010" and 2010-2015 labelled "2017", unless otherwise stated in a footnote.

Source of the data: United Nations Population Division, New York, "World Population Prospects: The 2017 Revision", last accessed June 2017.

Population using improved drinking water sources is the percentage of the population in urban and rural areas, according to national definitions, who use any of the following types of water supply for drinking: piped water, public tap, borehole or pump, protected well, protected spring or rainwater. Improved water sources do not include vendor-provided water, bottled water, tanker trucks or unprotected wells and springs. Use of an improved drinking water source is a proxy for the use of safe drinking water, see www.wssinfo.org for further information.

Source of the data: World Health Organization (WHO) and United Nations Children's Fund (UNICEF), Geneva and New York, the WHO/UNICEF Joint Monitoring Programme for the Water and Sanitation database, last accessed October 2015.

Population using improved sanitation facilities refers to the percentage of the population in urban and rural areas, according to national definitions, with access to facilities that hygienically separate human excreta from human, animal and insect contact. Facilities such as sewers or septic tanks, poor flush latrines and simple pit or ventilated improved pit latrines are assumed to be adequate, provided that they are not public. To be effective, facilities must be correctly constructed and properly maintained. Sanitation facilities are not considered improved when shared with other households, or open to public use. Use of an improved sanitation facility is a proxy for access to basic sanitation, see www.wssinfo.org for further information.
Source of the data: World Health Organization (WHO) and United Nations Children's Fund (UNICEF), Geneva and New York, the WHO/UNICEF Joint Monitoring Programme for the Water and Sanitation database, last accessed October 2015.

Refugees and others of concern to the Office of the United Nations High Commissioner for Refugees (UNHCR): The 1951 United Nations Convention relating to the Status of Refugees states that a refugee is someone who, owing to a well-founded fear of being persecuted for reasons of race, religion, nationality, political opinion or membership in a particular social group, is outside the country of his or her nationality and is unable to, or owing to such fear, is unwilling to avail himself or herself of the protection of that country; or who, not having a nationality and being outside the country of his or her former habitual residence, is unable or, owing to such fear, unwilling to return to it. In this series, refugees refer to persons granted a humanitarian status and/or those granted temporary protection. Included are persons who have been granted temporary protection on a group basis. The series also includes returned refugees, asylum-seekers, stateless persons and persons displaced internally within their own country and others of concern to UNHCR.
Source of the data: United Nations High Commissioner for Refugees (UNHCR), Geneva, UNHCR Population Statistics Database, last accessed March 2017.

Region is based on macro geographical regions arranged according to continents and component geographical regions used for statistical purposes as at 31 July 2017.
Source of the data: United Nations Statistics Division, New York, Statistical Yearbook 2017 edition (60th issue) Annex I - Country and area nomenclature, regional and other groupings (based on Series M49: Standard Country or Area codes and Geographical Regions for Statistical Use), a forthcoming publication.

Research & Development expenditure (% of GDP) refers to expenditure on creative work undertaken on a systematic basis in order to increase the stock of knowledge,

Technical notes (*continued*)

including knowledge of humanity, culture and society, and the use of this stock of knowledge to devise new applications. It is the total intramural expenditure on R&D performed on the national territory during a given period. It includes R&D performed within a country and funded from abroad but excludes payments made abroad for R&D.

Source of the data: United Nations Educational, Scientific and Cultural Organization (UNESCO) Institute for Statistics, Montreal, the UNESCO Institute for Statistics database, last accessed February 2017.

Seats held by women in national parliaments refer to the number of women in the lower chamber of national parliaments expressed as a percentage of total occupied seats in the lower or single House, situation as of 1 February 2017.

Source of the data: Inter-Parliamentary Union (IPU), Geneva, Women in National Parliament dataset and the Millennium Development Goals Indicators database, last accessed March 2017.

Sex ratio is calculated as the ratio of the medium fertility projected population of men to that of 100 women as of 1 July 2017, unless otherwise stated in a footnote.

Source of the data: United Nations Population Division, New York, World Population Prospects: The 2017 Revision; supplemented by data from the United Nations Statistics Division, New York, Demographic Yearbook 2015 and Secretariat for the Pacific Community (SPC) for small countries or areas, last accessed June 2017.

Surface area refers to land area plus inland water, unless otherwise stated in a footnote.

Source of the data: United Nations Statistics Division, New York, Demographic Yearbook 2015 and the demographic statistics database, last accessed June 2017.

Threatened species represents the number of plants and animals that are most in need of conservation attention and are compiled by the World Conservation Union IUCN/ Species Survival Commission (SSC).

Source of the data: World Conservation Union (IUCN) / Species Survival Commission (SSC), Gland, Switzerland and Cambridge, United Kingdom, IUCN Red List of Threatened Species publication, last accessed May 2017.

Tourist/visitor arrivals at national borders is any person who travels to a country other than that in which he or she has his or her usual residence but outside his/her usual environment for a period not exceeding 12 months and whose main purpose of visit is other than the exercise of an activity remunerated from with the country visited, and who stays at least one night in a collective or private accommodation in the country visited (see Recommendations on Tourism Statistics of the United Nations and the World Tourism Organization). The data refer to arrivals of non-resident tourists at national borders, unless otherwise stated in a footnote.

Source of the data: World Tourism Organization (WTO), Madrid, the WTO Statistics Database, last accessed December 2016.

Unemployment refers to persons above a specified age who during a specified reference period were: "without work", i.e. were not in paid employment or self-employment as defined under employment; "currently available for work", i.e. were available for paid employment or self-employment during the reference period; and "seeking work", i.e. had taken specific steps in a specified recent period to seek paid employment or self-employment (see ILO's current International Recommendations on Labour Statistics). The data refer to the 15 years and over age group and are based on ILO's modelled estimates, unless otherwise stated in a footnote.
Source of the data: International Labour Organization (ILO), Geneva, Key Indicators of the Labour Market (KILM 9th edition) and the ILOSTAT database, last accessed March 2017.

United Nations membership dates: The United Nations is an intergovernmental organization whose members are the countries of the world. Currently there are 193 Member States of the United Nations, some of which joined the UN by signing and ratifying the Charter of the United Nations in 1945; the other countries joined the UN later, through the adoption of a resolution admitting them to membership. The process usually follows these steps: first, the country applies for membership and makes a declaration accepting the obligations of the Charter; second, the Security Council adopts a resolution recommending that the General Assembly admit the country to membership and finally the General Assembly adopts a resolution admitting the country.
Source of the data: United Nations, New York, Member states and date of admission, last accessed June 2017.

Urban population is based on the number of persons at the mid-year defined as urban according to national definitions of this concept. In most cases these definitions are those used in the most recent population census.
Source of the data: United Nations Population Division, New York, "World Urbanization Prospects: The 2014 Revision".

Urban population growth rate is based on the number of persons defined as urban according to national definitions of this concept. In most cases these definitions are those used in the most recent population census. The data are an average over five-year ranges; 2000-2005 labelled "2005", 2005-2010 labelled "2010" and 2010-2015 labelled "2017", unless otherwise stated in a footnote.
Source of the data: United Nations Population Division, New York, "World Urbanization Prospects: The 2014 Revision".

Statistical sources and references

Statistical sources

Carbon Dioxide Information Analysis Center, Oak Ridge, Tennessee, Global, Regional, and National Fossil-Fuel CO_2 Emissions, available at _http://cdiac.ornl.gov/trends/emis/overview 2014.html_.

Food and Agriculture Organization of the United Nations, Rome, FAOSTAT database, available at _http://faostat3.fao.org/home/E_.

International Labour Organization, Key Indicators of the Labour Market, 9th edition software, available at _http://www.ilo.org/global/statistics-and-databases/research-and-databases/kilm/lang--en/index.htm_.
_____, LABORSTA Internet database, available at _http://laborsta.ilo.org/_.
International Monetary Fund (IMF), Washington, Balance of Payments (BOP) database, available at _http://data.imf.org/bop_.
_____, International Financial Statistics (IFS) database, available at _http://data.imf.org/ifs_.

Inter-Parliamentary Union, Women in National Parliaments, available at _http://www.ipu.org/wmn-e/classif.htm_.

International Telecommunication Union (ITU), Geneva, the World Telecommunication/ICT Indicators Database, available at _http://www.itu.int/en/ITU-D/statistics/Pages/default.aspx_.

International Union for Conservation of Nature (IUCN), The 2015 IUCN Red List of Threatened Species, available at _http://www.iucnredlist.org/about/summary-statistics_.

Organisation for Economic Co-operation and Development (OECD) Development Assistance Committee (DAC) statistics, available at _http://stats.oecd.org/_.

Secretariat of the Pacific Community (SPC) Statistics and Demography Programme, Population and demographic indicators, available at _http://sdd.spc.int/en/_.

United Nations Educational, Scientific and Cultural Organization (UNESCO) Institute for Statistics, Montreal, UNESCO statistics database, available at _http://data.uis.unesco.org/_.

United Nations High Commissioner for Refugees, Geneva, UNHCR Mid-Year Trends 2015, available at _http://www.unhcr.org/en-us/statistical-yearbooks.html_.

United Nations, Department of Economic and Social Affairs, Population Division, New York, Trends in International Migrant Stock: The 2015 Revision (United Nations publication POP/DB/MIG/Stock/Rev.2015/Age), available at _http://www.un.org/en/development/desa/population/migration/data/index.shtml_
_____, World Population Prospects. The 2017 Revision, available at _https://esa.un.org/unpd/wpp/_.

Statistical sources and references (*continued*)

_____, World Urbanization Prospects: The 2014 Revision, available at https://esa.un.org/unpd/wup/.

United Nations, Department of Economic and Social Affairs, Statistics Division, New York, Commodity Trade Statistics Database (COMTRADE), available at http://comtrade.un.org/db/default.aspx.
_____, Demographic Yearbook 2015 (United Nations Publication, ST/ESA/STAT/SER.R/45), available at http://unstats.un.org/unsd/demographic/products/dyb/dyb2.htm
_____, Energy Statistics Yearbook (Series J, United Nations publication), available at http://unstats.un.org/unsd/energy/yearbook/default.htm.
_____, International Trade Statistics Yearbook (Series G, United Nations publication), available at http://comtrade.un.org/pb/.
_____, National Accounts Statistics: Analysis of Main Aggregates (Series X, United Nations publication), available at http://unstats.un.org/unsd/snaama/introduction.asp.
_____, Standard Country or Area Codes for Statistical Use and United Nations Statistical Yearbook (Annex I) available at http://unstats.un.org/unsd/methods/m49/m49.htm http://unstats.un.org/unsd/publications/statistical-yearbook/.

United Nations Member States website, available at http://www.un.org/en/members/.

United Nations Sustainable Development Goals database available at https://unstats.un.org/sdgs/indicators/database/.

United Nations Office on Drugs and Crime, Vienna, Homicide Statistics website, available at https://www.unodc.org/unodc/en/data-and-analysis/crime-and-criminal-justice.html.

United Nations World Health Organization (WHO), Geneva, Global Health Observatory Data Repository available at http://www.who.int/gho/en/.
_____, Global Health Expenditure database available at http://apps.who.int/nha/database.

WHO / UNICEF Joint Monitoring Programme (JMP) for sanitation and water supply, available at www.wssinfo.org.

United Nations World Tourism Organization (UNWTO), Madrid, UNWTO statistics database, Yearbook of Tourism Statistics available at http://www.e-unwto.org/loi/unwtotfb.

World Intellectual Property Office (WIPO) Intellectual Property statistics data centre available at http://ipstats.wipo.int/ipstatv2/?lang=en.

Statistical sources and references (*continued*)

References

Food and Agriculture Organization of the United Nations (2010). Global Forest Resources Assessment 2010 (Rome), available at *http://www.fao.org/forestry/fra/fra2010/en/*.

International Labour Organization (2000). Current International Recommendations on Labour Statistics, 2000 Edition (Geneva), available at *http://www.ilo.org/public/english/bureau/stat/publ/currrec.htm*.

United Nations (1951 and 1967). Convention relating to the Status of Refugees of 1951 (United Nations, Treaty Series, vol. 189 (1954), No. 2545, p. 137), art. 1) and Protocol relating to the Status of Refugees of 1967 (United Nations, Treaty Series, vol. 606 (1967), No. 8791, p. 267), available at *https://treaties.un.org/doc/Publication/UNTS/Volume%20189/volume-189-I-2545-English.pdf* and *https://treaties.un.org/doc/Publication/UNTS/Volume%20606/volume-606-I-8791-English.pdf*.

United Nations (1982). Concepts and Methods in Energy Statistics, with Special Reference to Energy Accounts and Balances: A Technical Report. Statistical Office, Series F, No. 29 and Corr. 1 (United Nations publication, Sales No. E.82.XVII.13 and corrigendum), available at *http://unstats.un.org/unsd/publication/SeriesF/SeriesF_29E.pdf*.

United Nations (2008). Principles and Recommendations for Population and Housing Censuses Rev. 2. Statistics Division, Series M, No. 67, Rev. 2 (United Nations publication, Sales No. E.07.XVII.8), available at *http://unstats.un.org/unsd/publication/SeriesM/Seriesm_67rev2e.pdf*.

United Nations (2008). International Standard Industrial Classification of All Economic Activities (ISIC), Rev. 4. Statistics Division, Series M, No. 4, Rev.4 (United Nations publication, Sales No. E.08.XVII.25), available at *http://unstats.un.org/unsd/publication/SeriesM/seriesm_4rev4e.pdf*.

United Nations (2004). International Merchandise Trade Statistics: Compilers Manual, Statistics Division, Series F, No. 87 (United Nations publication, Sales No. E.02.XVII.17), available at *http://unstats.un.org/unsd/publication/SeriesF/seriesf_87e.pdf*.

United Nations (2010). International Merchandise Trade Statistics: Concepts and Definitions, Statistics Division, Series M, No.52, Rev.3, (United Nations publication, Sales No. E.10.XVII.13), available at *http://unstats.un.org/unsd/publication/SeriesM/SeriesM_52rev2E.pdf*.

United Nations (2011). International Recommendations for Energy Statistics (IRES), Statistics Division, available at *http://unstats.un.org/unsd/statcom/doc11/BG-IRES.pdf*.

Statistical sources and references (*continued*)

United Nations (2015). 2012 Energy Balances, Statistics Division, Series W, No. 21 (United Nations Publication, Sales No. E.15.XVII.13), available at http://unstats.un.org/unsd/energy/balance/2012/01.pdf.

United Nations, European Commission, International Monetary Fund, Organisation for Economic Cooperation and Development and World Bank (2009). System of National Accounts 2008 (SNA 2008), available at http://unstats.un.org/unsd/nationalaccount/sna2008.asp.

United Nations and World Tourism Organization (2008). International Recommendations for Tourism Statistics 2008, Series M, No. 83/Rev.1 (United Nations publication, Sales No. E.08.XVII.28), available at http://unstats.un.org/unsd/publication/SeriesM/SeriesM_83rev1e.pdf.

World Health Organization (WHO, 2007). International Statistical Classification of Diseases and Related Health Problems, Tenth Revision (ICD-10), (Geneva), available at http://www.who.int/classifications/icd/en/.

Related statistical products

The World Statistics Pocketbook can also be viewed online in PDF format as well as an app for Android and Apple devices at http://unstats.un.org/unsd/pocketbook/ and in UNdata at http://data.un.org/CountryProfile.aspx.

Other statistical publications offering a broad cross-section of information which may be of interest to users of the World Statistics Pocketbook include:

1. The Monthly Bulletin of Statistics (MBS) in print and the Monthly Bulletin of Statistics Online, available at http://unstats.un.org/unsd/mbs/.

2. The Statistical Yearbook (SYB) in print and online in PDF format, available at http://unstats.un.org/unsd/publications/statistical-yearbook/.

Both publications are available for sale in print format (see below for instructions on how to order). For more information about other publications and online databases prepared by the United Nations Statistics Division, please visit: https://unstats.un.org/unsd/publications/. For additional information about the work of the United Nations Statistics Division, please visit http://unstats.un.org/unsd. To order United Nations publications, please visit www.un.org/publications or contact:

United Nations Publications
300 East 42nd Street
New York, NY 10017
Tel: 1-888-254-4286 / Fax: 1-800-338-4550 / E-mail: publications@un.org

Please provide the Statistical Dissemination Section – which is responsible for producing the World Statistics Pocketbook, the Monthly Bulletin of Statistics and the Statistical Yearbook – your feedback and suggestions regarding these statistical products, as well as the utility of the data, by contacting statistics@un.org.